Determining Our Environments

Determining Our Environments

The Role of Department of Energy Citizen Advisory Boards

WALTER LEE WILLIAMS, JR.

PRAEGER

Westport, Connecticut
London

Library of Congress Cataloging-in-Publication Data

Williams, Walter Lee, 1960–
Determining our environments : the role of Department of Energy citizen advisory boards / Walter Lee Williams, Jr.
p. cm.
Includes bibliographical references and index.
ISBN 0–275–97207–0 (alk. paper)
1. Environmental policy—United States—Citizen participation. 2. Environmental policy—Economic aspects—United States. I. Title.
HC110.E5 W537 2002
333.7'0973—dc21 2001021645

British Library Cataloguing in Publication Data is available.

Library of Congress Catalog Card Number: 2001021645
ISBN: 0–275–97207–0

First published in 2002

Praeger Publishers, 88 Post Road West, Westport, CT 06881
An imprint of Greenwood Publishing Group, Inc.
www.praeger.com

Printed in the United States of America

The paper used in this book complies with the Permanent Paper Standard issued by the National Information Standards Organization (Z39.48–1984).

10 9 8 7 6 5 4 3 2 1

This book is dedicated to my parents Walter L. Williams, Sr. and Barbara Williams, and to my brother Robert Victor Williams. Without their support, this book would not have been possible.

Contents

Preface

I am forever indebted to Dr. Otis Stephens, Dr. John Scheb, Dr. Patricia Freeland, Dr. David Houston, and Dr. George Bowen. These persons were all unfailingly supportive, unendingly patient, and thoroughly professional. Special appreciation is due, of course, to my mentor and major professor Dr. Michael R. Fitzgerald. I will always be in his debt and treasure his friendship. Most of all, I wish to express appreciation to my family. Their support, inspiration, and faith made this and all things possible for me.

Abbreviations

AEC	U. S. Atomic Energy Commission
APA	Administrative Procedure Act of 1946
ASI	Advanced Services, Incorporated
ATSDR	Agency for Toxic Substances and Disease Registry
AWWTP	Advanced Waste Water Treatment Plant
BNFL	British Nuclear Fuels Limited
CAC	Citizen Advisory Committees
CDC	Center for Disease Control
CLN	Community Leaders Network
CRO	Community Reuse Organization
CWA	Clean Water Act of 1972
CERCLA	Comprehensive Environmental Response, Compensation, and Liability Act of 1980
CPSC	Consumer Product Safety Commission
DOE	U.S. Department of Energy
DOI	Department of Interior
DOJ	Department of Justice
EEOC	Equal Employment Opportunity Commission
EM	Environmental Management
EOA	Economic Opportunity Act of 1964
EPA	U.S. Environmental Protection Agency

ERDA	Energy Research and Development Administration
ERMC	Environmental Restoration Management Contractor
FAC	Fernald Advisory Committee
FACA	Federal Advisory Committee Act of 1992
FATLC	Fernald Atomic Trades and Labor Council
FBI	Federal Bureau of Investigation
FCAB	Fernald Citizens Advisory Board
FCRO	Fernald Community Reuse Organization
FCTF	Fernald Citizens Task Force
FDF	Flour Daniel, Fernald
FEMP	Fernald Environmental Management Project
FERMCO	Fernald Environmental Restoration Management Corporation
Fernald SSAB	Fernald Site Specific Advisory Board
FF	Flour Fernald
FFCA	Federal Facilities Compliance Act of 1992
FFERDC	Federal Facilities Environmental Restoration Dialogue Committee
FHEAC	Fernald Health and Environmental Advisory Committee
FHES	Fernald Health Effects Subcommittee
FLHP	Fernald Living History Project
FMPC	Feed Materials Production Center
FOIA	Freedom of Information Act of 1966
FRB	Federal Reserve Board

FRESH	Fernald Residents for Environmental Safety and Health
FTC	Federal Trade Commission
FWPCA	Federal Water Pollution Control Act Amendments of 1972
GAO	General Accounting Office
GSA	General Services Administration
HHS	U.S. Department of Health and Human Services
ICC	Interstate Commerce Commission
IEER	Institute of Energy and Environmental Research
ITC	International Technology Corporation
LDR	Land Disposal Restriction
NEPA	National Environmental Policy Act of 1969
NLO	National Lead of Ohio, Incorporated
NLRB	National Labor Relations Board
NOAA	National Oceanic and Atmospheric Administration
NRC	Nuclear Regulatory Commission
OEO	Office of Economic Opportunity
Ohio EPA	Ohio Environmental Protection Agency
OMB	Office of Management and Budget
ORAU	Oak Ridge Associated Universities
OSDF	On-Site Disposal Facility
OST	Office of Science and Technology
PAC	Political Action Committee

PETI	Petro Environmental Technologies, Incorporated
PNNL	Pacific Northwest National Laboratory
RAC	Radiological Assessments Corporation
RCRA	Resource Conservation and Recovery Act of 1976
RIFS	Remedial Investigation and Feasibility Study
SSAB	Site Specific Advisory Board
STP	Site Treatment Plan
TKC	The Keystone Center
TSCA	Toxic Substances Control Act of 1976
USDA	United States Department of Agriculture
WEMCO	Westinghouse Environmental Management Company of Ohio
WMCO	Westinghouse Materials Company of Ohio

Introduction

Many citizens feel that they have no meaningful input or influence on public policy decisions affecting them that are made by government agencies. They believe that by the time a government agency announces a policy decision, that agency has already decided on its course of action. In many cases, these citizens may hold demonstrations or file lawsuits to delay or stop the implementation of the policy. The impact of these demonstrations and lawsuits has been detrimental for agencies, resulting in increased expenses and costly delays. Negative media reports about the actions of government agencies have also contributed to an increasing distrust and lack of confidence in government. In an attempt to remedy these negative perceptions, many agencies have tried to increase stakeholder involvement in their policy process activities. The practice of increasing stakeholder involvement is an acknowledgement of the belief that, in a democracy, citizens should have meaningful participation in the creation and implementation of policies that affect them.

Rosenstone and Hansen observe that: "Distinct among the world's political systems, democracies offer citizens opportunities to participate in their own governance" (1993: 1). This is a study of the effort of public agencies to better incorporate citizen participation in the administrative process. Its focus is the continuing effort of the U.S. Department of Energy (DOE) to use *citizen advisory boards* composed of *stakeholders* (those who stand most to gain or lose from policy implementation) in its economic transition, waste management, and environmental restoration programs.

The stakeholder involvement group examined was the *Fernald Citizens Advisory Board* at Fernald, Ohio. The board was established by DOE to give the agency advice and recommendations on environmental cleanup activities at its facility in Fernald, Ohio. The facility, the Feed Materials Production Center, produced uranium fuel from 1951 to 1989 for the nuclear weapons program. As a byproduct, the facility also produced significant volumes of hazardous and toxic wastes. The resulting pollution posed a significant and persistent threat to humans and the ecosystem in the surrounding area.

The research found that the DOE adoption of the stakeholder involvement model at Fernald was effective; for the advisory board was expeditiously organized, reached consensus on critical issues, and accomplished its primary mission. In fact, the board's performance was such that the Clinton Administration considered it a major example of how federal agencies could be reinvented to produce a government that works better and costs less.

1

The Changing Regulatory Process

Introduction

The distinguished political scientist Charles O. Jones observes that in America "the very terms of governance are changing" (1998: 4). At the core of this transformation, according to Jones, is a "more open governing process." On an optimistic note, Jones concludes that this "change must, can, and will be absorbed in a democracy (4)." This study investigates a critical feature of this change—the effort of public agencies better to incorporate direct citizen participation in the policy process much more successfully. The study focuses especially on stakeholder involvement as a technique of citizen participation. This is accomplished by reviewing the roots of the citizen participation movement and the resulting impact of the movement on the public policy process—with emphasis on the administrative process. Then, the emergence and nature of a more open model of the process is detailed so as to frame the investigation of how effectively more open governance works in actual implementation. The test case is the long-term, continuing effort of the U.S. Department of Energy (DOE) to foster and employ citizen advisory boards in its economic transition, waste management, and environmental clean-up programs.

The emergence of an interest group society over the last half-century has affected the American public policy process in many ways, but one especially troubling manifestation is its growing tendency toward policy gridlock. This tendency is investigated explicitly by focusing on the nature and impact of recent regulatory process innovations designed to avoid or break gridlock. One of the most significant recent regulatory process innovations designed to break or avoid gridlock is stakeholder involvement. Models of the changing regulatory process, as it has shifted from the closed-traditional system to an open-participatory system, are presented in this study. The single case study, framed by the open-participatory model, is employed to answer the basic research question: How have recent innovations affected the process by which government seeks to regulate American society?

The purpose of this study is to examine the changes that have occurred in the regulatory process in recent years. These changes include the use of traditional stakeholder involvement groups in administrative decision making. Traditional stakeholder involvement includes persons and groups maintaining contact with legislators and consulting with public administrators after the administrators have implemented a public policy. Stakeholders are defined as *specific persons, organizations, and groups who are affected in some way by a specific public policy.* Stakeholders can be residents, businesses, elected officials, interest groups, professional groups, workers, and other persons who are affected by a specific public policy.

In the traditional regulatory process, the political process establishes a policy agenda and Congress formulates legislation. Once legislation is formulated, Congress delegates authority to an agency to carry out a policy. In this process, there is no direct public participation in an agency's decision making activities. This traditional approach is still used by some agencies. In the traditional process, the public hearing is the first opportunity for citizen participation. Indeed, for most citizens, it is the first time they become aware of the proposed policy decision. Increasingly, many citizens believe the hearing stage is too late in the process effectively to influence a government policy.

Many contacts between affected stakeholders and agency officials occur under what is referred to as the Contemporary Administrative Process Model or the Decide-Announce-Defend Model. In the Decide-Announce-Defend Model, an agency decides that it needs to create a policy to resolve a specific public policy problem. The agency then announces the creation of the new policy at a public hearing and defends its new policy during the public hearing.

A newer approach has been developed that attempts to enhance citizen participation in the creation and implementation stages of public policies. This newer approach is known as the Stakeholder Involvement Model, which will be tested in this book. In this model, various groups of persons who are affected by a particular policy remain in constant contact with the officials whose agency is responsible for the policy's creation. In the Stakeholder Involvement Model, affected stakeholder groups remain in constant contact with agency officials from the time that a public policy is created until that policy is implemented.

A focused inquiry into how the U.S. Department of Energy employs stakeholder involvement will yield important information regarding the nature and impact of expanding citizen participation innovations in the administrative process. This study's hypothesis was that the Stakeholder Involvement Model is a more effective means of citizen participation than the Decide-Announce-Defend Model. The stakeholder involvement group being studied is the Fernald Citizens Advisory Board, which was organized to provide environmental management and cleanup oversight at a Department of Energy facility located approximately twenty miles northwest of Cincinnati, Ohio.

Chapter 1 discusses the evolution of the traditional regulatory process, policy implementation gridlock, the citizen participation movement, the theoretical framework, and research design used to conduct this study. The chapter also discusses the history of the Department of Energy's (DOE's) Nuclear Weapons Complex and DOE's reasons for establishing citizen advisory boards at its facilities.

Chapter 2 discusses the history of the Fernald Environmental Management Project site and the current cleanup activities at the site. It also formally presents a Stakeholder Involvement Model, and provides the research design and case methods used in this study.

Chapter 3 discusses the creation, operation and recommendations of the Fernald Site Specific Advisory Board.

Chapter 4 gives an assessment of the Fernald Site Specific Advisory Board's effectiveness.

Chapter 5 discusses the results of a survey given by DOE to the members of its site specific advisory boards in 1997.

Chapter 6 discusses the summary, conclusions, and implications of the study.

The Traditional Regulatory Process:
The Regulatory State Rises

Over time, the federal government has greatly expanded its role in the United States. During the late nineteenth century, the United States became a more industrialized nation. Many businesses and industries formed interest groups to obtain or preserve benefits that occurred because of industrialization. Many businesses, such as railroads and oil companies, engaged in monopolistic business practices. For example, one railroad would buy up other railroads and would become the exclusive railroad for a particular area—forming a monopoly. Since that railroad company was the only one in that area, it would be in a position to charge excessive rates that customers would have little choice but to pay since there were no other competing railroads. These practices included charging excessive rates and discouraging competition. To regulate business practices, the government created several new agencies during the late nineteenth and early twentieth centuries.

The Interstate Commerce Commission (ICC) was created in 1887. The ICC's purpose was to prevent industries and businesses from engaging in monopolistic practices. Its initial focus was upon the regulation of railroad rates and practices. Congress passed the *Sherman Antitrust Act of 1890* to prohibit companies from forming trusts or monopolies—i.e., forming exclusive control of particular industries. An example of a monopoly was the Standard Oil Company that controlled the oil industry during the late nineteenth and early twentieth centuries. Several corporations formed trusts that controlled market prices and destroyed competition. The Sherman Antitrust Act was passed in response to public demands for reducing the giant business mergers and buyouts that threatened to monopolize many American industries. Other agencies created during this era included the Federal Reserve Board (FRB) in 1913 and the Federal Trade Commission (FTC) in 1914 (Gordon, 1986: 499). These agencies were the precursors of the current regulatory system, which was created between 1930 and the mid-1970s.

To confront the severe economic effects of the Great Depression, the federal government created a variety of new agencies during the 1930s. These included such major regulatory agencies as the Securities and Exchange Commission (SEC) and the National Labor Relations Board (NLRB) (Gordon, 1986: 499).

A third period of government expansion occurred during the 1960s and 1970s. During the 1960s and 1970s, the government created several new agencies. These agencies were created in response to the demands of the civil rights movement, the environmental movement, and the consumer movement. Some of these agencies were part of the Great Society and the War on Poverty programs. Such agencies included the Equal Employment Opportunity Commission (EEOC), the Environmental Protection Agency (EPA), and the Consumer Product Safety Commission (CPSC). The creation of these agencies and other government agencies during the late nineteenth century and the twentieth century led to an increase in the government's regulation of American society (Gordon, 1986: 499).

The Emerging Citizen Role

This study investigates changes that have occurred in the policy making process in recent years, including use of stakeholder involvement by many local, state, and federal agencies. Before the emergence of stakeholder involvement, many agencies used the decision making process called the traditional regulatory process. The basic elements of this model are provided in Appendix B.[1] The process involves virtually no direct public participation in agency decision making. The traditional approach to public participation is still being used by some agencies. But, as will be shown, it is now subject to severe criticism and is changing significantly toward a more open model.

In the traditional regulatory process, the political process establishes the policy agenda and the Congress, once a given problem has been socialized and incorporated into the ambit of the national government, formulates legislation. Eventually, and increasingly in the modern era, this meant the delegation of authority to an agency. With the explosion of federal activity and the proliferation of executive agencies in the New Deal era, an administrative state of gigantic proportions was created. The laws that created these agencies frequently contained very broad wording that described the agencies' goals and missions. Congress delegated a significant amount of authority to these agencies as issues became more complex, and legislatures delegated even more authority to them. This process continued until Congress passed the Administrative Procedure Act in 1946. This law was designed primarily to regularize the decision making procedures followed by federal agencies. An important component was the enhancement of public participation through requirements for public notification, comment, and hearings. Informal rule making was another statutory device for increasing public participation. Thus, in part, the APA sought to provide an opportunity for citizens more directly to influence the public policies proposed by federal agencies.

The APA refined the traditional process to better incorporate citizen concerns. Thus, public involvement activities were formally added to the decision making process. But, because public involvement came so late in the process, and was so constrained, the weight of decision making power remained largely in the hands of agencies. In essence, agencies tended to *decide, announce, and defend* policies rather than to have their decisions significantly affected by the public.

In the traditional process, stakeholder involvement activity involves persons and groups maintaining contact with legislators and consulting with public administrators after the administrators have implemented a public policy. These public administrators, persons, and groups maintain contact with each other on a regular basis. Under the traditional regulatory process, there is limited citizen involvement in public policy making activities. In many cases, the citizens involved are members of powerful interest groups affected by the policy. Citizens who are not members of influential interest groups often are not involved in the public policy making process until an agency has already decided to implement a policy. Usually after a public agency has decided to implement a policy, that agency holds public hearings to receive citizen input and concerns regarding the policy.

There is also a heavy reliance on scientific and technical experts by the public sector as public administrators and agencies rely frequently on scientific and technical experts to tell them the benefits of a policy if it is enacted. Finally, the public sector is heavily regulated by "sunshine laws" and laws such as the Administrative Procedure Act of 1946, which require government agencies to hold public hearings to give people the opportunity to express their concerns about a public policy. Still, these fledgling efforts to promote more inclusive and open agency decision making have a limited effect on public participation. The center of power remains as before, essentially within bureaucratic agencies that themselves are subject to *capture* by narrow interests (Wilson, 1980: vii-xii).

The Decline of Public Confidence in Authority

In 1946, Congress passed the Administrative Procedure Act (APA). This act requires government agencies to hold public hearings before they can officially implement any new public policies or changes in existing policies. The purpose of the law was to increase the accessibility of public agencies to citizens who have concerns about the agencies' policies. During the hearings, the citizens tell the agencies their concerns about public policies that the agencies proposed or announced. The intention of the APA was to increase citizen participation by giving citizens the opportunity to speak to the agencies about their concerns regarding these policies.

Some people felt that accessibility to public officials was still inadequate. Many of the persons who spoke at hearings were members of interest groups affected by the proposed policies. These interest groups often had close ties to the public agencies and were able to influence these public agencies to implement policies that benefited these interest groups. As a result, members of the interest groups were more likely to have access to agency personnel than were persons who did not belong to influential interest groups. Many persons felt that by the time the agencies held public hearings, these agencies had already decided to implement their proposed policies. Many individuals felt that agencies held public hearings *only* because local, state, and federal laws required them to do so. Thus, reluctant agencies incorporated citizen participation in a very narrow sense. As Harold Seidman and Robert Gilmour observe: "Citizen participation is a very slippery term and means different things to different people. If participation is measured by the number of citizens who participate at public hearings or vote for members of citizen boards, it rests on a very narrow base" (1986: 207). Seidman and Gilmour also noted that in many cases that:

> The "citizen participant" is generally the representative of an interest group. Citizen participation can be and has been used as a means for transferring power from officials who have at least some political responsibility to the community at large to self-perpetuating local cliques or the bureaucracy. It can operate in ways that provide symbolic citizen participation, but minimal individual citizen influence and maximum citizen frustration. (207)

Federal agencies are constrained by the requirement of the Administrative Procedure Act, which establishes uniform procedures for actions such as formal and informal rule making. *Formal* rule making applies to adjudication and trial proceedings. *Informal* rule making pertains to public notice, comment, and hearings. There are three significant objectives for informal rule making: First, the APA is to provide an opportunity for affected parties to submit comments on proposed rules; second, an agency must publish significant decisions in the *Federal Register* and hold public hearings to obtain public comment before implementing specific plans (Ryan, 1994: 2); third, the deliberations, rules, and procedures must be a matter of public record (Petersen, 1994: 44).

Proponents hoped the APA would induce agencies to become more responsive to public opinion when creating and implementing policies. This assumes, of course, that adjustments in proposed rules would occur as a result of the process. In practice, in the view of agency critics, public hearings often are mere formalities. Often, the agency is committed to policy implementation before public meetings are held. Some also contend that the agencies are more responsive to the concerns of powerful interest groups than to the concerns of individual citizens--including persons who attend public hearings. The interest groups meet with agency officials at meetings that occur away from public view.

In 1969, political scientist Theodore Lowi described the interaction of interest groups, congressional committees, and agencies as "interest group liberalism" (1969: 5). Interest group liberalism refers "to the tendency of agency officials to support policy demands of interest groups that have a stake in a policy. Interest-group liberalism constitutes a partial abdication by government of its authority over policy to the demands of interest groups" (Patterson, 1999: 289).

The relationships involving interest groups, congressional committees,

and agencies are also known as "iron triangles" (1999: 277). Other terms used to describe these relationships include "triple alliances and subgovernments" (Chandler, 1987; 162). Under these relationships, interest groups contribute money to the campaigns of congressional representatives, and lobby the members of Congress on behalf of the agencies. Because of this support, the agencies and congressional members are more likely to respond to the concerns of the interest groups than to those of individual citizens. Persons and groups who do not possess significant political power or financial resources are less likely to have the ability to form interest groups. Consequently, these persons and groups are largely excluded from opportunities to influence policies that affect them.

Jeffrey Berry summarizes the view that less affluent groups and persons often do not have the resources to form powerful interest groups to lobby their interests:

> The government should ensure that disadvantaged sectors of society that are inadequately represented by interest groups receive support to improve their representation in the political process. For the poor, minorities, and the disabled, there are interest groups active on their behalf, but they are few in number and do not have the resources to fund the kind of advocacy efforts they need. (1997: 238)

This view largely is shared by Seidman and Gilmour who posit:

> If our democratic system is to be responsive to the needs of all our people, organization structure and administrative arrangements need to balance the competing interests within given program areas so that none of the competing interests are immune to public control and capable of excluding less powerful segments of our society from effective participation in the system and an equitable share of its benefits. (1986: 16)

In part, this happens, according to Seidman and Gilmour, because "organizational arrangements are not neutral and tend to give some interests and perspectives more effective access to those with decision making authority" (1986: 15). In 1980, James Q. Wilson opined that agencies have been affected by what he referred to as "capture theory." He defines capture theory as the condition resulting when "agencies have been 'captured' by the interests that they are supposed to regulate" (Wilson, 1980: ix). This occurs when the agencies and interest groups have close ties to each other, and the agencies pursue public policies that benefit narrow interest groups more than the general public—or less well-organized stakeholders.

Jonathan Rauch (1994) found that the number and power of interest groups were growing dramatically with a variety of negative implications for the policy process—most especially policy gridlock. Rauch believes that it is relatively easy for any group affected by a public policy to form an interest group. Numerous new interest groups have emerged in Washington, DC, since the 1960s. He observes that the majority of interest groups that have lobbyists in Washington, DC, are relatively effective in pressuring members of Congress to create and maintain policies that benefit them. Further, Rauch believes that most interest groups are relatively influential within the policy domains that most affect them. Rauch believes that the emergence of numerous and powerful interest groups has contributed to the policy gridlock currently present in Washington. This reality makes innovations, changes, and terminations of public policies difficult to achieve.

Interest groups are also willing to file lawsuits to delay or eliminate policies that do not suit their interests. From the late nineteenth century until the 1960s, many individuals and organizations deferred to the expertise of the politically neutral public administrator. However, after the Vietnam War and the Watergate scandal, many citizens lost confidence in the government—especially in the federal government (Hibbing and Theiss-Morse, 1995; Lipset and Schneider, 1983; Nye, Zelikow, and King, 1997). This loss of confidence in government, to be sure, did not begin with the Vietnam War and the Watergate scandal; Robert Nisbet (1975) remarked upon the long "twilight of authority" that has settled on the West. The loss of confidence in government has been accompanied by a loss of confidence in business, labor unions, the news media, and other institutions in Western society. This decline of confidence in government, business, and other institutions also occurred in other Western democracies "such as Great Britain, Italy, France, the Netherlands, and the Scandinavian countries. Reports of citizen unrest, indifference, alienation, and hostility to government are similar to those in the United States" (Nisbet, 1975: 6).

Indeed, the Panel on Civic Trust and Citizen Responsibility (1999) published a report titled: *A Government to Trust and Respect: Rebuilding Citizen-Government Relations for the Twenty-first Century*. The report states that: "For many Americans, government is a large and distant entity from which they feel disconnected and disaffected. Americans love their country and Constitution, but many dislike and distrust their government" (1999: 4).

During the period of industrialization, many individuals moved from small towns and farms into cities to find jobs. After moving into cities, there was a loss of a sense of community and feeling of belonging that was present in rural areas. Persons turned to labor unions and political parties to meet their economic and community needs. People expected political parties to provide them with a sense of belonging and community that had been present only in the small towns and villages. After a weakening in the power of political parties and a decline in the influence of labor unions, individuals began to lose confidence in government, business, labor unions, and other institutions. The Vietnam War and the Watergate scandal merely focused attention on attitudes that had emerged over a period of several decades.

Mary M. Timney (1998) comments that: "In many cases, communication is a one-way street for administrator to citizens. The basic assumption of many public administrators is that citizens have, at best, marginal expertise, not essential information, and thus are best left out of the process until the important decisions have been made and they can do little damage" (1998: 98). While describing the tools necessary for practicing public administration, Dolores Foley (1998) states that: "What we often see at public hearings, is that, too often, citizen input is requested after a decision has been made. Deliberation is a way of making decisions, but it is of no use when a decision has already been made. In many cases, the solutions posed have been predetermined by the way the issues have been framed" (1998: 156).

Many persons and organizations became less likely to defer to public administrators' expertise and decisions after the 1960s and 1970s. Individuals became more distrustful and cynical about the government's intentions and justifications for enacting policies. Russell J. Dalton (1988) states that "not only do citizens expect more from their government, they are also more assertive in demanding a greater say in government decision making. Contemporary publics are less deferential to political elites and more likely to challenge the political establishment through citizen action groups and other direct-action techniques" (1998: 225). Persons are more likely to file lawsuits, lobby politicians, and make demands to stop or delay the implementation of policies that they oppose. As a result, more citizens are using litigation to resolve public policy disputes. Indeed, the spread of litigation rooted in citizen discontent with government may be said to have assumed epidemic proportions during the past three decades: "Former Attorney General William French Smith stated that the number of lawsuits in which the U.S. government was a party has increased significantly. In 1970, there were approximately 25,000 cases in which the federal government was sued. In 1980, the number of cases in which the government was sued had risen to 64,000 cases" (Grassley and Pou, 1992: 3). This is especially apparent in the regulatory process. The result is significant delays in policy implementation—usually it takes several years to resolve cases. Litigation is also very expensive for private businesses and federal, state, and local governments, as well as for individuals.

The time, money, and resources diverted to litigation activities have had a major impact on the regulatory process. Implementation of public policies is often delayed by lawsuits filed by individuals, interest groups, businesses, and other organizations that oppose these policies. Agencies must spend considerable time, money, and resources to deal with litigation suits filed against their organizations.

The Changing Regulatory Process:
The Deregulation Environment

When Ronald Reagan was elected president of the United States in 1980, the nation was suffering from a recession and from inflation. Reagan and other conservatives felt that government regulation was excessive and hindered the economic development of the United States. The belief was that if government regulations were reduced or eliminated, businesses and industry could expand, hire more workers, end the recession, and place inflation under control. During the 1980s, the belief was that government regulations hindered the efficiency of the private sector. Reagan and his supporters believed in the idea of New Federalism. Under New Federalism, state and local governments are given an expanded role, while the federal government's regulatory role is reduced. Reagan wanted to transfer more power to the state governments. These powers also included environmental regulatory responsibilities.

Reagan and his supporters believed that federal environmental laws hindered the efficiency and development of business and industry. The state and local governments would decide which government programs they wished to retain and which programs they wished to eliminate. Reagan and other conservatives believed that it was also expensive for business and industry to comply with federal environmental laws. Many conservatives who shared these viewpoints sent financial contributions to Reagan's presidential campaign. After Reagan's election, these conservative supporters expected Reagan to reduce enforcement of federal environmental laws.

During Reagan's first term, the federal government reduced funding for environmental programs such as water pollution, air pollution, hazardous waste management, pesticide regulations, and safe drinking water. Some states were able to expand their environmental regulatory activities. However, other states were unable or unwilling to do so. Some states did not have the financial resources or the personnel to increase their environmental regulatory activities. Environmental lobbies were strong in some states and weak in others. Other states feared that increased enforcement of environmental laws would discourage business and industry from relocating in their states.

After Reagan became president, he appointed Anne Gorsuch Burford as EPA administrator. Burford shared Reagan's views about environmental laws and regulations. During his presidency, Reagan significantly reduced budget appropriations for EPA. Burford transferred many of EPA's personnel to other EPA offices. As a result, many of EPA's personnel left the agency. Burford reduced funding for EPA's enforcement activities programs. Burford also reduced EPA's enforcement of existing federal environmental laws. These federal laws included the Resource, Conservation, and Recovery Act of 1976 (RCRA), the Toxic Substances Control Act of 1976 (TSCA), and Superfund, which had provisions requiring citizen participation activities. During this period, the Reagan administration significantly reduced funds for public participation programs. The reduction of citizen involvement activities involved several actions:

- A complete elimination of the citizen participation budget and all of the staff members associated with public participation activities in the program offices responsible for RCRA and TSCA regulations.

- EPA eliminated the position of Special Advisor to the Administrator for Public Participation.

- All EPA program offices lost the authority to award contracts for public participation workshops. These public workshops were similar to a "Waste Alert" program previously administered under TSCA. Public interest groups and environmental groups previously assumed responsibility for the TSCA program.

- EPA significantly reduced the funding and personnel needed to produce public information materials on hazardous waste. EPA's Office of Public Affairs was the office responsible for producing the public information materials. In the past, this office was a primary source for public information on hazardous waste.

- A stipulation in the proposed 1983 budget significantly reduced the fees that the federal government paid to lawyers for public interest groups. The attorneys worked for public interest groups that filed lawsuits against EPA for failing to enforce federal environmental laws. The reduced fees were allowed under TSCA and several other environmental laws. These regulations were a method of encouraging public participation within the administrative process by persons and groups who could not afford to litigate, but represented potentially significant opinions. Environmental groups used these regulations to acquire a significant advantage when influencing EPA's previous policies on hazardous waste.

During the early 1980s, EPA significantly reduced the human, financial, and material resources that previously sustained its public participation activities. These actions resulted in the dismantling of the administrative structure necessary to maintain the agency's public participation activities. In addition to its public participation programs, the actions taken by EPA also helped to significantly reduce the agency's environmental enforcement activities.

A second method employed by the Reagan administration to hinder environmental regulation was the use of cost-benefit analysis to justify agency activities. On February 17, 1981, Reagan signed Executive Order 12291 into law. This executive order required that federal agencies' proposed activities pass a cost-benefit analysis conducted by the Office of Management and Budget (OMB). The cost-benefit analysis was the standard used to justify environmental standards and health standards. The OMB wanted agencies to implement their policies by using the least costly public policy actions that were available. The cost-benefit analysis mandate required the agencies to justify their programs. In many cases, it was difficult if not impossible for the agencies to employ tangible measurements that could prove that their programs could bring forth results more desirable than the unrestrained operation of private markets. The primary goal of hazardous waste regulation was to make policy decisions that were often costly. Often, agencies such as EPA based their policy decisions on technical and scientific information that was frequently uncertain and subject to dispute. The implementation of EPA's enforcement policies was often expensive and thus conflicted with the OMB's objectives. As a result, the OMB cost-benefit analysis reviews of agency activities made citizen participation activities largely irrelevant. This created a veritable firestorm of protest among environmental groups and stimulated a nationwide movement for stakeholder involvement in the environmental policy process.

The Contemporary Regulatory Process

To summarize the argument to this point: over the past quarter-century the traditional regulatory process has ceased to function as designed. Indeed, it has shown signs of growing dysfunction as it increasingly manifests a strong tendency toward implementation gridlock. The emergence of interest groups and the decline of political parties have helped to increase implementation gridlock. The expansion of congressional subcommittees has given interest groups more opportunities to influence legislation. The interest groups contribute money to the reelection campaigns of subcommittee members in return for supporting legislation favorable to the interest groups. Interest groups also have more access to agency officials than do many individuals. Often, the interest groups are able to see that their interests are protected before a policy is implemented. The interest groups often meet with agency officials behind closed doors and away from public scrutiny. Strong, flexible, enduring relationships among congressional subcommittees, interest groups, and bureaucratic agencies have lessened access and influence for persons who do not belong to these networks.

The emergence of candidate-centered campaigns has weakened the role of political parties in election campaigns. Candidates now have their own organizations that manage their campaign activities. The candidates often hire professional campaign managers to run their campaigns. As a result, there is less management of political campaigns left for party organizations. In this type of election campaign, a candidate-centered campaign is dependent on fund raising. The national political parties contribute money to support the candidates and spend money to support the candidates. However, the financial role of the political parties is not as prominent as in the past. Interest groups and personal contributions now have a more influential financial role in election campaigns than the national political parties do. Candidates receive much of their funding from interest groups and their political action committees. Interest groups now contribute more money to fund congressional campaigns than the national political parties contribute. These activities have increased access and influence of interest groups and have diminished access and influence for citizens who do not belong to these interest groups.

Protests, Litigation, and Gridlock

In the *contemporary* regulatory process, the steps from agenda setting to policy implementation rooted in the *Decide, Announce, and Defend Model* often are proving insufficient to bring closure. That is to say, after the agency decision is promulgated, there is now a strong tendency for stakeholders to organize against implementation—typically producing significant delays and sometimes derailing implementation altogether. Figure 2 presents a model of this process. Thus, for example, the agenda is set when the president, Congress, or an agency decide that there is an existing problem in society that needs a public policy to resolve it. Policy formulation occurs when the new policy is promulgated. This is done through statutes, executive orders, and agency discretion. The agency establishes a program and rules that form the new policy. The agency then holds public hearings as required by law. Citizens express their concerns about the policy during these hearings. The public hearings are the first opportunity in which the public directly becomes involved in the decision making process. Usually by the time that these public hearings occur, the agency has already made an administrative decision to implement the policy. The agency announces its intention to implement the new policy during the hearings. The agency then defends its decision against critics during these hearings.

If all goes well, the new policy is implemented by the agency. The policy has an impact on the existing problem and then the process repeats itself when another problem occurs and the president, Congress, or an agency decides that this new problem needs a policy to resolve it. However, the new policy is often not implemented by the agency. Organizations and citizens who are critical of the new policy react negatively to it. This group reaction to the policy sustains itself for a long time. These groups frequently hold protests and file lawsuits to delay or stop the agency from implementing the policy. These actions lead to policy gridlock. Policy gridlock is expensive and time consuming for the agency.

Policy gridlock occurs with growing frequency and intensity in contemporary American society. Citizens often feel that by the time that public hearings are held, it is too late for them to have any influence on whether a policy is implemented. They are often resentful that they are first consulted about their opinions during the later stages of the policy process. As one observer has noted:

> A major factor in the enactment of the original *Administrative Procedure Act of 1946* and in most subsequent mandates for citizen involvement was the perception that the interests of most citizens were being disregarded by a group of decision making institutions that increasingly affected important aspects of their lives. The pattern of co-optation and domination of administrative agencies by particular clientele groups began during the postwar era. (Rosenbaum, 1978: 45)

In many cases, citizens believe that the agency has already decided to implement the policy regardless of the public's concerns. The citizens feel that often the only way that they can have any impact on an agency's implementation decision is to hold protests and to file lawsuits. Lawsuits are frequently filed to delay and stop a policy from being implemented, which often does happen. What follows is a study of the recent attempt to incorporate citizen participation, as stakeholders, in the regulatory process as an effective means to avoid and or overcome this gridlock.

The Quest for Public Participation

The citizen participation movement began after World War II. The Administrative Procedure Act of 1946 required federal agencies to give public notices that announced upcoming public hearings where citizens could express their concerns about proposed policies that would affect the public. However, many citizens felt that by the time that the public hearings were held, the agencies had already decided to implement the policies.

The citizen participation movement continued into the 1960s after Congress passed several legislative acts that required federal agencies to allow citizen participation in the agencies' decision making activities. The emphasis on citizen participation was focused toward people who benefited from the agencies' programs. This participation is based on the tradition in American democracy that the people who are most affected by a policy should have a voice in creating, implementing, or changing the policy. During the 1960s, the local governments of several major cities established citizen advisory boards that focused on the policies of municipal agencies. These municipal agencies were responsible for handling policies that focused on school systems, police departments, public housing, welfare, and so on. During the 1960s, these local citizen advisory boards were created in response to the urban riots that occurred in many cities.

Citizen participation in environmental decision making activities emerged during the 1970s. This citizen participation occurred because Congress passed several laws that required federal agencies, such as the EPA, to inform people about the effects of proposed environmental policy changes. These laws required agencies such as the EPA to encourage, provide for, and assist public participation activities.

Stakeholder involvement occurs when an agency involves and consults groups of stakeholders who are affected in some way by the agency's policies. Stakeholders include residents, businesses, interest groups, professional groups, elected officials, citizens, and so on. Stakeholder involvement now is taken to include the establishment of citizen advisory boards that provide advice to local, state, and federal governments and their respective agencies regarding public policies.

The Citizen Participation Movement: Changes Since the 1940s

The purpose of the Administrative Procedure Act (APA) of 1946 was to give citizens an opportunity to tell agencies their concerns about policies proposed by government agencies. Citizens would tell the agencies their concerns in public hearings. The APA required agencies to give public notices regarding upcoming public hearing meetings at which citizens could express their concerns regarding proposed policies that would affect the public. At these hearings, each person who wished to speak was granted a limited amount of time to express his or her concerns. Agency officials often would justify the proposed policy using the agency's own experts. The experts would often use technical data and technical language to describe why the policy would be beneficial to the public. Frequently, the hearings were dominated by members of interest groups who were familiar with the agency's policy making processes and often had their own experts. These interest groups often had the financial and legal resources to challenge the agencies' perspectives on any proposed policies. Many citizens felt that by the time that public hearings were held, the agencies had already decided to implement a policy. This is a primary reason that many citizens lost confidence in institutions such as government and business.

A second act of legislation that aided the citizen participation movement was the Freedom of Information Act of 1966 (FOIA). The FOIA enabled persons to request records held by the federal government. The only records exempted from the FOIA were records that the government felt could not be released because of national security considerations. The FOIA enabled many citizens and interest groups to obtain information from the government that otherwise would have been unavailable to them.

The citizen participation movement began during the 1960s after Congress passed several acts of legislation. Congress passed several federal laws that required several federal agencies to allow citizen participation in their decision making activities. These acts included the Economic Opportunity Act (EOA) of 1964, and the Demonstration Cities and the Metropolitan Development Act of 1966 (or Model Cities Act). These acts of legislation were passed as part of President Lyndon Johnson's War on Poverty program to eliminate poverty in the United States—with particular emphasis on urban areas. The EOA created the Office of Economic Opportunity (OEO). The purpose of the OEO was to establish anti-poverty programs in low-income urban areas, work with low-income citizens in urban areas, and help these persons become politically organized. The EOA stated that its community action programs should involve "maximum feasible participation" of the local residents who were affected by its programs (Moynihan, 1969: 3). The Model Cities Act "required the Department of Housing and Urban Development to effect the widespread participation of the community" (Fiorino, 1989: 525). In these acts of legislation, citizen participation was considered a right and not a privilege. The emphasis on participation focused toward persons who were the beneficiaries of these programs. This participation is based on the tradition in U.S. democracy that local citizens who are the persons most affected by a problem or public policy should organize themselves to confront the problem or change the policy.

Citizen Participation in Environmental Policy Issues

During the 1960s and 1970s, public confidence in the government declined significantly. An important consequence of the loss of faith in Washington was an explosion of local activism:

> Since the 1960s, an emerging feature of the American political landscape has been the proliferation of a variety of community-based grassroots organizations designed to bring about a more just and democratic political system for their constituencies through their influence on local political conditions and structures. Together, these grassroots organizations may be viewed as part of a broader social movement whose general goal is "redemocratizing the United States political system." (Cable and Cable, 1995: 117)

According to these scholars, environmental grassroots organizations first emerged in 1978, when the Love Canal Homeowners Committee was organized in response to contamination problems that occurred in the Love Canal neighborhood of Buffalo, New York. Environmental grassroots organizations are neighborhood-based environmental organizations that emerged because of environmental problems that existed within a particular neighborhood. Since 1978, several grassroots environmental organizations have emerged and have had a significant influence on the environmental movement. Norman J. Vig and Michael E. Kraft (1997) mention that "over the past two decades, public concern and support for environmental protection has risen significantly, spurring the development of an expansive array of new policies that substantially increased the government's responsibilities for the environment and natural resources, both domestically and internationally" (1997: 26).

During the 1970s, the citizen participation movement emerged in environmental decision making activities. In 1969, Congress passed the National Environmental Policy Act (NEPA). NEPA required federal agencies, such as the EPA, to inform citizens of the effects of proposed environmental policy changes. The NEPA also required federal agencies to publish an environmental impact statement (EIS) that would identify any proposed actions that may affect the environment. NEPA contained a provision that authorized judicial review of an agency to determine if the agency complied with the EIS requirement. These characteristics enabled the NEPA to serve as a means of popular control instead of executive control over the decisions of the agency. The two provisions allowed environmental factors and noneconomic factors to have a significant role in EPA decision making activities. The NEPA provisions were regarded as a form of citizen participation because they allowed the public to have a voice in the agency's environmental decision making activities.

Environmental interest groups and advocates used the NEPA to oppose and challenge public works projects and private projects that were dependent on federal funds. Environmental advocates and interest groups also made use of sympathetic federal courts to oppose the public and private projects that were dependent on federal funds. As a result, this created a perception that citizen participation in environmental decision making activities was merely a pretext for environmental interest groups to oppose, confront, and file lawsuits to stop projects that they opposed.

A second law that promoted citizen participation in environmental decision making activities was the Federal Water Pollution Control Act of 1972 (FWPCA). Section 101(e) of the FWPCA established "procedures for EPA and the states to create and implement plans for controlling sources of water pollution. This provision directed that public participation shall be encouraged, provided for, and assisted by the EPA administrator and the states" (Fiorino, 1989: 527). This section of the FWPCA is known as the "208 program." The 208 programs established a system to enhance public involvement. The public involvement activities conducted under FWPCA included: newsletters, slide shows, public hearings, and workshops.

Other federal environmental laws that required some type of citizen participation included the TSCA, RCRA, and the Comprehensive Environmental Response, Compensation, and Liability Act of 1980 (CERCLA or the Superfund Act). EPA established the public participation programs. The citizen participation activities included public hearings, newsletters, slide presentations, and public workshops.

Several studies have been conducted that measure the impact that citizen advisory boards have had on environmental policy and management decisions. Frances M. Lynn and George J. Busenberg, after surveying the extant literature conclude:

> The U.S. experience with the use of citizen advisory committees (CACs, also known as citizen advisory boards), for environmental issues, spans at least thirty years. CACs were used primarily by local and state governments. In the past few years, there has been an increased interest in the use of citizen advisory committees by the federal government. An example is DOE's establishment of SSABs [Site Specific Advisory Boards] at several of its nuclear facilities. (1995: 147)

Lynn and Busenberg reviewed fourteen empirical studies of CACs involved in environmental policy decisions dating from 1976 to 1994. These empirical studies included case studies, large-scale surveys, and consultant reports. Lynn and Busenberg's study concluded that the influence of CACs on environmental policy outcomes varied from case to case, with some CACs accomplishing little and other CACs having significant impacts on policy (147).

The increases in citizen participation were largely limited to members of public and environmental interest groups. Environmental and public interest group members were primarily from well-educated, middle income, and upper income socioeconomic groups. These were individuals who had the time, financial resources, and desire to participate in citizen participation activities. Helen Ingram and Steven Rathgeb Smith summarize the situation in this fashion:

> The participation resulting from the new environmental and consumer laws has been limited, for the most part, to the staff-dominated Washington "public interest" groups that have sufficient expertise to overcome barriers to participation erected by the highly esoteric nature of environmental and other forms of judicial and bureaucratic regulatory proceedings. This failure was caused by the inability of participatory politics to cope successfully in a political world dominated by administrators. (1993: 40)

Stakeholder Involvement as Citizen Participation

Stakeholder involvement is defined as *the involvement of individuals and organizations that are affected in some way by a particular public policy decision.* These individuals and organizations will "either receive benefits or bear costs as a result of a policy decision" (Ozawa and Susskind, 1985: 26). Stakeholders include businesses, interest groups, elected officials, professional groups, individual citizens, and others. Activities conducted to influence policy include voting, litigation, demonstrating, lobbying legislators, contacting the news media, and maintaining contact with agency officials.

One example of stakeholder involvement is the citizen advisory board (also known as a citizen oversight committee). These bodies provide advice and recommendations to local, state, and federal governments and their respective agencies on specific public policies. William H. Stewart, Jr. (1976) stated that one benefit of citizen participation is that "a freer exchange of ideas occurs between officials and citizens with the expectation being that perceived differences in thinking between the agency officials and citizens would lessen. Increasing the levels of citizen participation would improve communication between citizens and public administrators" (1976: 22). Stewart also believes that citizen participation is "supposed to meet the need for bona fide links to specific communities (e.g., the elderly, young persons, and other groups of stakeholders) within the total community" (1976: 22).

Citizen advisory boards were first created during the 1960s. The boards were created in response to urban riots that occurred in many American cities during the 1960s. The advisory boards often consisted of individuals who lived in the economically depressed areas affected by the riots, and of officials of a particular local, state, or federal agency. The agencies usually had their own public policy experts. The advisory boards were often completely dependent on the information given to them exclusively by policy experts who worked for the agencies. The agencies often disclosed only the information that was advantageous to them. The citizens often did not have the economic, financial, or political resources to hire their own policy experts who could monitor and evaluate the information revealed to them by agency personnel. The citizens often did not have the policy expertise to verify the accuracy of the information given to them by agency members of an advisory board. As a result, the citizen members often found that although they were members of an advisory board, in many cases, they had little power to influence public policies that affected their communities. Because of these conditions, many of the advisory boards were disbanded after a few years.

There are a variety of concerns regarding the efficacy of citizen advisory boards that arose from the citizen participation efforts of the 1960s (Arnstein, 1969; Cunningham, 1972; Kweit and Kweit, 1981; Moynihan, 1969; Zimmerman, 1972 and 1986). First, the use of citizen advisory boards as a method of stakeholder involvement tends to favor more powerful interest groups. Powerful interest groups are more likely to have their own policy experts. The policy experts of a powerful interest group have a greater ability to evaluate the policy information given to them by a public agency. When an interest group has significant power and resources, it has an increased possibility of influencing a policy. Also, in practice, the involvement of a citizen advisory group often occurs after the policy has *already reached the implementation stage*. Citizen advisory groups can be effective only if they are involved in both the policy formulation and policy implementation stages of the public policy process. Also, the agency could co-opt the members of the advisory group into the agency's organizational culture, and the advisory group's viewpoints might reflect those of the agency more than the groups they represent. It is also possible that citizen advisory boards may not be representative of the populations that they are supposed to represent. Participation on a citizen advisory board requires a significant amount of time and resources. Many persons do not have the time, resources, or inclination to serve on an advisory board. As a result, many of the persons who are able and willing to serve on an advisory board often tend to be highly educated and are from higher income socioeconomic groups. These persons might not be representative of the individuals that a citizen advisory board is supposed to represent. Moreover, citizen advisory boards may have little power to make significant policy changes. Many persons perceive citizen advisory boards as public relations efforts by agencies to justify and legitimize their actions. The advisory boards may be perceived as an agency effort to minimize the problems and actions that originally led to criticism of the agency's actions. Finally, the members of citizen advisory boards may not have the background necessary to understand the scientific and technical issues that are prevalent in policy issues such as environmental policy. There is concern among many agencies that many advisory board members may have difficulty understanding policy issues that require a significant amount of scientific and technical knowledge. A major concern of this study is the extent to which the problems that plagued the citizen participation programs in the past continued to burden the DOE's stakeholder involvement efforts in the 1990s.

Theoretical Framework and Research Design

The theoretical model used to frame the study is presented. This stakeholder involvement model is produced by contemporary efforts to force a more open and inclusive regulatory policy process. It is currently being implemented in a variety of federal agencies, most notably the EPA and DOE. The basic purpose of this study is to investigate how and to what effect the new model is being employed in environmental management and cleanup activities at DOE facilities. Also presented in this chapter are the case methods, basic research questions, and overview of the case being studied for this research project.

Theoretical Framework: The Contemporary Model Revisited

Two models of the regulatory process have been discussed so far in this study. The first model, presented as Figure 1, is the traditional regulatory policy process and features little if any public participation in the process. The second model, presented as Figure 2, and is of the contemporary regulatory process and encompasses the growing tendency toward implementation delay and gridlock. This is also referred to as the Decide-Announce-Defend Model (McCabe, Colglazier, and Fitzgerald, 1993: 250). Both models are currently used by public agencies as a framework for developing and implementing their policies. In recent years public participation activists have promoted a third model: the Stakeholder Involvement Model presented as Figure 3. All figures can be found in Appendix B.[2]

In the Contemporary Regulatory Process Model, an agency decides to create a new policy to resolve a public policy problem that exists within a society. The agency announces to the public that it has already created a new policy and intends to implement it. The agency then holds public hearings and defends its new policy during these public hearings.

This entire process begins when an agency determines that a public policy problem exists within society and believes that a new public policy is needed to resolve this existing problem. The agency creates or formulates a policy to solve the problem. A program is designed and rules are created which comprise this new policy. The agency holds public hearings so that individuals can make comments and express their concerns about the proposed policy to the agency's personnel.

At this point, the Decide-Announce-Defend phase of this model occurs. The agency has created a policy and has already decided to implement it. The agency then holds public hearings because local, state, and federal laws require the agency to do so. The agency tries to defend its new policy during the public hearings. Often, the agency attempts to justify its decision with arguments and technical information. After holding public hearings and comments, the agency often makes an administrative decision to adopt the new policy.

Once a decision has been made to adopt a new policy, there are two possible reactions to it. The first possible reaction is that the public will immediately approve it. If this happens, the agency immediately implements the policy. After a certain amount of time has elapsed, the agency determines if the policy is having an impact on the problem. If the problem is resolved, the agency and society will determine if there is another problem that needs a new public policy to resolve it. The agency sets an agenda, and repeats the process.

The second possible reaction to the new policy is that certain groups will oppose it and will react negatively to it. The groups react by organizing activities to oppose the policy. The groups continue their opposition activities for a sustained time. The groups hold protests, hold press conferences, and file lawsuits against the agency to delay or eliminate the implementation of the policy. The protest and litigation activities result in policy gridlock. Policy gridlock keeps the policy from being implemented by the agency, essentially preventing the administrative process from continuing. Note, in Figure 2, that the two lines that pass through the arrow that points from Administrative Decision to Implementation are placed there to indicate that the process has been terminated because of protests and litigation by groups who are opposed to the policy.

The Stakeholder Involvement Model

The Stakeholder Involvement Model, in its present incarnation as an innovation in federal agency operations, emerged as a result of the recommendations of a report produced by the Federal Facilities Environmental Restoration Dialogue Committee (FFERDC). This was an interim report published in February 1993 by the Keystone Center, a public policy research center based in Keystone, Colorado. This interim report is also referred to as Keystone I. The reason for this name is to distinguish this report from a final report that the Keystone Center and the FFERDC published in April 1996. The FFERDC "was established by EPA and was a national advisory committee comprised of forty representatives from federal, state, tribal, environmental, community, and labor organizations that were stakeholders affected by environmental pollution at government facilities such as those operated by DOE, and the Department of Defense (DOD)" (English et al., 1993: 5). The Keystone I report "recommended improving stakeholder involvement in key federal facility environmental restoration decisions, and that federal agencies establish citizen advisory boards to assist in the decision making process" (English et al., 1993: 5). The citizen advisory boards and improved stakeholder involvement would help to facilitate cleanup efforts at the federal facilities. The Keystone I report states that these actions are necessary to restore public confidence and trust in these agencies. The recommendations of the Keystone I report were a major impetus for the DOE to establish its Site Specific Advisory Board (SSAB) program. The establishment of SSABs and other citizen advisory boards that included stakeholders resulted in the eventual creation of the Stakeholder Involvement Model. According to Mary English and associates:

> Stakeholder involvement mechanisms are meant to augment citizen participation models and to counterbalance trends toward centralized, bureaucratic decision making. They place increased emphasis on two aspects: first, they emphasize that all people (officials as well as lay public) have different and sometimes conflicting "stakes" in the outcomes of a decision making process; and second, they emphasize that stakeholders should be fully involved early on, well before decisions are made. (1993: 4)

The breakdown of the efficacy of the decide-announce-defend model has created a situation in which stakeholders mobilize and force themselves into the process whenever possible. Thus, "the fundamental assumption of this [stakeholder involvement] model is that stakeholders today are inevitably involved in implementation. The idea is to provide for stakeholder involvement that by its nature facilitates rather than inhibits effective policy implementation" (McCabe, Colglazier, and Fitzgerald, 1993: 247). In their explication of stakeholder involvement in agency operations, Amy McCabe, William Colglazier, and Michael Fitzgerald proceed to elaborate in this fashion:

> Early stakeholder involvement broadens the range of alternatives considered and provides early warnings about the costs and benefits of a given approach from the standpoint of those most likely to support or oppose implementation later. It also significantly reduces the basis for later claims by disgruntled stakeholders that they were denied access to the process at a point where their participation could affect the decision. (1993: 247-248)

McCabe, Fitzgerald, and Colglazier also said that:

> Early and meaningful involvement of stakeholders provides the persons making and implementing decisions with an early warning of where key potential opponents are likely to stand later in the process. Perhaps the most significant result is that a sense of trust and confidence in the process—and thus the policy—should [increase] over time based on stakeholder experience rather than on assurances from agency officials. (1993: 248)

The Stakeholder Involvement Model begins when an agency recognizes that a problem exists and that society believes that a new public policy is needed to resolve the problem. The agency sets an agenda to resolve the problem. The agency consults, involves, and accommodates stakeholders. Stakeholders are defined as interest groups, businesses, legislators, individuals, and others who may be affected by the new policy. The agency consults the stakeholders about their opinions on the new policy, attempts to involve the stakeholders, and tries to accommodate the stakeholders' concerns and interests. The stakeholders remain in constant contact with agency officials. The agency makes a decision to formulate a policy to resolve the problem. Stakeholders contact the agency's officials and tell the officials about their reactions to the newly formulated policy.

The agency then designs a program and creates rules that comprise the agency's new policy. The stakeholders inform the agency of their approval or disapproval of the newly designed policy's program and rules. The agency holds public hearings so that individuals can make comments and express their concerns to agency personnel. During the public hearings, members of stakeholder groups also tell the agency about their concerns about the policy. After holding the public hearings, the agency makes an administrative decision to adopt the new public policy. The agency implements the new policy and remains in constant contact with the stakeholders who are affected by it. Unlike the previous model, the Stakeholder Involvement Model places emphasis on consensus building between all the affected stakeholder groups and agency personnel. This consensus building attempts to address all the interests and concerns of the stakeholders and agency officials. Consensus is reached when none of the stakeholders or agency officials can suggest an alternative that better meets the objectives of all of the affected groups (Susskind, 1994: 4).

Once the policy is implemented, the agency may decide to support the new policy. At this stage, the stakeholders may decide to approve the new policy and to support it. After a certain amount of time has elapsed, the agency determines if the policy is having an effective impact on the problem. If the problem is resolved, the agency and society may determine that there is another societal problem that needs a newly formed public policy to resolve it. This action repeats the policy process according to the Stakeholder Involvement Model.

The Differences Between the Models

There are some major differences between the Contemporary Regulatory Process and the Stakeholder Involvement Models. In the Stakeholder Involvement Model, stakeholder groups that are affected by a policy are supposedly less likely to resort to litigation in order to delay or stop a policy that they believe is in conflict with their interests. The perception is that stakeholders are less likely to file lawsuits if they play a role in creating and implementing a policy. *The agency meets with the stakeholder groups that it believes will be affected by the new or changed public policy during each stage of the public policy process.* However, it is often difficult to identify all the groups affected by a policy. During the meetings, the agency and the stakeholder groups discuss their differences and agree to compromise on those differences. During these discussions, the agency and the affected groups discuss their opposing viewpoints, compromise their positions, and reach a consensus. Once a consensus is reached, all of the parties reach a formal agreement. This agreement includes changes in the existing public policy that originally led to the dispute. The bureaucracy then implements a new or revised public policy, which has meet the approval of the agency and the affected groups. The agency meets with the stakeholder groups at every stage of the policy process. In contrast, in the Contemporary Regulatory Process Model, the agency meets with stakeholders only after the policy has reached the implementation stage.

Research Design and Case Methods

The research design involved studying a case involving the use of stakeholder involvement in the regulatory process. The type of stakeholder involvement studied in this project was a *site-specific advisory board* (SSAB). This is the name given to the committees established to provide DOE with advice regarding the environmental cleanup activities at its facilities.

A total of 46 people were interviewed for this research project.[3] A significant number of the participants agreed to be interviewed in exchange for confidentiality. The people were contacted through personal interviews and telephone interviews. These interviews included 23 personal interviews and 38 telephone interviews. Twelve people were interviewed twice. Five people were interviewed three times. The interviews occurred in 1996, 1998, 2000, and 2001. The persons interviewed either worked or lived in the following metropolitan areas: Knoxville, Tennessee; Cincinnati, Ohio; Dayton, Ohio; Miamisburg, Ohio; Chicago, Illinois; Atlanta, Georgia; and Washington, DC. DOE's Oak Ridge Reservation facility is located in the Knoxville metropolitan area and the Fernald site is located in the Cincinnati metropolitan area. Personal interviews were conducted in the Knoxville and Cincinnati metropolitan areas. When personal interviews could not be arranged, telephone interviews were used. Telephone interviews were used to contact persons in the Dayton, Ohio; Chicago, Illinois; Miamisburg, Ohio; and Atlanta, Georgia, metropolitan areas. Telephone interviews were also used to contact persons in the Cincinnati area when personal interviews could not be arranged. Electronic mail was used to communicate with interviewees to ask them additional questions after they had been interviewed in person.

The research activities of this study also involved traveling to Harrison, Ohio, and other towns within the Cincinnati metropolitan area to interview stakeholders who were involved with the Fernald SSAB. The personal interviews were arranged with the key actors involved in the case (e.g., DOE administrators, members of the Fernald SSAB, and Fluor Daniel Fernald [FDF] personnel), who participated in the Fernald SSAB's activities or otherwise had an interest in the Fernald SSAB activities. Fluor Daniel Fernald was the company awarded a contract by DOE to clean up the Fernald site.

The EPA, DOE, and Agency for Toxic Substances and Diseases Registry (ATSDR) administrators interviewed included persons who were assigned to their respective agency's local, regional, and national offices, and who worked with the Fernald SSAB. Telephone interviews were conducted with key actors at the EPA's Region V office in Chicago, Illinois; the Agency for Toxic Substances and Diseases office in Atlanta, Georgia; DOE's regional office in Miamisburg, Ohio; and the Ohio Environmental Protection Agency, Office of Federal Facilities Oversight, Southwest District Office in Dayton, Ohio, to ask them about their involvement with the Fernald Citizens Advisory Board and Fernald's cleanup program.

Case Methods

The research method employed in this study is the single case study. This is a study of the experience of the United States Department of Energy as it sought to apply the Stakeholder Involvement Model to environmental management, remediation, restoration and future land use at its Fernald, Ohio, facility. Informed sources with knowledge about the case and key actors involved in the case were asked open-ended questions in unstructured interviews regarding the following: their degree of satisfaction with their stakeholder involvement agreements; the strengths and weaknesses of these processes; the differences between these processes and the traditional regulatory processes for resolving disputes; and recommendations for improving the processes. Implications and conclusions based on this type of case method study were also discussed. Personal interviews were made with key actors and informed sources. All relevant public law documents, regulations, executive orders, memoranda, documents, agency reports, official statements, and media coverage regarding U.S. DOE adaptation, design, and implementation of stakeholder involvement in environmental restoration and cleanup programs were reviewed. Public hearing transcripts were analyzed to determine what happened, why, and what the effects were in the case.

This research intensively studied why, how, and to what effect the

Stakeholder Involvement Model is employed in contemporary federal agencies, specifically focusing on the U.S. Department of Energy's adoption of the Stakeholder Involvement Model. The unit of analysis is the Fernald SSAB. The investigation of this single-case is justified by the revelatory nature of the study, by its empirical application of a theoretical model, and as a prelude to further inquiry (Yin, 1989: 46-50). A *multiple-case* design would be even more robust, given the expanding use of stakeholder involvement at numerous DOE and DOD sites around the world. But, the extensive resources and time required for multiple-case design, unfortunately, were beyond the means of this research investigator. It is expected, however, that the present endeavor will provide a basis for replication in subsequent multiple-case research.

Stakeholder involvement in administrative decision making is the most recent manifestation of the citizen participation movement. Stakeholder involvement represents a significant attempt to reform the public policy process to counter an increasing tendency toward policy gridlock. A focused inquiry into how the U.S. Department of Energy employs stakeholder involvement yielded important information regarding the nature and impact of expanding citizen participation innovations in the administrative process. Site specific advisory boards are a type of stakeholder involvement that was implemented by DOE at several of its facilities. The present study is limited in scope but important in its implications. Tremendous time, resources, and energy are being spent in operationalizing stakeholder involvement. Close attention, therefore, to how and how well this reform actually works is appropriate and timely.

Basic Research Questions

This research is an intensive study of the DOE attempt to apply the Stakeholder Involvement Model to its environmental management and restoration efforts at its facilities around the nation. The basic research questions for this inquiry are:

> How has the U.S. Department of Energy sought to adopt, design, and implement specific citizen participation innovations, such as site specific advisory boards, into its environmental management and restoration programs?
>
> What conclusions can be drawn from a systematic inquiry into the adoption, design, and implementation of site specific advisory boards in the U.S. Department of Energy's environmental restoration and cleanup programs?
>
> What implications for the public policy process flow from these conclusions?

These questions are answered by conducting an intensive case analysis of the DOE SSAB program in Fernald, Ohio.

Overview of the Fernald Citizens Advisory Board Case

This is the study of a case involving a citizen advisory board established by DOE to provide advice and recommendations to DOE regarding the agency's environmental cleanup efforts at the Fernald Environmental Management Project facility, a DOE facility in Fernald, Ohio, located approximately twenty miles northwest of Cincinnati, Ohio. The Fernald SSAB is the advisory board being studied for this project. In 1951, the construction of the Fernald facility was completed and the facility began its production activities. In 1953, full production operations began at the Fernald facility.

The facility operated from 1951 until 1989, producing uranium products that were used in nuclear weapons. During its years of operation, the plant released large amounts of uranium dust into the atmosphere. Radioactive wastes and other hazardous substances were buried on the plant site, causing the contamination of soil, ground water, and well water in the surrounding area. In 1985, several local residents filed a lawsuit against DOE and the company that operated the Fernald plant. The suit alleged that the radioactive waste and other hazardous substances leaked into the local underground water supply and contaminated the well water used by many residents. The suit also alleged that residents suffered from emotional distress and that their property values had declined because of DOE's actions. In 1989, DOE and the local residents settled the case out of court.

In 1990, several workers at the Fernald plant filed a lawsuit against DOE and National Lead Industries of Ohio, Incorporated—the company that operated the Fernald plant for DOE. The lawsuit alleged that several workers were exposed to radiation at the plant and suffered from increased cancer rates as a result. Many of the workers were alleged to have died from the long-term radiation exposure. The plaintiffs also alleged that the radiation dangers were intentionally hidden from them. In July 1994, DOE and the Fernald workers settled the case out of court.

In December 1992, DOE awarded a contract to a company to manage the cleanup of the facility. In August 1993, DOE established the Fernald Citizens Task Force. The Fernald Citizens Task Force was the former name of the citizen advisory board given responsibility for making recommendations about the cleanup of radioactive and hazardous waste from the Fernald facility. In July 1995, the Fernald Citizens Task Force published a report that described its recommendations for future uses and environmental cleanup activities for the Fernald site. In July 1997, the Fernald Citizens Task Force changed its name to the Fernald Citizens Advisory Board. In this book, the citizen advisory board will be referred to as the Fernald SSAB.

Rationale for the Study

In response to the decline of public confidence and deference and the rise of citizen activism and the interest group society, the federal government is instituting reforms to increase the amount of stakeholder involvement in the formulation of public policy. The increased amount of stakeholder involvement includes the use of citizen advisory boards. Citizen advisory boards are frequently used in the public sector. The citizen advisory boards established by DOE are known as site-specific advisory boards (SSABs). The activities of stakeholder involvement are based on the traditional models of the public policy process. However, the use of SSABs by public administrators may have a major impact on the traditional public policy models and the traditional activities of the regulatory process. The purpose of stakeholder involvement is to help restore confidence, reduce conflict, and increase trust in the government and the public policy process. In many cases, stakeholder involvement is used in the public sector and is based on the democratic ideal that citizen involvement in the democratic process should be maximized to the greatest extent possible. Stakeholder participation by persons and groups in the policy process is also based on this democratic ideal. Because site specific advisory boards were established only a few years ago, little research exists on citizen advisory boards that focus exclusively on environmental activities such as hazardous waste cleanup activities at DOE facilities.

There are several reasons why this case was chosen as a research project. First, this case was the first example in which DOE awarded a contract to a private company to clean up the hazardous and radioactive wastes at one of its nuclear facilities. The first company to ever receive a contract under DOE's newly created Environmental Restoration and Management Contractor (ERMC) program was Fluor Daniel, Incorporated. Fluor Daniel, Incorporated is the company that received a contract from DOE to manage and clean up the Fernald facility. An ERMC is a company awarded a contract by DOE to clean up one of the agency's nuclear facilities. Fernald is a test site for DOE's ERMC program. Second, the Fernald SSAB was the first citizen advisory board to be created by DOE. Because Fernald is a relatively small facility, it was the first DOE site where the agency established a site-specific advisory board. DOE has since established SSABs at several of its nuclear facilities. DOE has undergone intense public scrutiny and has received public pressure to clean up its facilities. This pressure was a factor in DOE's decision to create SSABs at several of its facilities. The agency hopes that the SSABs will help to restore public confidence in the agency. Third, the Fernald site covers 1,050 acres and is one of DOE's smaller facilities. The relatively small size of the Fernald site makes it easier to determine if the environmental cleanup activities at Fernald are being effective. Fernald's smaller size means that cleanup activities may be completed more quickly there than at a larger DOE site, which cover thousands of acres as do DOE's Hanford Reservation, which covers 360,000 acres; the Idaho National Engineering Laboratory, which covers 580,000 acres; and the Savannah River Plant, which covers 192,000 acres.

A study of this case is essential to determine the effectiveness of a site-specific advisory board in overseeing the cleanup activities at a DOE facility. A study of this case is also necessary to determine if the site-specific advisory board has had a positive or negative impact on the cleanup efforts at Fernald.

History of the Department of Energy

The nuclear weapons complex was created during World War II. Intelligence agencies in the United States and Great Britain discovered that Nazi Germany was working to construct nuclear weapons to be used against the Allied nations such as the United States, Great Britain, and the Union of Soviet Socialist Republics (USSR). The Allies feared that if the Nazis developed atomic weapons first, the Nazis would have the opportunity to use these weapons against the Allies and win the war. Consequently, the U.S. decided to establish its own atomic weapons program and try to construct nuclear weapons before the Nazis could do so. In 1942, the United States established the Manhattan Project. The Manhattan Project was the name of the United States government's program to construct nuclear weapons during World War II. Facilities such the Oak Ridge Reservation in eastern Tennessee, the Los Alamos National Laboratory in New Mexico, and the Hanford Reservation in Washington state were constructed to manufacture parts for the atomic bombs that were later dropped on Japan in August 1945.

After World War II, relations worsened between the United States and the USSR. This period marked the beginning of the Cold War. The two countries had been allies during World War II. After the war ended, the USSR and the United States were the only remaining superpowers. The USSR then began constructing nuclear weapons, vowed to spread communism throughout the world, and vowed to overthrow capitalism. Ideologically opposed to communism, the United States vowed to stop, reverse, or at least contain the spread of communism among the world's nations. In response to the USSR's nuclear weapons building program, the U.S. expanded its nuclear weapons complex. During the late 1940s and early 1950s, nuclear facilities such as the Rocky Flats Plant in Colorado and the Savannah River plant in South Carolina and others were constructed as part of DOE's Nuclear Weapons Complex, which at its peak consisted of sixteen major facilities in thirteen states. These facilities consisted of weapons testing facilities, national laboratories, 'warehouses, and weapons production facilities.

History of DOE's Nuclear Weapons Complex

After the war, the U.S. Congress acted to place atomic energy and nuclear weapons under civilian control. In 1946, Congress passed the Atomic Energy Act of 1946 that created the Atomic Energy Commission (AEC). The AEC's mission was to administer and regulate both commercial and military uses and production of nuclear power. The AEC administered the government-operated nuclear facilities from 1946 until 1974. In 1974, Congress abolished the AEC, in 1975, the federal government created two new agencies to replace the AEC. One of these agencies was the Nuclear Regulatory Commission (NRC). The NRC's mission was to license and regulate the civilian uses of nuclear power. The civilian uses of nuclear power consist primarily of commercially operated nuclear power plants. The second federal agency created to replace the AEC was the Energy Research and Development Administration (ERDA). The AEC's research operations were transferred to the ERDA. In 1977, Congress created the Department of Energy. DOE was established as a federal department with cabinet-level status. After Congress created DOE, DOE assimilated the ERDA. DOE also assimilated two other independent agencies, the Federal Energy Commission and the Federal Power Commission. DOE's primary mission was to manage its complex of nuclear weapons facilities and to create nuclear weapons for the military.

In the past, the AEC and DOE were not open about the activities at their facilities. The agencies justified this practice because of national defense and security considerations. The main purpose of DOE was to develop and produce nuclear weapons for the military. As a result, much of DOE's work was classified and was not subject to public scrutiny. During this period, many persons agreed with this policy and believed that it was justified by the existence of the Cold War with the USSR.

DOE also felt that its unique mission and the Atomic Energy Act of 1946 allowed the agency to be exempt from federal, state, and local environmental laws. As a result, DOE buried large amounts of radioactive and hazardous materials at its nuclear facilities. In many cases, the radioactive and hazardous wastes contaminated local water supplies. DOE also released large amounts of radioactive and hazardous wastes into the atmosphere. DOE felt that national security considerations necessary for producing nuclear weapons took priority over issues such as safe working conditions and obeying federal and state environmental laws. Because of these actions, the facilities in DOE's nuclear weapons complex became polluted with large amounts of radioactive and hazardous wastes that were produced, buried, and stored at these facilities. These large amounts of wastes are dangerous to the health of DOE employees who work in the facilities and residents who live near DOE's facilities.

The Legislative Significance of the Federal Facilities Compliance Act of 1992

Between 1972 and 1980 the Congress enacted major legislation creating a complex web of environmental regulation. Among these were the Resource Conservation and Recovery Act of 1976 (RCRA), the Federal Water Pollution Control Act of 1972 (FWPCA), the Clean Water Act of 1972 (CWA), and the Comprehensive Environmental Response, Compensation, and Liability Act of 1980 (CERCLA or Superfund Act). It soon became apparent that federal facilities were among the most polluted sites covered by these statutes and tended to be the worst violators—especially those run by the DOD and DOE. Well into the 1980s, a battle raged among environmentalists, the EPA, and DOE as to whether or not government agencies were subject to such regulation.

In 1984, a federal court decision ruled that DOE was not exempt from obeying federal, state, and local environmental laws. The federal court decision was *Legal Environmental Assistance Foundation, Incorporated v. Hodel* (586 F. Suup. 1163; 20 ERC [BNA] 2246; 14 ELR 20425). In 1983, local newspapers in Knoxville, Tennessee, and Oak Ridge, Tennessee, reported that DOE's Oak Ridge Reservation facility had released mercury into the East Poplar Creek for several years. The East Poplar Creek is located near DOE's Y-12 Plant, which is part of DOE's Oak Ridge Reservation facility located approximately thirty miles northwest of Knoxville, Tennessee. The media's reports resulted in two environmental interest groups, the Legal Environmental Assistance Foundation and the National Resources Defense Council, filing a lawsuit against DOE in U.S. District Court for the Eastern District of Tennessee, Northern Division in Knoxville. Donald Hodel was named as the plaintiff since he was the current DOE Secretary. In the lawsuit, the environmental interest groups alleged that DOE was not exempt from obeying federal environmental laws. DOE argued that the Atomic Energy Act of 1946 exempted the agency from obeying state and federal environmental laws. On April 13, 1984, the federal judge in the U.S. District Court in Knoxville ruled that the Atomic Energy Act of 1946 did not exempt DOE from obeying federal environmental laws such as the Resource Conservation and Recovery Act, the Clean Water Act, and the Federal Water Pollution Control Act Amendments. The judge also ruled that DOE "had violated its national pollutant discharge permit"

(Environmental Law Reporter, May 1984: 10209) while operating the Y-12 plant. This permit was granted to DOE under the Federal Water Pollution Control Act. The judge ruled that DOE was not exempt from obeying state environmental laws. DOE decided not to appeal the court's decision.

Because of the federal court decision, other environmental groups and citizens' groups began filing lawsuits against DOE. The lawsuits also accused DOE of violating federal environmental laws. In many of these cases, the courts ruled against DOE, while DOE settled other cases. The litigation associated with the lawsuits became expensive for DOE.

In many cases, the federal courts ruled in favor of DOE and stated that the agency was exempt from obeying federal, state, and local environmental laws because of federal *sovereign immunity*. An example of this dispute is the case of *U.S. Department of Energy v. Ohio* (112 S.Ct. 1627 [1992]). In 1986, the state of Ohio filed a lawsuit against DOE. The suit alleged that DOE violated state and federal environmental laws while operating the Fernald facility. DOE stated that since it was a federal agency, sovereign immunity exempted DOE from obeying federal and state environmental laws. The suit was appealed to the U.S. Supreme Court, which heard the case. On April 21, 1992, the Supreme Court ruled in a 6 to 3 vote that "Congress had not explicitly exempted federal facilities" (Congressional Quarterly Almanac, 1992: 261) from obeying federal and state environmental laws.

During 1992, the House Congressional Committee on Energy and Commerce held congressional hearings and listened to testimony that described the inability of federal agencies to reach agreements regarding environmental cleanup activities at federal facilities. The congressional committee's examination of hazardous waste compliance problems at federally operated facilities had occurred for several years. The committee received testimony from "the GAO [General Accounting Office], EPA officials, state attorney generals, state environmental agencies, state legislators, and environmental organizations that federally operated facilities present some of the worst RCRA compliance problems" (United States Code Congressional and Administrative News, 1992: 1288). The committee found: "Two federal agencies, DOE and DOD, together generate approximately 20 million tons of hazardous and radioactive wastes annually" (United States Code Congressional and Administrative News, 1992: 1288). The committee also noted that on May 16, 1988, while campaigning for president in Seattle, Washington, President George Herbert Walker Bush said that there were serious environmental compliance problems at federal facilities and that federal agencies were some of the worst environmental polluters in the country. Bush said that the federal government should abide by environmental laws that it requires others to obey.

The GAO conducted several investigations that led the agency "to conclude that the federal government has been slow to comply with hazardous waste management laws. In a May 1986 report, the GAO reviewed compliance with the RCRA at 17 federal agencies in 12 states and found that almost half of the 72 hazardous waste handlers inspected by EPA were cited for violations" (United States Code Congressional and Administrative News, 1992: 1288-1289). In its investigation, the GAO found that: "Data provided by the EPA to the committee during the One hundred and Second Congress indicate that DOE and DOD compliance rates still lag behind those of private industry, ranging from 10% to 15% lower than the compliance rates of private industry" (United States Code Congressional and Administrative News, 1992: 1289).

Congressional committees at the same time were confronted with mounting evidence of tremendous levels of DOE noncompliance with environmental regulations. For example:

> The House Subcommittee on Oversight and Investigations and the Subcommittee on Transportation and Hazardous Materials received testimony from EPA and state environmental officials regarding their frustration with attempts to obtain compliance with hazardous waste regulations at DOE facilities such as the Fernald plant in Ohio; the Rocky Flats, Colorado facility, and the Hanford Reservation in Washington state. (United States Code Congressional and Administrative News, 1992: 1290)

Later, congressional hearings revealed that DOE facilities such as Fernald and Rocky Flats had a long history of environmental violations and attempts to conceal those violations. On June 6, 1989, approximately 70 agents from the Federal Bureau of Investigation (FBI) and the EPA entered the Rocky Flats facility. The agents who entered the facility had a search warrant. This action was part of a criminal investigation into alleged environmental violations at the Rocky Flats facility. Testimony before the Subcommittee on Transportation and Hazardous Materials also revealed that:

> DOE admitted that, since 1951, the agency knew of pollution problems at Fernald and conceded that Fernald released more than 300,000 pounds of radioactive uranium particles into the air during its years of operation—even though the contractor operating the plant warned DOE of the danger. Instead of acting on the contractor's warnings, federal officials covered up the problem and ordered the contractor not to put future warnings in writing. (United States Code Congressional and Administrative News, 1992: 1290)

Additional testimony revealed that three wells near the Fernald plant had been contaminated. Four large storage silos at the Fernald site were "filled with radium and other radioactive materials that were mixed with hazardous wastes. The radium and the radioactive and hazardous wastes had leaked from the silos into the soil for several years and may still be contaminating the area surrounding the Fernald site" (United States Code Congressional and Administrative News, 1992: 1290-1291).

The governors of several states also testified before the committee and subcommittees and told the congressional members of the problems their states faced in getting federal agencies to clean up federal facilities in their respective states, and getting the agencies to obey state and federal environmental laws. On October 14, 1988, the Subcommittee on Transportation, Tourism and Hazardous Materials, House Energy and Commerce Committee held hearings on DOE's pollution problems at Fernald. Three members of the Fernald Residents for Environmental Safety and Health (FRESH), an environmental watchdog group comprised of residents who lived near the Fernald plant, testified before the subcommittee. One person who testified was Lisa Crawford. Lisa Crawford,

who was the president of FRESH and eventually became a member of the Fernald Citizens Advisory Board. The members of FRESH told of their experiences and concerns with environmental pollution at the Fernald site to the subcommittee members.

The Subcommittee on Transportation and Hazardous Materials held hearings on March 3 and March 10, 1988. The subcommittee heard testimony from the state attorney generals from Ohio, Maine, and Colorado; representatives from GAO, EPA, Department of Justice (DOJ), DOE, and DOD; and witnesses representing state agencies, environmental organizations, and citizen groups (United States Code Congressional and Administrative News, 1992: 1304). During the sessions of the One Hundred and First Congress, the subcommittee held hearings on March 14 and April 12, 1989. Testimony was heard from the state attorney generals from Colorado, Idaho, Nevada, and Washington state; state environmental officials from Kentucky, New York, North Carolina, Ohio, and Pennsylvania; representatives from EPA, DOE, DOD, and DOJ; and representatives of the Sierra Club, National Audubon Society, National Resources Defense Council (United States Code Congressional and Administrative News, 1992: 1304).

Various groups and officials testified before congressional committees and subcommittees to persuade Congress to enact a federal law that required federal agencies to obey federal and state environmental laws. The testimonies of federal officials, state officials, federal agencies, state agencies, environmental interest groups, the National Conference of State Legislators, and residents; the conflicting rulings of different federal district courts when determining if federal agencies were exempt from obeying state and federal environmental laws; and the Supreme Court's decision in the *Department of Energy v. Ohio* case influenced Congress to enact a law requiring federal agencies to obey state and federal environmental laws. Congress realized that state and local governments were excluded as stakeholders from DOE's decision making process.

In order to rectify the situation, Congress passed the Federal Facilities Compliance Act (FFCA) of 1992 (PL 102-386) on October 6, 1992. President George Herbert Walker Bush signed the FFCA into law on the same date. The purpose of the FFCA is to "bring all federal facilities into compliance with federal and state hazardous waste laws" (U.S. DOE, January 1993: I-71). The FFCA also waives federal sovereign immunity from the federal and state hazardous waste laws and allows the EPA to impose fines and penalties for violating those laws. The FFCA includes provisions concerning DOE's compliance with RCRA land disposal restrictions (LDRs) for mixed waste (waste that contains both hazardous and radioactive components). Sovereign immunity is waived for facilities that are subject to an LDR administrative or judicial order agreement, or permits as of October 6, 1992. Facilities are not subject to fines or penalties as long as they remain in compliance with the order or agreement. For facilities that are not subject to an LDR order or agreement, fines and penalties for LDR violations are delayed for three years as long as the mixed waste is managed in compliance with all other FFCA requirements (U.S. DOE, January 1993: I-71).

Mixed wastes are generated and stored at many of DOE's facilities.

Historically, DOE has stored large amounts of wastes at its facilities because of limited options for waste disposal and the treatment of wastes. The FFCA prohibits DOE and other federal facilities from storing hazardous wastes at their facilities for more than a year. However, the FFCA allows these facilities to extend the storage time without facing fines or penalties for violations of hazardous waste laws. During this extended period, DOE and other federal facilities are not subject to fines as long as they remain in compliance with the RCRA land disposal restrictions' orders, permits, or agreements. The FFCA requires these federal facilities to develop new site-specific compliance plans within a three-year period.

The FFCA also required DOE to develop a detailed mixed waste inventory report within 180 days after October 6, 1992, the date that the FFCA law was passed. DOE was required to send this mixed inventory report to the governor of each state where DOE has a facility. The mixed waste inventory report was to describe the volume of mixed waste, characteristics of the mixed waste, existing capability for treatment, and technologies available for waste treatment and disposal. In addition, DOE is to update the inventory information on a yearly basis. DOE must also create Site Treatment Plans (STPs) for creating the necessary capacity to treat mixed waste at its facilities. The STPs are to be developed for each DOE site where mixed waste is generated or stored. Each of the STPs is to serve as a guide for implementing methods of waste treatment.

The passage of the FFCA strengthened the cases of state governments and the EPA when they file lawsuits against DOE for failure to obey state and federal environmental laws. The law also enabled the EPA and state governments to impose fines and compliance orders against DOE and other federal departments for failure to obey federal environmental laws, especially provisions of the RCRA of 1976. One social scientist, who wishes to remain anonymous and is familiar with environmental policy and DOE operations, commented that:

> Laws such as RCRA and CERCLA required the federal government to establish public participation programs. DOE was exempted from complying with local, state, and federal environmental laws until Congress passed the Federal Facilities Compliance Act of 1992. This happened because the maintenance of national security received priority over obeying environmental laws. (Personal interview, Oak Ridge, Tennessee, April 19, 1996)

In 1989, DOE established the Office of Environmental Restoration and Waste Management (EM). This office is responsible for DOE's cleanup activities at its nuclear weapon complex facilities.

DOE's Justifications for Establishing Citizen Advisory Boards

In February 1989, the House Armed Services Committee's Subcommittee on Procurement and Military Nuclear Systems Procurement held a hearing to listen to testimony about the procedures that DOE used to conduct cleanup and restoration activities at its nuclear facilities. The hearing included testimony from DOE, GAO, and the National Resources Defense Council. In April 1989, the governors of ten states sent the Secretary of Energy a letter that called for decisive federal action in establishing a comprehensive national program for the cleanup of all of DOE's facilities. The proposal made by the governors contained a discussion of several main elements for a national program. One of the elements was the need to develop a national priority system for ensuring that appropriate priorities for DOE cleanup activities were developed (Keystone II, 1996: C1).

The EPA administrator also sent the director of OMB a letter that discussed the concerns of several federal departments. The letter said that there was a need to establish environmental priorities and funding priorities for cleaning up federal facilities. In the letter, the EPA administrator proposed convening a formal dialogue on the issues concerned with the establishment cleanup priorities for federal facilities. In July 1989, additional support for a national dialogue on priority setting for federal facility cleanups occurred when 49 state attorney generals sent an open letter to the U.S. House of Representatives. The letter said that the attorney generals supported a dialogue on federal facilities' cleanup issues as a method of strengthening relationships between state and federal governments (Keystone II, 1996: C1).

In February 1991, the U.S. Congress Office of Technology Assessment published a report titled *Complex Cleanup: The Environmental Legacy of Nuclear Weapons Production.* This report recommended that DOE establish citizen advisory boards to enhance the environmental cleanup processes at its facilities. The report also recommended that DOE create a structure that establishes public participation in important cleanup and technical decisions. This policy initiative could be executed by Congress establishing citizen advisory boards at each of DOE's sites. Congress would provide the citizen advisory boards with full-time technical staff. The staff would "provide technical and environmental policy advice to DOE, EPA, the Department of Health and Human Services (HHS), and state governments" (Scrimgeour and Hanson, April 1993: 9). The advisory boards could examine the following issues: environmental cleanup; risks to public health; and the disposal and storage of radioactive wastes and hazardous wastes. Because of the citizen advisory boards' access to technical support staff, information, and other necessary resources, effective participation in environmental cleanup decision making activities could occur. As a result, the advisory boards could promote "openness, public trust, and cooperation among the interested stakeholders. Currently, openness, public trust, and cooperation do not exist between the interested stakeholders and the federal agencies" (Scrimgeour and Hanson, April 1993: 9).

In April 1992, EPA established the Federal Facilities Environmental Restoration Dialogue Committee (FFERDC) as an advisory committee under the Federal Advisory Committee Act to address federal environmental cleanup issues (Keystone I, 1993: 4). The FFERDC was also known as the Keystone Committee and will be referred to as the Keystone Committee hereafter. The primary force behind the creation of the Keystone Committee was informal information and consensus-building discussions that were initiated in 1991. These informal discussions focused on exchanging information on the various approaches that federal agencies were using to set priorities for cleaning up their facilities (Keystone I, 1993: 5).

The purpose of the Keystone Committee was to provide a forum for identifying and refining issues related to environmental restoration facilities at federal facilities. The Keystone Committee was intended to be a forum for the exchange of information and ideas among persons representing organizations and agencies that had an interest in or responsibility for managing or overseeing environmental cleanup activities at federal facilities (Keystone I, 1993: 4). The Keystone Committee's goal was to reach a consensus on policy recommendations intended to improve the process "by which federal facility environmental cleanup decisions are made in such a fashion that these decisions reflect the priorities and concerns of all stakeholders" (Keystone II, 1996: vii). The EPA Deputy Administrator appointed 40 persons to the Keystone Committee. The members of the Keystone Committee included persons from the following agencies and organizations: "EPA, USDA [Department of Agriculture], DOI [Department of the Interior], DOE, DOD (and its military services), the National Oceanic and Atmospheric Administration (NOAA), and the Agency for Toxic Substances and Disease Registry (ATSDR); state, tribal, and local governments; and numerous other nationally, regionally, and locally based environmental community, environmental justice, labor, and Native American organizations" (Keystone II, 1996: viii). The members of the Keystone Committee did not participate in the dialogue activities as official representatives of their respective organizations, but participated as individual citizens.

In February 1993, the Keystone Committee released the *Interim Report of the Federal Facilities Environmental Restoration Dialogue Committee: Recommendations for Improving the Federal Facilities Environmental Restoration Decision making and Priority-Setting Processes.* EPA, DOE, and the Keystone Center (TKC) published this report. The Keystone Center is a "non-profit environmental conflict management organization located in Keystone, Colorado. In late 1990, EPA asked TKC to convene a policy dialogue on federal facility environmental restoration priority-setting" (Keystone II, 1996: C1). The staff members of TKC conducted "discussions and interviews with stakeholders to determine if there was enough support for the idea of a national environmental policy dialogue, to determine which specific environmental policy issues should be the focus of the proposed dialogue" (Keystone II, 1996: C1), and to decide which individuals should participate in the proposed dialogue.

The Keystone Committee was created under the Federal Advisory Committee Act (FACA) of 1972 (PL-92-463) which was passed by Congress on October 6, 1972. The FACA is a law that provides operational guidelines to federal advisory boards, committees, and other groups that are created by federal agencies to provide advice to the federal government. The FACA "requires agencies to follow certain formalized procedures including chartering and maintaining balanced memberships, providing public notices of meetings, and holding meetings open to the public" (Keystone II, 1996: 53-54).

In addition to the FACA's statutory requirements, federal agencies that establish advisory boards "must comply with their own implementing regulations, with the administrative guidelines of the U.S. General Services Administration (GSA), and with getting the approval of the Office of

Management and Budget (OMB)" (Keystone II, 1996: 54). The FACA also enables the chartering agency "with the authority to adjourn meetings and approve agendas—powers that some communities believed could be abused" (Keystone II, 1996: 54). Requirements also stipulate that the advisory board meetings must be open to the public and that notices regarding the time and location of advisory board meetings must be published in the *Federal Register*.

After the release of the Keystone I report, the Clinton administration placed limitations on the creation of new FACA committees. In response to this action, federal agencies have approached advisory boards in at least two ways: as Technical Review Committees and as Restoration Advisory Boards. DOD expanded on the approach it had taken with its Technical Review Committees (TRCs). TRCs were a predecessor to DOD's Restoration Advisory Boards (RABs). RABs are citizen advisory boards established by the Defense Department to advise the agency on its environmental cleanup activities at DOD military bases (Keystone II, 1996: 54). As of January 1996, DOD had established approximately 200 RABs at its bases (Keystone II, 1996: 48). At that time, DOD had not charted its RABs as federal advisory committees. In September 1996, DOE created a single FACA charter that applied to all of its SSABs (Keystone II, 1996: 54).

The Keystone I report stated that there was a deep distrust and a lack of public confidence in DOE. The report described several strategies for including stakeholders such as local residents, environmental interest groups, local governments, state governments, public interest groups, Native American tribes, low-income communities, and minorities in the processes of making government environmental cleanup decisions.

Keystone I recommended that DOE establish citizen advisory boards to assist the agency in its environmental cleanup activities and to restore trust between DOE and the public. The citizen advisory boards that were created by DOE are known as site specific advisory boards (SSABs). DOE began establishing SSABs at its facilities in 1993 when advisory boards were established at the following sites: the Fernald Environmental Management Project, Fernald, Ohio; Hanford Reservation, Washington state; Idaho National Engineering Laboratory, Idaho; Rocky Flats Plant, Golden, Colorado; and the Savannah River Plant, South Carolina. As of 1997, DOE had established SSABs at a total of 13 of its facilities. These additional facilities are: Los Alamos National Laboratory, New Mexico; Monticello Millsite, Utah; Nevada Test Site, Nevada; Oak Ridge Reservation, Tennessee; Paducah Plant, Kentucky; Pantex Plant, Texas; St. Louis Airport Site, Missouri; and the Sandia National Laboratories, New Mexico. In January, 1996, DOE published a document called *Site Specific Advisory Board Guidance.* This book provides procedures and guidelines for creating and operating SSABs. The Keystone I report also indicated that studies of citizen advisory groups showed that such groups can improve the decision making process in the following ways:

1. Provide a setting for direct, regular contact between agencies and a diverse set of stakeholders.

2. Provide a forum for stakeholders and agencies to understand the competing needs and requirements of the government and the affected communities.

3. Provide a forum for discussing citizen issues and concerns, thus enabling the development of a more complete and satisfactory plan or decision.

4. Enable citizen review and an evaluation of plans and their technical adequacy to allow more opportunities for public participation than is possible in most single opportunity public participation efforts such as public hearings.

5. Permit a more detailed consideration of issues to occur than is possible as a result of the minimum legal requirements identified in various state and federal laws—e.g., public hearings.

6. Broaden the consideration of issues to include the values of stakeholders as well as facts regarding the environmental cleanup process. (Colorado Center for Environmental Management, 1993: 9-10)

Keystone I also encouraged DOE and other federal agencies to be more open in releasing information about their activities to the public. Keystone I encourages all federal agencies to establish citizen participation policies and to make sure that public participation occurs early, frequently, and continuously throughout the decision making process. The report also mentions strategies for dealing with shortages of funds that may occur when the budget appropriations of federal agencies are reduced. This action has happened to DOE in recent years. These strategies are designed to assure that the interests of the stakeholders are not shortchanged and are also designed to reduce the possibility of disputes occurring between the advisory boards and the federal agency over cleanup enforcement disputes.

The Keystone I report stated that some stakeholders criticized the method in which federal agencies released information regarding its cleanup programs. One criticism was that stakeholders felt that they were consulted late in the decision making process after the federal agencies had already ended their investigative work before beginning the cleanup activities. A second criticism listed in Keystone I was that stakeholders perceived that their requests for information were treated by federal agency officials as burdensome and an obstruction to management instead of an entitlement of citizenship. A third criticism was that the release of agency information and exchange efforts were inconsistent between federal agencies and between federal facilities.

The most important recommendation of the Keystone I report was the establishment of citizen advisory boards such as SSABs and RABs at federal facilities. The Keystone I report recommended that federal agencies establish citizen advisory boards to improve the distribution of information on federal facilities' cleanup activities, to provide independent policy advice, and to provide technical advice to federal agencies regarding cleanup decisions (Keystone II, 1996: 47). The report advised that the establishment of advisory boards might increase trust and public confidence in the agencies. Therefore, Keystone I recommended that agencies establish advisory boards at major federal facilities. Thus, as of 1997, DOE had established advisory boards at 13 of its facilities. As of January 1996, DOD had established about 200 RABs at its military bases.

After the release of Keystone I, the Keystone Committee held eight regional briefings to discuss the Keystone I report and to receive comments. At the regional briefings, many people stated that the viewpoints of local governments and the environmental justice community were not adequately included in the Keystone I report's recommendations. In response to these concerns, the Keystone Committee added new members to the committee during the fall of 1993 and during January 1995. This increase in membership brought the Keystone Committee's total membership to 50 individuals (Keystone II, 1996: C3).

In April 1996, the Keystone Committee released the *Final Report of the Federal Facilities Environmental Restoration Dialogue Committee: Consensus Principles and Recommendations for Improving Federal Facilities Cleanup.* (Keystone II). DOE, EPA, and the Keystone Center also published this report. The Keystone II Report recommended that DOE and other federal agencies use citizen advisory boards such as SSABs to involve the public in the decision making processes for making environmental cleanup decisions. The SSABs are also encouraged to network and share information, particularly technical and legal information with each other. These practices may lead to quicker solutions and may save more time and financial expenses than when the SSABs work alone. Keystone II recommended that the SSABs place notices of upcoming meetings in the *Federal Register.* The SSABs also place notices of upcoming meetings in local newspapers to inform the public about their activities, as they believe that placing notices in local newspapers is more likely to reach the public than placing them in the *Federal Register.*

The Keystone II Report stated that federal agencies must do a more effective job of assuring that low-income persons, persons of color, and members of local governments are adequately represented in their stakeholder involvement programs. The report encouraged federal agencies to assist minorities, Native Americans, and low-income communities in developing the technical and analytical expertise that is necessary to become effective participants in the stakeholder involvement programs. The policy information requirements of minority and low-income communities may, in some cases, be more extensive than the policy information requirements of other communities, such as the regulatory community. Examples of policy information requirements might include environmental impacts resulting from proposed cleanup actions, employment opportunities, and the development of businesses.

The report mentioned that federal agencies sometimes do not include local government officials early enough in the cleanup process to make sure that local government officials can identify matters of concern regarding environmental cleanups, federal facility layoffs, and the closure of federal facilities. The Keystone II Report stated that in some cases, the public perceives the community involvement programs to be public-relations efforts enacted by the agencies to present the agencies' actions in a favorable manner and to minimize or hide problems. The report indicated that a limited number of federal agency personnel have expertise in including persons in stakeholder involvement programs and in the decision making process.

Keystone II also stated that Freedom of Information Act (FOIA) exemptions are applied by some federal agencies in an extremely broad and cautious mode. Sometimes, these exemptions are used to justify withholding documents from the public. An entire document may be withheld from release because portions of the document are confidential. However, other portions of the document may be eligible for release to the public.

The Keystone II report encouraged federal agencies to make extensive use of the news media and computer networks such as the Internet and the World Wide Web. In addition, the report encourages federal agencies to publish a newsletter that focuses on the issues involved in federal facility cleanups. The report recommends that EPA develop a public stakeholders' guide to federal facilities' cleanup activities. The guide could be a video, a written document, or some other type of media that would describe basic information about the Keystone Committee's recommendations and the cleanup processes for federal facilities. The guide would also describe information concerning regulatory and legal processes for initiating cleanup activities.

The Keystone reports were the result of unprecedented interagency and environmental group cooperation to confront the monumental problems facing DOD and DOE facilities in environmental management and remediation. This cooperation was, to be sure, fostered by the Clinton administration's emphasis on the environment and the congressional prod to federal agencies provided by the FFCA.

Other Reasons for the Establishment of DOE's SSAB Program

The FFCA and the Keystone initiative were major factors impelling the DOE to move to the Stakeholder Involvement Model, but other factors were also involved. For example, a social scientist who has extensively studied citizen participation in environmental regulation observed that:

> A primary reason that DOE established the SSAB program was the expenses from lawsuits and settlements resulting from litigation against DOE. Many local residents, environmental interest groups, state governments, and nuclear workers have filed lawsuits against DOE. There was publicity regarding DOE's releasing radioactive and hazardous materials into the atmosphere, burying radioactive and hazardous material at its facilities, and polluting ground water and surface water with its radioactive and hazardous wastes. (Personal interview, Oak Ridge, Tennessee, April 19, 1996)

The expenses resulting from litigation encouraged DOE to establish citizen participation programs such as SSABs. The belief was that persons would be more likely to support policies that they helped create and implement and are not as likely to file lawsuits against the agency. It was hoped that the establishment of SSABs would help to restore public confidence in the agency.

Another reason for the establishment of the SSAB program was widespread and growing negative publicity. DOE received a significant amount of negative media publicity as a result of the lawsuits filed against the agency and of the revelation that DOE released radioactive and hazardous materials into the atmosphere and buried millions of tons of radioactive and hazardous waste at its facilities. Monitoring indicated that radioactive and hazardous wastes often seeped into and contaminated surface water and ground water. DOE was slow to respond to many of these allegations and in many cases denied them. Consequently, DOE has lost public trust and confidence among many individuals. In the past, DOE did not publicly discuss the discharging of waste into the environment. It was only after the media revealed them that this practice began to change. The agency hopes that the establishment of the SSAB program will help restore public confidence and trust in DOE.

A third reason was that DOE was downsizing many of its operations. This meant layoffs at facilities such as Hanford and Oak Ridge. The employee layoffs at DOE occurred as a result of the fall of communism. The fall of Communism led to the fall of the Berlin Wall in 1989, the breakup of the USSR in 1991, and the fall of Communist governments in several Eastern European countries during the early 1990s. The breakup of the Soviet Union left the United States as the world's only remaining superpower. As a result, many Americans believed that it was no longer necessary for the United States to continue maintaining a huge military force and a large number of nuclear weapons. The federal government closed many military bases. Many defense contractors and DOE facilities laid off thousands of workers. In order to remain in operation, some defense contractors and DOE facilities have been converting some of their facilities to develop and produce items that can be used in the civilian world. Some DOE research laboratories are now considering changing their mission to doing research on peaceful uses of nuclear power or on products that can be used in the civilian world. Because the military has been reduced in size and the former Soviet Union is currently not seen as a future military threat to the United States, fewer nuclear weapons are needed by the military. Therefore, fewer nuclear weapons are produced and the DOE has laid off many of its workers. After the fall of communism, DOE had its budget appropriations significantly reduced by Congress. The United States and the former Soviet republics of Russia, Belarus, the Ukraine, and Kazakhstan are also trying to destroy some of their nuclear weapons. DOE currently has fewer personnel and resources than in the past. DOE hopes that the SSAB program will help the agency more efficiently use its remaining personnel and resources. The agency believes that it is less expensive and more efficient for DOE to consult with a citizen advisory board to help speed up the cleanup activities at its facilities.

A fourth reason was that many members of Congress wanted to significantly reduce DOE's budget and eventually eliminate DOE as a government agency. For example, an article in the *Cincinnati Enquirer* stated that, in April 1993, the Clinton administration announced that the amount of money appropriated to the Fiscal Year 1994 budget for DOE's cleanup activities would be reduced by $70 million. The Clinton administration had appropriated $300 million in the Fiscal Year 1994 budget for Fernald's cleanup activities, which was more than the $295.5 million allocated in the 1993 budget but significantly less than the $365 million originally requested by DOE to continue its cleanup activities at Fernald (Barton, October 1, 1993: C2).

The *Enquirer* article also mentioned that, in September 1993, the Senate voted 89 to 10 to approve an energy-appropriations bill that reduced environmental cleanup funding by $600 million below the amount of funding requested by the White House. The amount of money allocated to cleanup operations at DOE facilities was reduced by $360 million below the amount of money requested by the Clinton administration. The House voted to cut funding for defense activities by $280 million below the amount of funding requested by the White House (Barton, October 1, 1993: C2).

A third example of reduced funds for environmental cleanup programs is that President Clinton's fiscal year 1998 budget included $268.3 million for Fernald's cleanup activities, whereas DOE officials had requested $276 million for that year. During the 1997 fiscal year, Fernald received $269.9 million for cleanup programs. Ohio governor George Voinovich expressed concern that the proposed 1998 budget was about $10 million less than the amount needed in 1998 to maintain Fernald's environmental cleanup schedule. Voinovich and the Ohio EPA believed that the reduced budget "could delay Fernald's cleanup by at least two years past the 2005 cleanup goal established under DOE's ten-year cleanup plan for Fernald" (Barazia, February 7, 1997: A1).

Although Congress and the Clinton administration threatened to significantly reduce DOE's budget, the agency's environmental cleanup budget has not actually suffered. Indeed, in several instances, DOE's cleanup budgets have increased over the years. As one local DOE official who was interviewed summarized the situation:

> Since 1991, Congress has increased Fernald's cleanup budget every year. For the past five or six years, Fernald's cleanup budget has increased with the rate of inflation. DOE's cleanup budget has been stable. Ohio's two senators and the local congressional representatives from the Cincinnati area have been supportive of Fernald's cleanup program and see to it that Fernald receives the amount of money it needs to continue its cleanup activities. (Personal interview, Harrison, Ohio, July 15, 1998)

In an interview, an environmental engineer familiar with DOE's operations observed: "Congress decreased DOE's funding over the last few years, but not by as much as they originally threatened. Congress always threatens to cut DOE's budget, but doesn't cut much. Fernald has done all right when it comes to funding" (Personal interview, Oak Ridge, Tennessee, May 28, 1998).

In many cases, the newspaper articles written about Fernald often mentioned that Congress was threatening to cut Fernald's budget or had already reduced Fernald's budget. When asked about the articles, several Fernald SSAB members and DOE officials disputed the claims made by the newspaper articles. In any event, DOE is constantly operating under the threat of budget cuts that sooner or later are bound to affect environmental management and restoration at its facilities. SSABs provide a mechanism for incorporating stakeholder advice on establishing program priorities in this eventuality.

The impetus for DOE's adoption of the stakeholder involvement model was provided by a variety of forces—protests, litigation, legislative initiatives, and interagency cooperation. In the end, however, one thing was certain— DOE was compelled to become and had to learn to operate as a regulated agency. No longer did concerns for national security and military secrecy exempt the agency from the inexorable pressure for citizen participation in its environmental management and restoration decision making.

Conclusion

The emergence of the grassroots environmental movement largely coincided with the loss of energy in the community power movement. Thus, environmentalists eventually were successful in persuading Congress to incorporate public participation in the new environmental laws—especially the National Environmental Policy Act of 1969 (NEPA). The complex regulatory structure shaped by post-NEPA environmental statutes in the 1970s accelerated this trend. Environmental laws passed by Congress required federal agencies such as the EPA to establish public participation programs. These efforts flowered in the 1980s and culminated in the focus on *stakeholder involvement* in the 1990s. This form of participation occurs when government organizations, especially regulatory agencies, remain in constant contact with stakeholders who are affected in some way by a policy. The stakeholders are contacted during every stage of the policy process from when a policy is created to after a policy is implemented.

It is important to note that the limited accessibility and influence of persons affected by policies implemented by public agencies produced by the rise of the technocratic administration is not easily overcome. Studies, for example, of the citizen advisory boards formed to work with public agencies during the 1960s and 1970s generally found that these did not increase the power of individuals to influence public policies implemented by public agencies (Arnstein, 1969; Cunningham, 1972; Kweit and Kweit, 1981; Moynihan, 1969; Zimmerman, 1972 and 1986). Citizen advisory boards created to provide public input on environmental policy and regulatory decisions have produced a mixed record: sometimes they appear to have had no impact on policy decisions, and in other instances they have had significant impacts on policy decisions (Lynn and Busenberg, 1995).

This chapter examines how the citizen advisory board came to be an acceptable feature of policy implementation within the U.S. Department of Energy. The major focus, beyond describing the path by which the DOE and other federal agencies arrived at the adoption of the Stakeholder Involvement Model, is upon the actual application of the model in the field. This should contribute to a better understanding of the promises and pitfalls of citizen participation in the regulatory process.

This chapter also reviewed the history of DOE's nuclear weapons complex and DOE's previous emphasis on weapons production, national security, and secrecy at the cost of environmental management and cleanup. The FFCA, recommendations of the Keystone reports, burgeoning litigation, widespread negative publicity, and budgetary uncertainty provided the impetus for the DOE to establish the SSAB program. DOE hopes that the establishment of the SSAB program will help restore public trust and confidence in the agency. With fewer resources, a reduced budget, and fewer employees, DOE hopes that the SSAB program will efficiently use the agency's remaining personnel and resources. DOE believes that the use of SSABs will be a more efficient use of the agency's remaining personnel and resources.

Thus, by the mid-1990s the DOE was moving, albeit not always voluntarily, from its former status as a closed, technocratic, and essentially unregulated agency toward becoming more open and inclusive in its environmental management and restoration programs. It is one thing, however, formally to adopt the Stakeholder Involvement Model; it is another thing entirely to make it work. The history of the Fernald Environmental Management Project (FEMP) is presented in the next chapter and its legacy of environmental problems is detailed. The establishment and the activities of the Fernald Citizens Advisory Board are described. This is done in order to begin a systematic assessment of how the DOE Stakeholder Involvement Initiative was implemented and how well it actually worked in the field.

NOTES

1. All figures are found in the Appendix B.

2. All figures are found in Appendix B.

3. Additional information on interviews is presented in Appendix C.

2

From Production to Cleanup: A History of the Fernald Facility

Introduction

This chapter presents the history of the U.S. Department of Energy Feed Materials Production Center in Fernald, Ohio, and of the environmental problems engendered by its operations. Also discussed are the burgeoning citizen protests and lawsuits and the governmental disputes that eventually stymied the DOE at this site.

The Fernald Site Specific Advisory Board, an SSAB within the DOE weapons complex, is the public participation mechanism for monitoring the progress of environmental management and remediation (most especially for hazardous wastes) at DOE's Ohio facility. A chronology of significant events in Fernald's operations in general and of the Fernald facility SSAB in particular is provided in the Table in Appendix A.[1] This facility was originally known as the Feed Materials Production Center (FMPC). The Feed Materials Production Center was a nuclear weapons plant that produced uranium fuel elements for nuclear reactors and other uranium products for the U.S. nuclear weapons program. The uranium products were then taken to other DOE facilities for further assembly into nuclear weapons (Abramson, May 11, 1991: A19). The uranium fuel was taken to other DOE facilities where it was converted into plutonium—the primary ingredient in nuclear weapons. The operation of this facility over time yielded significant volumes of hazardous and toxic wastes on the site. It also resulted in pollution on-site and in the surrounding area that posed a significant and persistent threat to humans and the ecosystem.

The Fernald Feed Materials Production Center: Location and Demographics

The Fernald facility is located on 1,050 acres of land in southwestern Ohio, and is approximately 20 miles northwest of Cincinnati, Ohio. The Fernald site is located within the boundaries of three local townships: Crosby Township, Morgan Township, and Ross Township. However, "90% of the Fernald site lies within the boundaries of Crosby Township" (Personal interview, Harrison, Ohio, July 15, 1998). As Figure 4 shows, the Fernald site is located in a rural area within two counties—Hamilton County and Butler County, Ohio—which have a combined population of approximately 1.2 million persons.[2] The Cincinnati metropolitan area contains approximately 1.7 million persons and consists of counties in Ohio, Kentucky, and Indiana (Fernald Citizens Task Force, July 1995: VIII-3). Cities located near the Fernald site that have significantly large populations include Cincinnati, Fairfield, and Hamilton. In detail:

> Cincinnati has a population of approximately 364,000 people, while Fairfield has a population of approximately 39,800 persons, and Hamilton has a population of approximately 61,400 persons. Hamilton and Fairfield are approximately 6 to 8 miles northeast of Fernald. Approximately 14,600 persons live within 5 miles of Fernald, and approximately 2.74 million persons live within 50 miles of the Fernald site. (Fernald Environmental Restoration Management Corporation, June 1996: 19)

Hamilton County has a population of 866,228 people, while Butler County has a population of 291,479 persons. Many of the communities around the Fernald site are unincorporated towns. Most of the communities are characterized as agricultural or as "bedroom" communities for commuters living within the Cincinnati area (Fernald Citizens Task Force, July 1995: VI-2).

Fernald was one of several facilities that are part of DOE's nuclear weapons complex where nuclear components were constructed for assembly into nuclear weapons made for the military. The environmental legacy of its operations poses, in the absence of effective and timely management and restoration, significant risk to large numbers of people and future generations.

Operational History

In 1951, DOE granted a contract to National Lead of Ohio, Incorporated (NLO), and its parent company, National Lead Industries, Incorporated, to construct and manage the Fernald facility. Fernald's primary mission was to produce uranium products to be used as components in nuclear weapons. After the uranium products were produced at Fernald, they were sent to other facilities on DOE's nuclear weapons complex for further assembly into nuclear weapons. NLO began constructing the facility and completed construction in 1951. During 1951, some production activities began at Fernald. In 1953, full production operations began at the Fernald facility. NLO operated the facility from 1953 until 1985. In 1985, NLO decided against renewing its contract with DOE, and DOE granted a contract to the Westinghouse Corporation to operate the Fernald facility. In 1986, the Westinghouse Materials Company of Ohio (WMCO), a subsidiary of the Westinghouse Corporation, took over the Fernald site's operations. In July 1989, DOE stopped production at the Fernald plant. In June 1991, DOE officially ended all production operations at Fernald. In July 1991, WMCO was renamed the Westinghouse Environmental Management Company of Ohio (WEMCO).

The Establishment of the Fernald Health and Environmental Advisory Committee

In 1985, NLO established the Fernald Health and Environmental Advisory Committee (FHEAC). The mission of the FHEAC was to provide recommendations and advice to NLO regarding worker health and safety issues at Fernald and the environmental impacts of NLO's activities on the surrounding community. The FHEAC's charter stated that the organization's purpose was to provide independent assessment, evaluation, and advice to NLO regarding health and environmental issues, programs, and policies. The FHEAC consisted of nine members who were chosen by NLO's plant director at Fernald. This practice was continued by WMCO after it took over NLO's Fernald contract. The senior environmental staff member at Fernald appointed the FHEAC chairperson from the organization's membership. FHEAC members represented local residents; Fernald Residents for Environmental Safety and Health (FRESH), a local environmental group; the Sierra Club; doctors; local school officials; university professors; and business leaders. Members received compensation of $350 per day and reimbursement for travel expenses. The chairperson could obtain temporary assistance from specialists who were not members of the FHEAC. The FHEAC's objectives and functions were to review documents pertaining to Fernald, familiarize itself with the areas of expertise of each member, and become familiar with a wide range of fields that pertained to problems at Fernald. These fields included radiation, physics, radiobiology, geology, hydrology, economic issues, and political issues. The FHEAC also identified problems at Fernald and suggested recommendations (Scrimgeour and Hanson, April 1993: C-2 and C-3).

The FHEAC's impact and accomplishments included advising DOE on potential emergency situations at Fernald. DOE and WMCO responded to FHEAC's recommendations. DOE purchased and installed warning sirens and radio units at Fernald. WMCO identified and replaced faulty detection and alarm systems. WMCO, DOE, county, and state officials organized an evacuation plan and held joint emergency response drills. The FHEAC identified and recommended solutions for problems regarding environmental pollution and worker and resident safety and health issues resulting from Fernald's operations. According to the staff of Fernald Environmental Restoration Management Corporation (FERMCO was DOE's Fernald contractor in 1990), DOE disbanded the FHEAC at the suggestion of the FHEAC. The FHEAC existed from 1985 until 1990 (Scrimgeour and Hanson, April 1993: C-3 and C-4).

Environmental Contamination

The Fernald facility was constructed over an underground water source that is referred to as the Great Miami Aquifer, which is a well water source for many residents who lived near the plant. Ground water from the aquifer was also a major source of drinking water for persons living in the region. The Great Miami Aquifer is one of the largest drinking water aquifers in the country, containing almost 10 trillion gallons of water (Fernald Citizens Task Force, July 1995: 6). Some of the water from the Great Miami Aquifer flows into the Fernald site from areas to the west and to the northwest of the facility. This water flow from the aquifer continues flowing in a southeasterly direction through the Fernald site. Radioactive and hazardous wastes buried at the Fernald site have leaked into the Great Miami Aquifer. The water flow comes into contact with contaminated radioactive wastes, and hazardous wastes that were buried at Fernald and have seeped into the aquifer's water.

The most contaminated area of the aquifer is an area located immediately south of the Fernald site known as the *south plume*. The ground water in this area is contaminated with significant levels of uranium. Residents living within this area had obtained their water from wells that received water from the Great Miami Aquifer. Studies by DOE, EPA, and the Ohio EPA indicate that "as much as 5.8 billion gallons of water or 0.062% of the total aquifer has been contaminated above background levels of uranium as a result of releases from the Fernald site" (Fernald Citizens Task Force, July 1995: 6). In 1993, a DOE study revealed that radioactive materials and toxic materials leaked from six waste pits located at the Fernald site and threatened the groundwater supplies in the Fernald area. These radioactive materials include uranium and thorium. Other toxic substances included solvents and heavy metals. EPA has designated the Great Miami Aquifer as a "sole source aquifer." EPA gives this designation to underground aquifers that the agency has determined would pose a significant health risk to humans if contaminated by radioactive wastes and hazardous wastes.

There are two bodies of water that flow through or near the Fernald site. Paddy's Run Creek flows through the western portion of the Fernald site. Approximately one and a half miles south and east of the Fernald site, Paddy's Run Creek flows into the Great Miami River. The Great Miami River flows into the Ohio River approximately 25 miles downstream from the Fernald site. The area of the Great Miami River between the Fernald site and the Ohio River is not a designated source of public drinking water for local residents. Also, approximately a mile east of the Fernald facility, the Southwest Ohio Water Company operates a production well water field.

During the facility's years of operation, large amounts of uranium dust were released into the atmosphere. Radioactive and hazardous waste materials were buried in pits on the plant site, causing the contamination of soil, ground water, and well water in the surrounding area. Storm runoff water from Fernald contaminated the ground area around the facility. Buildings, equipment, materials, and metals used at Fernald were also contaminated with radioactive wastes and hazardous wastes. Exposure to the radioactive and hazardous wastes can occur through direct contact, ingestion, and inhalation of contaminants. The most common method for ingesting contaminants from Fernald is to drink contaminated water that originated from the Great Miami Aquifer. Another way of ingesting contaminants is the inadvertent consumption of foods contaminated by radioactive and hazardous wastes, especially foods grown in contaminated soil. Health risks from radioactive wastes and hazardous wastes include cancer, burns and injuries from flammable or explosive materials, and radiation. Some of the radioactive wastes that caused contamination at Fernald include uranium, plutonium, radon, thorium, technetium-99, mercury, strontium-90, radium, and dilute hydrogen fluoride. Some of the hazardous wastes that caused contamination at the site include asbestos, polychlorinated biphenyls (PCBs), "sulfuric acid, methanol, hydrochloric acid, laboratory chemicals, nitric acid, sodium hydroxide, processed wastes, and heavy metals" (Fernald Environmental Restoration Management Corporation, June 1996: 8).

The contamination problems at Fernald were discussed in an article in the October 31, 1988 issue of *Time* magazine (Cramer, Leavitt, and Nash, 1988: 60-65). The article discussed the contamination problems at Fernald and several other DOE sites. In the article, local resident Marvin Clawson and several members of his family said that they lived near the Fernald site and that some members of the family underwent cancer surgery because of the contamination problems at Fernald. The Clawsons believed that living in proximity to Fernald's wastes caused these family members to develop cancer. Marvin Clawson and three members of his family were pictured on the cover of the issue. The headline on the cover was "The Nuclear Scandal: The Clawsons of Ohio Blame the Fernald Uranium Plant for Cancer in Their Family: They Are Not Alone." In 1993, Marvin Clawson became a member of the Fernald SSAB.

Extensive contamination has occurred at the Fernald site. Because of these contamination problems, DOE and its contractors have spent millions of dollars trying to clean up Fernald and other DOE sites. The contamination problems have also resulted in lawsuits filed by local residents, DOE workers, and subcontractors and in a loss of public trust and confidence. Problems such as these influenced DOE to establish its SSAB program.

The Genesis of Conflict—Health and Environmental Problems

While the Fernald facility was operating, the news media reported that massive amounts of uranium dust were released into the atmosphere. There were also reports of workers at Fernald dying of bone, liver, and brain cancer (Hamilton, 1990: 31). The plant workers had died from cancer after being exposed to radioactive and hazardous wastes at the facility over a period of several years, according to media reports.

During the 1980s, uranium was buried on the Fernald plant site. The uranium leaked into Fernald's underground well water supply, spreading contamination beyond the confines of the plant site. In 1984, a local journalist reported that the Fernald facility had released large amounts of radioactive dust into the atmosphere and that several local wells were contaminated with uranium. This report caused an uproar among the local residents. During 1984, Lisa Crawford, a resident who lived near the Fernald site, discovered that uranium buried at the Fernald site had seeped into the ground and contaminated the water of a well that was located on her farm. Crawford and her husband discovered that DOE was aware that their well water had been contaminated since 1981, but sent annual reports to the Crawford's landlord that stated that tests had proved that the well water was not contaminated. In 1984, after discovering the contaminated water in her well, Crawford founded the Fernald Residents for Environmental Safety and Health (FRESH). FRESH is a community organization consisting of local residents who monitor the activities of the Fernald site. Crawford is the president of this organization.

In January 1985, Crawford and four other Fernald residents filed a $300 million lawsuit on behalf of 14,000 persons who lived within a five-mile radius of the plant (Feinberg, 1990: 41). The lawsuit was filed against National Lead of Ohio, Incorporated, and the company granted a contract by DOE to operate the Fernald facility. Although the real target of the lawsuit was DOE, the residents filed the lawsuit against National Lead of Ohio. Stanley Chesley, a prominent Cincinnati attorney hired by the local residents, argued that Fernald's pollution problems were the responsibility of DOE's contractor and not the responsibility of DOE. Chesley devised this legal argument as the basis for the lawsuit. The attorney developed this legal strategy for the lawsuit because, during this time, all federal departments and federal agencies were protected from lawsuits because of sovereign immunity. The legal principle of sovereign immunity means that the federal government is immune from lawsuits unless it grants consent to be sued. In their lawsuit, the residents alleged that mismanagement of the Fernald facility resulted in decreased property values, emotional distress, and contaminated well water supplies.

In 1989, DOE settled the lawsuit for $78 million. Within a year of this court settlement, other law firms filed similar lawsuits against the contractors of several DOE facilities. These facilities included the Hanford Reservation in Washington state; the Mound Plant in Miamisburg, Ohio; and the Oak Ridge Reservation in Oak Ridge, Tennessee. When filing the lawsuits, the law firms also argued that the private contractors were responsible for the pollution problems at DOE facilities instead of DOE itself (Obmascik, April 7, 1996: 1A). In 1991, DOE paid $1.5 million to the Radiological Assessments Corporation (RAC) of Neeses, South Carolina, to conduct a study on the amount of uranium dust released into the atmosphere from Fernald. RAC conducted the study and prepared it for the Centers for Disease Control. RAC studied the releases of uranium dust from Fernald for three years: 1960, 1961, and 1962. The study concluded that "about 200,000 pounds of uranium were released. This amount represented 40% of the total amount of uranium dust that DOE said was released over a thirty year period" (Schneider, December 19, 1991: B22 [L]). The study's researchers said that, by the year 1993, they could more effectively determine the contamination risks faced by Ohio residents. The study's conclusions differed from previous studies conducted by DOE. In 1985, DOE conducted its first official study of Fernald's contamination. Then, DOE concluded that "no more that 192,000 pounds of uranium had been released from Fernald over a period of thirty-one years. In 1989, DOE conducted a second study and concluded that possibly as much as 550,000 pounds of uranium was released from Fernald" (Schneider, December 19, 1991: B22 [L]).

The Fernald residents who filed the lawsuit hired the Institute for Energy and Environmental Research (IEER) to conduct a study of the Fernald plant's releases of uranium into the water and atmosphere. The IEER is a private research firm based in Takoma Park, Maryland. In May 1989, the IEER completed its study. The study reached conclusions similar to those found in the RAC study.

In June 1989, the lawsuit was settled when DOE, on behalf of NLO, agreed to pay $78 million to the Fernald residents. The agency agreed to compensate Fernald residents as much as $5 million for decreased property values resulting from environmental harm. DOE also agreed to pay up to an additional $1 billion over the next six years to clean up the environment around the plant. The federal government further agreed to pay millions of dollars into a court-administered fund to pay for continual medical monitoring of the 14,000 residents for a five-year period (Feinberg, 1990: 41).

In 1986, the state of Ohio filed a lawsuit against the Department of Energy. The suit included a $206 million claim and alleged that while operating the Fernald facility, hazardous wastes and radioactive wastes were not properly disposed of by DOE. The agency, it was charged, released radioactive materials into the surface, air, and water and polluted surface water and ground water. The suit also accused DOE of violating state and federal environmental laws. The federal environmental laws included the Clean Water Act of 1972 (CWA) and the Resource Conservation and Recovery Act of 1976 (RCRA). The suit was filed in the federal district court in Cincinnati, Ohio. DOE moved to have the suit dismissed. On March 18, 1988, the United States District Court for the Southern District of Ohio denied DOE's motion to have the suit dismissed. The court found that the CWA and RCRA waived federal sovereign immunity from punitive fines. The case was appealed to the United States Court of Appeals for the Sixth Circuit in Cincinnati. On June 11, 1990, the Sixth Circuit Court of Appeals affirmed in part but found that immunity had not been waived in RCRA's citizen suit provision (U.S. Department of Energy v. Ohio, 112 S.Ct. 1627 [1992]). The Sixth Circuit Court of Appeals concluded that: (1) the waiver of sovereign immunity and the CWA extends to civil penalties under federal law or approved state water pollution laws, and (2) the citizen suit provision of the RCRA waivers sovereign immunity for civil penalties (904 F.2d. 1058 [6th Cir. 1990]). The suit was appealed to the U.S. Supreme Court, and on April 21, 1992, the United States Supreme Court ruled in a 6 to 3 vote that the federal government's sovereign immunity from liability from civil fines imposed by Ohio for past violations of CWA or RCRA had not been waived (U.S. Department of Energy v. Ohio, 112 S.Ct. 1627 [1992]). The Supreme Court found that Congress had "not explicitly exempted federal facilities from violating state and environmental laws" (*Congressional Quarterly Almanac*, 1992: 261).

On December 2, 1988, the state of Ohio signed a Consent Degree with DOE. A Consent Degree occurs when two or more parties agree to a settlement. The parties present the terms of the settlement to a judicial court, and a judge enforces the terms of the agreement. The court's duty is to make sure the agreement is enforced. The Consent Decree is legally binding for all of the parties involved. The Consent Degree signed by DOE and the state of Ohio requires DOE to upgrade the hazardous waste activities. The Consent Degree also requires DOE to control the wastewater and storm water runoff that accumulate at the Fernald facility. The Consent Degree required the completion of the RCRA and the CERCLA (or Superfund) cleanup. However, in March 1990, the state of Ohio cited DOE for contempt because the agency failed to comply with the terms of the 1988 Consent Decree. The portion of the Consent Decree that DOE failed to comply with involved the application of the RCRA regarding the storage of hazardous waste.

In July 1986, EPA and DOE agreed to establish a timetable for removing radioactive and hazardous wastes from the Fernald site. In December 1989, the Fernald site was placed on the EPA's National Priorities List, which made the Fernald facility a Superfund, or CERCLA, site. The Consent Decree signed between the state of Ohio and DOE also required DOE to complete the cleanup of the Fernald site under the Superfund requirements.

In June 1990, DOE and the EPA signed a CERCLA Consent Agreement. This agreement is legally binding for all of the involved parties. However, in 1990, the Fernald cleanup schedule was revised. In November 1990, EPA began imposing fines against DOE because DOE failed to meet the cleanup deadlines and failed to furnish information required by its cleanup agreement with EPA.

> On May 13, 1991, DOE agreed to pay $100,000 to EPA as a penalty for DOE's failure to meet deadlines and to provide information on cleanup activities. DOE also conceded EPA's authority to impose fines on another federal agency. The agreement settled a claim of nearly $500,000 against DOE. EPA began imposing the fine against the agency, and DOE was fined at the rate of $20,000 a week. (*The New York Times*, May 12, 1991: 19 [L])

DOE also agreed to pay $150,000 on cleanup activities at Fernald. This amount was above what DOE otherwise would have spent as long as Congress appropriated the money. DOE, which had a budget of nearly $20 billion, planned to spend $339 million on Fernald during the next fiscal year (Wald, May 14, 1991: A14 [L]).

On February 2, 1993, DOE officials informed EPA and the Ohio EPA that the agency could meet the cleanup goals of the May 1991 agreement. DOE was supposed to have cleaned up one of Fernald's sites by February 6, 1993. DOE requested an extension for cleaning up the Fernald site. The agency requested that the extension be granted for more than one year until April 1994. "Under DOE's revised schedule, a draft cleanup plan, or record of decision (ROD), that was originally due in December 1993 would not be finished until March 1, 1995. DOE also had other cleanup deadlines and reports on various sites at Fernald that were due in 1993" (Rubin, March 8, 1993: 24).

DOE had difficulty meeting EPA cleanup deadlines at many of its facilities. The agency had made several agreements with EPA to meet cleanup deadlines at several sites at Fernald and DOE's other facilities. Therefore, the EPA imposed fines on DOE for failing to meet cleanup deadlines.

During 1990, a group of Fernald workers and subcontractors filed a lawsuit against NLO and National Lead Industries which accused the two companies of intentionally subjecting the workers to radiation hazards at Fernald and deliberately concealing the dangers from them. The workers claimed that they suffered emotional distress from the fear of getting cancer or leukemia (*The Wall Street Journal,* July 27, 1994: B6 [E]). Stanley Chesley, a prominent

Cincinnati attorney, represented the Fernald workers in their lawsuit. In 1985, Chesley represented several Fernald residents when they filed a lawsuit against National Lead of Ohio and sought legal compensation because they felt that the contractor had allowed radioactive wastes buried at Fernald to seep into their underground well water supplies.

The Fernald workers who filed the lawsuit hired Dr. Peter S. Gartside, a professor of biostatistics at the University of Cincinnati, as a paid consultant. Gartside conducted a study involving individuals who worked at the Fernald plant.

> Gartside evaluated the causes of death for 1,371 Fernald workers who died between 1953 and 1991. He compared the cancer mortality rates of the Fernald workers to the cancer mortality rates of the U.S. general population. Gartside also found that the median life expectancy of Fernald workers was 58 years, five years less than the median life expectancy of all Americans from 1953 to 1991. (Schneider, April 13, 1994: A16 [L])

Gartside analyzed the medical records of the Fernald workers in his study and discovered that the workers had "died at significantly younger ages and suffered a higher incidence of lung, intestinal, and blood cancers than the U.S. population as a whole" (Schneider, April 13, 1994: A16 [L]). The results of Gartside's study were made public in April 1994. This was the first time that a study involving the health rates of Fernald workers was released to the public.

Not surprisingly, NLO criticized the findings of Gartside's study. NLO hired Dr. Geoffrey Howe of the National Cancer Institute of Canada to conduct a study for NLO. NLO wanted Howe to use data similar to the data that Gartside used for his study. Howe compared the cancer rates and death rates of Fernald workers to the cancer and death rates of the population of Ohio—not the U.S. population. Howe's study was also completed in 1994, and NLO claimed that the study showed that "there was nothing unusual about the health rates of Fernald workers or the incidents of cancer deaths" (Schneider, April 13, 1994: A16 [L]). Howe concluded there was not an excess of cancer rates among the Fernald workers. Tara O'Toole, a doctor who was an Assistant Secretary of Energy for Environment, Safety, and Health, also criticized Gartside's study. O'Toole said that there were too few subjects involved in Gartside's study to make conclusions about the cancer rates of Fernald workers, but that Gartside's findings merited further study. A partial explanation for the reasons that Gartside's and Howe's studies reached different conclusions is that Gartside compared the Fernald workers to the U.S. general population, while Howe compared the Fernald workers to the population of Ohio (Schneider, April 13, 1994: A16 [L]).

In 1986, a study conducted by the Oak Ridge Associated Universities (ORAU), a DOE contractor, reached conclusions similar to those found in Gartside's study. The ORAU researchers identified a trend involving what seemed to be unusually high rates of colon cancer among Fernald workers (Schneider, April 13, 1994: A16 [L]).

In July 1994, the lawsuit involving the Fernald workers and subcontractors who filed suit against NLO was settled. The federal government announced that it would pay for lifetime monitoring and provide $15 million in damages to settle the lawsuit by Fernald workers who claimed that they were unwittingly exposed to radiation at the Fernald plant. The agreement effectively ended the 1990 lawsuit that sought $500 million in damages. This class-action settlement covers about 6,000 former workers and subcontractors, and approximately 4,500 of those workers are still living. The settlement includes a $15 million fund to pay emotional distress claims and legal fees, and at least another $5 million was dedicated to medical monitoring (*The Wall Street Journal,* July 27, 1994: B6 [E]).

In August, 1996, Cincinnati attorney Stanley Chesley announced that he intended to file lawsuits on behalf of cancer victims or members of their families who believed that their cancer was linked to the Fernald plant.

During August 1996, the Radiological Assessment released the results of a study by the Radiological Assessment Corporation, an organization of scientists hired by the U.S. Centers for Disease Control. The Centers for Disease Control supervised the study. The Radiological Assessment Corporation conducted a six-year study of persons living near the Fernald plant. The study examined nine possible scenarios that were based on how long people lived near Fernald and how many miles they lived from Fernald. The study concluded that persons who lived near Fernald had a higher-than-average risk of developing lung cancer. The lung cancer resulted from radon gas and not from uranium dust. Chesley stated that the previous cases involving his lawsuits on behalf of Fernald residents and Fernald workers allowed only claims for emotional distress and declining property values. Chesley said that claims for cancer disease were not allowed in those lawsuits. The attorney said that the results of the study confirmed his beliefs and the beliefs of local residents (Petrie, August 24, 1996: 13A).

Several lawsuits were filed against DOE contractors who operated the Fernald facility. Local residents filed a lawsuit against NLO, DOE's Fernald contractor, in 1985. In 1986, the state of Ohio filed a lawsuit against DOE. In 1990, Fernald workers, contractors, and subcontractors filed a lawsuit against DOE. These lawsuits, filed by local residents, Fernald workers, contractors, and subcontractors, were eventually settled by DOE. The lawsuit settlements in these cases involved millions of dollars.

Several studies claim that Fernald workers have had higher cancer mortality rates and death rates than the U.S. general population. Findings in studies such Gartside's and the ORAU's have increased public distrust and decreased public confidence in DOE. Stanley Chesley has represented several Fernald residents, workers, and subcontractors in lawsuits filed against DOE's Fernald contractors. The frequency of these lawsuits filed against DOE and its contractors at several facilities reflect the loss of public trust and confidence in DOE. One of the reasons that DOE decided to establish the SSAB program was the filing of a significant number of lawsuits against the agency. These lawsuits have cost DOE millions of dollars in legal expenses, court settlements, and court decisions.

DOE and Environmental Agencies' Negotiations

In December 1992, DOE awarded a five-year, $2.2 billion contract (Aeppel, June 30, 1994: A2) to Fluor Daniel, Incorporated and Jacobs

Engineering to manage the cleanup of the facility. Fluor Daniel is a multinational corporation that has contributed thousands of dollars to the election campaigns of key congressional members and congressional committee members, both Republicans and Democrats. Fluor Daniel had formed a political action committee (PAC) to influence the campaigns of congressional members who could pass legislation that could affect the company. Members of Congress who belonged to congressional committees handling environmental issues often received campaign contributions from Fluor Daniel. For example, "the energy and water projects subcommittee of the Senate Appropriations Committee controls funding for Fernald and other similar projects. Since 1991, nearly all the members of this subcommittee have received contributions from Fluor Daniel" (Barton, December 26, 1996: B5). Fluor Daniel also contributes "soft money" to the national Republican and Democratic parties. During 1996, Fluor Daniel's political action committee spent hundreds of thousands of dollars on campaign donations, and also contributed more soft money to both political parties than any other construction firm. Because of these political activities, Fluor Daniel has often received federal contracts.

In addition to receiving federal contracts from DOE, Fluor Daniel has also received federal contracts from other cabinet departments and federal agencies. These departments and agencies include EPA, the Defense Department, the Commerce Department, and the Department of Health and Human Services. Fluor Daniel's work is conducted in states such as Texas, Florida, Maryland, Pennsylvania, Arizona, South Carolina, Missouri, Ohio, California, and Alaska (Barton, December 26, 1995: B5). Contractors who perform work in various parts of the country have an advantage when interacting with members of Congress because they become constituents for more congressional members. When a federal contractor has a presence within a congressional district, it becomes easier for the contractor to talk to a congressional member. Thus, Fluor Daniel has many supporters in Congress.

There were also several companies that became partners with Fluor Daniel in the environmental cleanup contract. Jacobs Engineering is a company based in Pasadena, California, and is Fluor Daniel's junior partner in the cleanup contract. Two additional companies that eventually became partners with Fluor Daniel and Jacobs Engineering in the cleanup contract are Halliburton NUS Environmental Services and Nuclear Fuel Services. Fluor Daniel, Incorporated, is also the head of a contractor group that is managing the cleanup efforts at Fernald. However, before receiving the contract, the company had no experience with working in nuclear weapons plants. In addition, Fluor Daniel has subcontracted much of the environmental cleanup work to approximately 1,000 other companies (Aeppel, June 30, 1994: A2).

After Fluor Daniel received the contract in 1992, the Fluor Daniel-led contractor group was renamed the Fernald Environmental Restoration Management Corporation or FERMCO. The Feed Materials Production Center (FMPC) was the original name of the Fernald facility when it was first constructed. After Fluor Daniel received the contract, the FMPC was renamed the Fernald Environmental Management Project (FEMP). This was the first time that DOE had awarded a contract to a company to clean up one of its nuclear facilities. DOE's purpose was to award a contract to a single

Environmental Restoration Management Contractor (ERMC) that would supervise and integrate the cleanup activities among the contractor and subcontractors. The Fluor Daniel contract was considered to be a test case for DOE. The Fernald plant, DOE's smallest nuclear weapons facility, has been inoperative since 1989. Other DOE facilities are considered to have more serious contamination problems.

The contract was awarded to Fluor Daniel to appease the agency's critics who were complaining that DOE was awarding cleanup contracts to the same firms that caused the contamination at its nuclear facilities. Thus, Fluor Daniel and other contracted companies did not have any previous experience in removing nuclear and hazardous waste from nuclear facilities.

Government auditors are concerned that the ERMC system might repeat many of the mistakes that were made under the previous system. In August 1992, GAO reviewed the new ERMC program. The GAO report found "limited evidence" that savings could result from the use of the ERMC program (Pasternak and Cary, December 14, 1992: 47). For example, the ERMC program calls for subcontracting all of the work except the management duties of the environmental cleanup activities. As a result, the "actual cleanup work is likely to be done by subcontractors who are not working under fixed-cost obligations to DOE" (Pasternak and Cary, December 14, 1992: 47).

Continuing Problems at the Fernald Site

It is possible that DOE is likely to be forced to rely on the same system of subcontractors under DOE's newly formed ERMC program. Fluor Daniel was the first company awarded an ERMC contract by DOE under the agency's ERMC program. Fluor Daniel has a $5 billion contract to clean up the Fernald plant. However, "over one thousand subcontractors are employed at Fernald, and DOE officials concede that many of the contractors who previously received contracts from DOE will find work under the Fluor Daniel contract" (Pasternak and Cary, December 14, 1992: 47). At Fernald and other cleanup sites, the contractors and subcontractors hired by DOE are often the same companies that were responsible for the pollution and contamination of DOE facilities. Officials at DOE believed that they had little choice but to hire the companies because these companies are the only ones who were completely knowledgeable about the contamination and pollution in the their facilities. There are few companies that have the expertise to operate nuclear facilities and to cleanup the radioactive and toxic materials in DOE facilities.

A few months after beginning work at Fernald, Fluor Daniel laid off persons who previously worked for Westinghouse. Fluor Daniel hired outside labor to perform the cleanup and dismantling of the facility. The previous workers wanted the cleanup jobs for themselves and accused the company of union busting. During the George Herbert Walker Bush presidency, DOE encouraged Fluor Daniel to subcontract out its work, so that the work could be completed more rapidly. However, under the Clinton administration, DOE ordered Fluor Daniel to halt the layoffs and to retrain the previous production workers for the environmental cleanup work (Aeppel, June 30, 1994: A2).

DOE and the contractor had been criticized for significant cost overruns during the cleanup process. "For example, the cost of a cleanup-feasibility study totaled $1.7 million during the study's first year of existence. However, the cost of the study has since grown to $107.8 million. A DOE inspector general's audit found that the original price estimates were unrealistic" (Pasternak and Cary, December 14, 1992: 35). Because of this error, the contract needed significant modifications, and DOE and Fluor Daniel did not have any experience in conducting the types of assessments that were needed in the cleanup project. This was the first time that DOE and a contractor had made assessments for an ERMC project. DOE and the contractor also received criticism for excessive overhead in the Fernald project.

> In 1993, DOE budgeted $105 million for materials and labor for the cleanup of Fernald; $203 million will go for contractor overhead and related costs. OMB reviewed DOE contracts and discovered that the DOE-approved overhead rates were more than twice as high as the overhead rates on similar contracts with the Army Corps of Engineers that also used commercial contractors for much of its work. (Pasternak and Cary, December 14, 1992: 36)

DOE's Inspector General criticized the agency for awarding a company called Advanced Sciences Incorporated (ASI), a $1.7 million contract to perform cleanup work at Fernald (Pasternak and Cary, December 14, 1992: 46). In 1986, ASI was an Albuquerque-based company awarded a subcontracting job by DOE to work at Fernald. ASI was awarded the contract as a Section 8(a) small business contractor when the magnitude of the Fernald cleanup project was not thoroughly understood. ASI's original contract was worth $1.7 million for the first year with four one-year options. The contract was later negotiated at $18.3 million. Later, contract costs increased to $72 million as EPA enforced RCRA and Superfund laws, and field studies revealed larger amounts of radioactive and hazardous wastes (Pasternak and Cary, December 14, 1992: 36).

DOE awarded ASI a contract to perform a site Remedial Investigation and Feasibility Study (RIFS) of the Fernald site. During this period, Westinghouse was the company to which DOE awarded a contract to operate the Fernald facility. Although Westinghouse officials stated they did not believe that ASI had the technical competence to perform the duties assigned to it, DOE defended its decision to award the contract to ASI. DOE's Inspector General discovered that DOE officials did not adequately monitor ASI's work at Fernald. "The costs of ASI's work at Fernald have risen to more than $100 million. At one point, ASI's financial health was in such poor condition that Westinghouse improperly paid ASI $16 million to assure that ASI did not go out of business and that ASI's work would continue" (Pasternak and Cary, December 14, 1992: 46). A Westinghouse official conceded that the ASI payment was improper. At present, ASI has established a support team with the International Technology Corporation (ITC), a subcontractor of ASI. In November 1991, "International Technology Corporation's Gerald W. Westerbeck, DOE's deputy site manager, said that ASI is now performing adequately at the Fernald site" (Pasternak and Cary, December 14, 1992: 36).

Cleanup management problems have not just been found by external sources. Internal auditors at DOE criticized agency management for serious time delays, cost overruns, and poor progress in cleaning up the Fernald site. At Fernald, DOE's Inspector General faulted the agency and its contractors for extensive cost overruns and time delays in performing the site's remedial investigation and feasibility study (Engineering News Record, May 24, 1993: 22).

The Inspector General's report stated that DOE's Fernald field office and its contractors "had no experience in planning, executing, and controlling remedial investigation and feasibility studies. The Inspector General is also asking DOE to recover $668,000 from the contractor for billings that exceeded the number of hours shown in drilling reports" (Engineering News Record, May 24, 1993: 22). The Inspector General also criticized DOE for spending "$2.3 million on preliminary design and budgeting another $178 million for further design and construction of forty-five waste storage buildings at Fernald, even though a disposal method had not been chosen. The report said that DOE assumed a major financial risk without any assurances that EPA would approve" (Engineering News Record, May 24, 1993: 22). The Inspector General "also noted that preliminary estimates for constructing the storage buildings at Fernald was $1,083 per cubic yard compared to $48.50 per cubic yard for similar structures at DOE's Weldon Spring, Missouri site. The Inspector General wanted to know if the cost difference was justified if the buildings were necessary" (Engineering and News Record, May 24, 1993: 22).

DOE received criticism for not having enough personnel assigned to facilities targeted for cleanups. Leo Duffy, a DOE manager who was responsible for environmental cleanups at DOE facilities, was appointed to this position in 1989. Duffy stated that when he began working at this position, DOE did not have an existing plan for spending money on cleaning its facilities. No staff existed to coordinate environmental cleanup activities at the 36 DOE sites targeted for cleanups. Few persons were assigned to such DOE sites as Fernald, the Savannah River Plant, and Hanford.

During 1991, Duffy wanted to hire new personnel to work at the cleanup sites; but this would create more costs for DOE, and the Clinton administration wanted to control costs. Duffy wanted to hire 707 new employees. Only 58 or 8% would be employed in the fields of cost estimation, accounting, budget review, and business management. However, the other personnel would perform no oversight duties whatsoever. DOE allocated money to hire only scientists, engineers, attorneys, administrators, and personnel managers (Pasternak and Cary, December 14, 1992: 46).

Fluor Daniel was also criticized for billing the government for items such as expensive company dinners, an Earth Day celebration, a company picnic, and ordering clothes for their community relations staff. The Fluor Daniel company picnic cost taxpayers approximately $108,000 (Aeppel, June 30, 1994: A2).

All of these incidents angered the House Energy and Commerce Committee, which is responsible for overseeing DOE. In December 1993, the committee held hearings in which it criticized Fluor Daniel for its past actions. During a December 1, 1993, congressional hearing, Thomas P. Grumbley, Assistant Secretary for Environmental Restoration and Waste Management, stated that he was dissatisfied with FERMCO's performance. He said that DOE was concerned because of the contractor's handling of labor disputes, costs, and safety concerns (Ichniowski and Rubin, January 3, 1994: 11). Congressional committee members warned Fluor Daniel that if the company did not improve its performance, its contract would be awarded to another company. Subcommittee Chairman John D. Dingell (D-Michigan) also criticized the contractor. Dingell contended that while FERMCO focused its attention on site cleanup, it failed to implement critical management systems (Ichniowski, December 13, 1993: 8). Nicholas C. Kaufman, FERMCO's president, responded that FERMCO inherited a 2,000 person workforce that had to be retrained from conducting nuclear weapons production to performing environmental cleanup activities, and that in April 1993, FERMCO was notified that DOE's Fernald budget was cut 30 %. As a result, these budget cuts forced FERMCO to reorganize plans for all the work they intended to perform. FERMCO's president also mentioned that Fernald had five different site managers since FERMCO took over the site on December 1, 1992 (Ichniowski, December 13, 1993: 9). On December 15, 1993, Fluor Daniel replaced Kaufman as the president of FERMCO. Fluor Daniel transferred the individual to another position within the company, and replaced the individual with three of the company's senior managers. DOE said that FERMCO's performance has improved, but that the contractor is still under close observation.

The awarding of a contract to Fluor Daniel was the first time that the agency awarded a contract to a company to clean up one of its nuclear facilities. DOE's purpose was to award a contract to a single Environmental Restoration Management Contractor (ERMC) that would supervise and integrate the cleanup activities involving the contractor and the subcontractors. Some federal auditors were concerned that the ERMC program system might repeat some of the mistakes made under the previous system. A GAO report concluded that there was little evidence that using the ERMC program would result in increased savings. Several reports by the news media criticized DOE, its contractor, and several subcontractors for incurring cost overruns and performing inadequate work. The House Energy and Commerce Committee criticized Fluor Daniel for the contractor's handling of labor disputes, safety concerns, cost overruns, and failure to implement critical management systems. The congressional committee threatened to award the contract to another company if Fluor Daniel did not improve its performance. DOE said that Fluor Daniel's performance has improved, but the agency is keeping the contractor under close observation.

Fernald Dose Reconstruction Study

Since 1990, the federal government's Centers for Disease Control and Prevention (CDC) has supervised a dose reconstruction study that is being conducted by the Radiological Assessments Corporation. This study estimated the amount of radioactive material released at Fernald from 1951 until 1988. The study then estimated the type of radioactivity and the amount of radioactivity the public may have been exposed to during this period. In this study, the public is defined as persons who lived and/or worked within a 6.2-mile radius of the Fernald facility. The CDC estimated that:

> As many as 1 million pounds of uranium was released into the environment from Fernald. Very high concentrations of uranium exist in soils at depths up to 20 feet in the former production area as a result of leaks, spills, and runoff during production. Airborne uranium has also resulted in widespread contamination in surface soils outside Fernald's former production area. (Fernald Citizens Task Force, July 1995: 8)

Although the CDC report focused on uranium releases, radon was the primary radioactive substance released from the facility that contributed to the public's health risks. The radon came mainly from the K-65 concrete silos that are situated along the western area of the Fernald site. The highest level of radioactivity at the Fernald site was found in three of the K-65 silos (Fernald Citizens Task Force, July 1995: 8). The silos were constructed in 1951 to provide temporary storage for waste materials. However, the waste materials were never removed from the silos. Silos 1 and 2 contain wet waste residues that resulted from processing high-grade uranium ores. High concentrations of radium were stored in silos 1 and 2, which resulted in the production of dangerous levels of radon gas (Fernald Citizens Task Force, July 1995: 9). Leaks eventually developed in the domes of silos 1 and 2. Large amounts of radon were released into the environment from the K-65 silos from 1951 until 1988. As a result, large amounts of radon gas were released into the atmosphere. Silo 3 contains cold metal oxide residues generated at Fernald from uranium extraction operations during the 1950s. Silo 4 was never used and remains empty except for rainwater (Fernald Citizens Task Force, July 1995: 10). The radon releases were highest during the 1960s and 1970s and decreased significantly after 1979. This decrease occurred because some openings in the domes of the K-65 silos were sealed. In 1991, the radon emissions decreased further when the Fernald facility installed a bentonite clay layer within the silos.

The Dose Reconstruction Study took into consideration that there were several ways that the public could become exposed to radiation. These ways included direct exposure to water, air, soil, vegetation, milk, and other food sources. The food sources received radiation doses through direct contact with the air, growing in contaminated soil, and milk produced by cows exposed to the radiation. The amount of radiation exposure that a person received depended upon the number of years a person lived in the area, how far away a person lived and worked from the Fernald facility, and whether an individual ate food that was exposed to radiation. The study examined nine hypothetical scenarios in which a person could receive doses of radiation that might cause cancer. The scenarios were based on how far a person lived from Fernald, and how many years a person had lived near Fernald. For example, a person who lived only one mile from Fernald received a median radiation exposure that was ten times greater than the median amount of radiation exposure received by a person who lived only six miles from the Fernald facility. The study did not cover persons who worked at Fernald and thus received higher doses of radiation during their working hours.

In August 1996, the study concluded that persons who lived near Fernald and worked at the Fernald plant had a higher-than-average chance of developing lung cancer. The *Fernald Dosimetry Reconstruction Project Study* (Radiological Assessments Corporation, August 1996) was the first government-sponsored study of cancer risks from Fernald that confirmed the beliefs of local residents. The reaction of local residents accepted the results of the study and stated that the study confirmed the fears and beliefs of many persons who lived near Fernald. The study stated that in the worst-case scenario, a Fernald area resident would had a 3% chance, and in some cases, possibly as high as a 9% chance of increased cancer risk over other Americans of developing lung cancer in his lifetime"(Van Sant, August 23, 1996: A7). The study considered radon gas to be the main health threat to the residents' health. Surprisingly, the study determined that the main health threat was not the thousands of tons of uranium dust that were released from Fernald during its years of operation, even for persons who might have ingested uranium by drinking water from underground wells located near Fernald. The study determined that radon gas emitting from the K-65 silos at the Fernald site "accounted for at least 70% of the local residents' radiation exposure" (Bonfield, August 23, 1996: A8).

In February 1997, several of the scientists who conducted the study said that they overestimated the cancer risks of local residents. The National Research Council, a division of the National Academy of Science, formed a 14-member panel to review the study. The National Research Council released a report stating that the study omitted several key factors that might cause an increase in the likelihood of lung cancer. The review panel stated that cigarette smoking was a factor that was not taken into account during the study. The review panel also stated that the study overestimated the amounts of the doses and the risks of cancer that threatened local residents. The Centers for Disease Control planned to review the study and the National Research Council's report before deciding whether it would conduct a study to determine if Fernald residents suffered from a cancer rate that was higher than average. Fernald SSAB member Lisa Crawford said that she was surprised by the release of the National Research Council's report. Crawford declared that it was unfair for the Fernald community to be told in August 1996 that it had a higher-than-average risk for cancer but, in February 1997, the same community was told that it has a much lower risk of cancer than previously thought.

In July 1997, scientists from the National Research Council retracted the report they released in February 1997, and confirmed the findings of the Radiological Assessment Corporation's August 1996 report. Previously, the National Research Council scientists had argued that the August 1996 study's "dose estimates for women, children, and non-smokers who lived near Fernald was four to six times too high. In July 1997, the scientists stated that the figures for women and non-smokers were accurate, and both the National Research Council and the Radiological Assessment Corporation agreed to decrease the estimate dosage for children" (Gallagher and Bonfield, July 11, 1997: A1).

Fernald residents and their supporters were pleased to hear that the National Research Council scientists now supported the findings of the August 1996 report. Many local residents, researchers, and scientists want the federal government's Centers for Disease Control to conduct a full epidemiological study. The government scientists' confirmation of the Fernald Dose Reconstruction Study's August 1996 report's findings gave new support to the persons who wanted the epidemiological study conducted. The epidemiological study would determine how many local residents contracted lung cancer due to radiation exposure from the Fernald plant. This study would also compare past and present cancer cases with estimated doses of radiation to determine if there is a connection between radiation dosages and increased cancer rates. The study would take many years to complete and would cost several million dollars.

Conclusion

The Fernald site was built in the 1950s as part of DOE's nuclear weapons complex. Fernald's mission was to produce uranium products that would be shipped to other DOE facilities for assembly into nuclear weapons. The production activities at Fernald also produced radioactive, hazardous, and toxic byproducts constituting a serious threat to humans and the environment. The DOE and its contractors buried large quantities of radioactive and hazardous wastes on the Fernald site. Significant quantities of uranium dust were also released into the atmosphere. Pollution problems, safety concerns, and worker health concerns resulted in several lawsuits being filed against DOE. Local residents, Fernald workers, and the state of Ohio have each filed lawsuits against DOE. All this bred a continuing legacy of distrust and controversy with which DOE must today contend in the Fernald region.

The nature of its operations, chronic problems with waste storage and disposal, and a legacy of environmental degradation at the DOE Fernald facility unfortunately is characteristic of the nuclear weapons complex as a whole. The quest for weapons production, with little regard for the progressively harmful long-term effects of its byproducts, occurred behind the veil of national security and military secrecy. This greatly exacerbated the problems of public access and accountability inherent in any closed, technocratic decision making agency. Eventually, the DOE faced an increasingly hostile political environment and found itself in gridlock. Under pressure from citizens' groups, local and state governments, the federal courts, other federal agencies, and the weight of congressional legislation, the DOE office at Fernald found itself with little choice but to move toward more systematic and comprehensive citizen participation. It was at this troubled facility that the *first* of DOE's SSABs became operational. The next chapter details that endeavor.

NOTES

1. This table is provided in Appendix A.
2. Figure 4 can be found in Appendix B.

3

Implementing the Model: The Creation of the Fernald Site Specific Advisory Board

Introduction

In this chapter, the creation and operation of the Fernald Site Specific Advisory Board is described. A third-party convener selected the members of the original SSAB. The convener endeavored to produce an SSAB membership representing the full spectrum of stakeholders.[1] The advisory board organized itself into committees, held meetings and workshops, voted on issues, and published reports including recommendations for waste disposal and land use at Fernald after the cleanup activities are completed. In 1993, shaped largely by the recommendations contained in the Keystone Report discussed earlier, and with adjustments for unique local conditions, the Fernald SSAB was the first full-scale DOE effort to implement the stakeholder involvement model in the weapons complex (U.S. DOE, January 1997: 1).

The Creation of the Fernald Site Specific Advisory Board: Steps Taken by DOE to Establish the Fernald

From May 1993 until August 1993, the creation of an SSAB was in the planning stages. The advisory group then was referred to as the Fernald Advisory Committee (FAC). In August 1993, this advisory group changed its name to the Fernald Citizens Task Force (FCTF). In July 1997, the Fernald Citizens Task Force changed its name to the Fernald Citizens Advisory Board (FCAB). By whatever name, the stakeholder group was an SSAB and was established by DOE to help design and monitor environmental management and remediation activities at the Fernald site. The goal of the SSAB is to increase stakeholder involvement and to improve the decision making process in the Fernald restoration activities. The SSAB was formed with the cooperation of the U.S. Environmental Protection Agency (U.S. EPA), the Ohio Environmental Protection Agency (Ohio EPA), and DOE. The SSAB consists of fourteen stakeholders and two alternates. Representatives from the U.S. EPA, Ohio EPA, and DOE are ex-officio members of the SSAB (Fernald Citizens Task Force, September 15, 1993: 3). The ex-officio members participate in the advisory group's discussions. Ex-officio members of the SSABs serve as advisors and are non-voting members on all the SSABs.

The SSAB members represent various stakeholders affected by Fernald's cleanup activities. The stakeholders represented on the SSAB include the following groups: local residents, labor organizations, a local environmental group, business organizations, a medical organization, and various local governments. The SSAB members were chosen in accordance with the requirements of the Federal Advisory Committee Act of 1972 (FACA). FACA requires that persons selected to participate on federal advisory boards must be representatives of stakeholder groups affected by a particular public policy. These advisory boards were established so that its members could discuss the concerns and recommendations of the affected stakeholder groups with the agency responsible for implementing the public policy. Some of the SSAB members live near the Fernald site. All of them live or work in the Cincinnati area. Members of the SSAB do not receive any pay for their service on the advisory board, but receive reimbursement for travel and other expenses. DOE provides funding and administrative support for the SSAB (Fernald Citizens Task Force, September 15, 1993: 3).

Board Mission

In August 1993, the DOE formally recognized the SSAB. The SSAB officially reports to the DOE Assistant Secretary for Environmental Management, the EPA Region V regional administrator, and the director of the Ohio EPA (Fernald Citizens Task Force, July 1995: 14). The SSAB was chartered to provide DOE, EPA, and the Ohio EPA with recommendations regarding four critical issues facing the Fernald facility in its effort to deal with the legacy of its production operations:

What should be the future use of the Fernald site?

What residual risk and remediation levels should remain following remediation?

Where should the waste be disposed?

What should be the priorities among remedial actions? (iii)

The reports subsequently issued by the SSAB provide stakeholder answers to these questions. When trying to answer these questions, the SSAB had to consider social, health, economic, and political issues at Fernald, and the consequences of cleaning up the Fernald site (29).

Board Recruitment

An independent consultant was hired to serve as the convener of the Fernald SSAB. The convener's primary task was to identify and select members for the SSAB. In May 1993, DOE, EPA, and the Ohio EPA worked through the Alliance of Ohio Universities to hire Dr. Eula Bingham, a professor of environmental health at the University of Cincinnati College of Medicine. Her qualifications for the job were impeccable.

At the time of her appointment, Dr. Bingham was the director of the Ohio Hazardous Substances Research, Education, and Management Institute at the University of Cincinnati. She served as a volunteer investigator for the National Institute of Environmental Health Sciences and had served on several local, national, and international committees that dealt with environmental and public health issues. From 1977 until 1981, Dr. Bingham also served as the administrator of the Occupational Safety and Health Administration during the Carter administration. Dr. Bingham, in an interview with a journalist, indicated that she considered the establishment of a local citizen advisory board "a critical step in ensuring that the democratic principles envisioned by the Founding Fathers are used to resolve the intractable problems of nuclear waste disposal" (Powers, June 9, 1993; 1A). Her job was to identify potential candidates for membership on the SSAB, interview the candidates, and deliver a list of recommendations to DOE. DOE gave the University of Cincinnati $15,000 to select the stakeholders for the advisory board. Bingham received no money from DOE or the University of Cincinnati as compensation for her work in selecting the advisory board members (Fernald Citizens Task Force, July 1995: 13-14). Reflecting on this work five years later, a person associated with the Fernald SSAB said that:

> Dr. Bingham wanted a free hand in selecting the advisory board members. DOE officials at Fernald wanted the job done quickly. She felt that she had to come up with a list of stakeholders who were affected by the activities at Fernald. These stakeholders included local residents, schoolteachers, local officials, labor union representatives, scientists, college professors, and environmental activists. (Telephone interview, September 22, 1998)

From May 1993 until August 1993, Bingham identified and selected potential stakeholders who could participate on the advisory board. The criteria used for selecting persons for the advisory board were that they should be residents who lived within a few miles of the Fernald site and were also members of stakeholder groups that were affected by the cleanup activities at Fernald. Many of the persons who were chosen to become members of the SSAB lived only a few miles from the Fernald site. Other persons selected for SSAB membership lived farther away from Fernald, but belonged to various stakeholders' groups affected by Fernald's cleanup activities.

During the summer of 1993, Bingham used a combination of public meetings, mass mailings, and personal recommendations from local officials and stakeholder groups to identify potential candidates for the board. DOE accepted all the recommended candidates. In August 1993, the advisory board was established as the Fernald Citizens Task Force—DOE's *first* SSAB now was in place (Fernald Citizens Task Force, July 1995: 13-14).

The convener was also asked by DOE to identify a potential chairperson for the SSAB and, in consultation with DOE, EPA, and the Ohio EPA, to develop a draft charter. Eventually Dr. Bingham recommended Mr. John Applegate, a professor of environmental law at the University of Cincinnati, for appointment as the chairperson of the SSAB. A Fernald SSAB member later applauded Dr. Bingham's work and gave her much credit for later SSAB credibility and success:

> Eula Bingham was an excellent choice as a convener because she was independent of DOE and was respected in the community. She had the political experience to be able to "read" the community to identify groups that needed to be represented and individuals who could work together. DOE accepted her recommendations. Once the convening process was complete, Bingham had no further role with the Fernald SSAB or the Fernald site. (Applegate, 1998: 936)

Eventually, Dr. Bingham recommended 14 members and 2 alternates to serve on the original Fernald SSAB. Two of the nominees declined—citing time constraints for their refusal. One person resigned after limited service and another switched places with an original alternate. Subsequently, an additional person petitioned the board for a seat on the SSAB. The SSAB members recommended that this person be appointed. DOE later made the appointment. To provide membership continuity over time, half of the members were given two-year terms, and half were given three-year terms. In addition to the regular SSAB members, representatives from DOE, EPA, and Ohio EPA were placed on the board as ex-officio members. In that capacity, they act as advisors to the board and are non-voting members.

When the SSAB members' terms expire, the board's steering committee proposes new members to fill the vacancies, and the entire board discusses and votes in the new members. In considering new appointees, the committee takes into account such factors as the SSAB's need for technical expertise, demographic balance, and diversity. Under the charter, the SSAB recommends replacements to DOE, and the DOE Secretary makes the appointment. The DOE Secretary selects the new board members in concurrence with DOE's Ohio Field Office and the Fernald DOE office (Telephone interview, November 18, 1998).

The 14 charter members of the SSAB represented a variety of interests and backgrounds that were crucial to the environmental management and restoration activities at Fernald. Eight members lived or worked in the vicinity of Fernald. The remaining SSAB members were selected to reflect a combination of skills, interests, and constituencies that are important to the remediation of the Fernald site. All the SSAB members live and work with the Cincinnati metropolitan area (Fernald Citizens Task Force, July 1995: 13-14).

Board Organization[2]

When the Fernald SSAB was first formed, it held monthly meetings, originally on weekday evenings and then on Saturday mornings to provide an opportunity for holding longer meetings. The SSAB made efforts to hold its meetings within the vicinity of the Fernald site. However, space requirements and a desire to reduce costs eventually resulted in meetings being held in a variety of locations around the region. Ultimately, a permanent facility used by the Fernald facility contractor was made available to the SSAB at no cost to the board. The SSAB's meetings are open to the public and are widely publicized in local newspapers and through mass mailings. Members of the public are invited to raise questions and express their concerns at these meetings. Information about forthcoming meetings is also posted on Internet sites that are maintained by DOE's Fernald field office. In 1996, after completing the tasks required in its original mission statement, the SSAB began holding its meetings only once every two months. These meetings are usually held on a weekday evening.

In December 1995, the SSAB formed four committees to address specific areas of environmental management and remediation activities at Fernald. The committees were formed to address issues such as technical support, membership, groundwater remediation standards, and waste disposition. Each committee had three to five members and a chairperson. The four committees were: Transportation, Natural Resources, Environmental Monitoring, and Waste Management. As the SSAB gained experience and the nature of its tasks became evident over time, the board changed its committee system. An environmental engineer familiar with the Fernald SSAB said that "as the Fernald SSAB gains experience and knowledge, it periodically reorganizes its committee structure to meet new and existing environmental cleanup issues" (Personal interview, Oak Ridge, Tennessee, June 19, 2000). Thus, in 1997, three additional committees were formed: the Efficiency Committee, the Steering Committee, and the Membership Committee. In February 1998, the SSAB reorganized its seven committees into four committees: the Off-Site Committee; the On-Site Committee; the Efficiency Committee; and the Steering Committee. In January 2000, the SSAB again reorganized into two committees: the Stewardship Committee and the Remediation Committee.

Besides serving on these committees, SSAB members also serve on other citizen advisory boards that address issues concerning Fernald. These advisory boards include the Fernald Community Reuse Organization (FCRO) and the Fernald Health Effects Subcommittee (FHES). The FCRO is a community group consisting of local residents and FDF employees. The FCRO addresses economic development issues that will occur at Fernald once the cleanup activities are completed. The FCRO also advises DOE on socioeconomic issues that will result from employee layoffs and Fernald's eventual closure after the cleanup activities are completed. The FHES is comprised of persons who are concerned about the effects of radioactive and hazardous wastes on the health of residents who live near Fernald. Thus, the SSAB provides stakeholder *representation* not only through its membership, but, due to its members having overlapping organizational memberships, it also integrates the board into a larger web of citizen participation mechanisms.

The SSAB also hired a technical consultant independently to verify and evaluate the information given to them by DOE and Fluor Daniel, Fernald (FDF). FDF provides the SSAB with clerical staff who work under the direction of the SSAB chairperson. In addition, FDF also provided the SSAB with a second technical consultant who is an FDF employee.

The Fernald SSAB also reviews the budget amounts received by DOE's Fernald site and contracts awarded by DOE to companies to perform environmental cleanup work at Fernald. If the SSAB feels that the budget amount is not sufficient to maintain Fernald's cleanup activities, then the SSAB consults with DOE officials, FDF officials, and members of Congress. The members of Congress consulted by the Fernald SSAB include Ohio's two senators and the congressional representatives from the Cincinnati area.

Administrative support for the SSAB was provided by FERMCO, DOE's site contractor for the Fernald facility. The administrative support staff consists of one full-time staff member and several clerical support staff members who work under the direction of the SSAB chairperson. The SSAB also hired a consultant independently to verify the technical information and other information given to them by DOE and FERMCO. This action also helps the SSAB to maintain its stature as a neutral and independent citizen advisory group. The SSAB hired Douglas Sarno, the president of Phoenix Environmental Corporation, to act as the advisory board's technical consultant. Phoenix Environmental Corporation is an environmental consulting firm based in Arlington, Virginia. In December 1993, Phoenix Environmental began working for the SSAB. The SSAB also obtained from DOE funds to contract with other experts on specific issues on an *ad hoc* basis.

The SSAB spent the first six months of 1994 increasing its knowledge on DOE site characteristics and environmental cleanup activities. Members felt these activities were necessary because of their widely differing backgrounds and experience and the acute variation in their level of technical knowledge on environmental public policy activities.

When making its decisions, the SSAB tries to discuss the issues in depth before taking a vote. The SSAB tries to reach a consensus on these issues and then makes its decisions by taking a vote in which the majority vote rules. One SSAB member commented on this by observing that: "The majority vote has nearly always been unanimous, but there have been a few cases in which there has been at least one no vote. The Fernald SSAB makes every effort to achieve a consensus on issues. We normally try to discuss an issue in depth before taking a vote so that we know whether there is a high degree of consensus" (Telephone interview, November 18, 1998).

Indeed, the degree of consensus attained by the SSAB has proven remarkable. As another SSAB member observed, "In the entire history of the Fernald SSAB, I can recall only one vote that was not unanimous" (Telephone interview, November 18, 1998).

Fernald SSAB Operations and Activities: Meetings, Workshops, and Hearings

The Fernald SSAB holds regular meetings. From 1993 until 1996, these meetings were held once a month. Since 1997, meetings have been held once every two months. Whenever possible, the SSAB holds these meetings within the vicinity of the Fernald site. Sometimes, the SSAB holds its meetings in various locations to give more people an opportunity to attend the meetings. A permanent site for meetings was eventually selected for all SSAB meetings. The meeting place and the SSAB office are located within a few miles of the Fernald site. All meetings are open to the public. Time for public comment is made available at each meeting. Sufficient space is made available for public attendance at the board meetings. Public notices of all board meetings are issued in local newspapers and through mass mailings.

During 1993, the SSAB held several meetings that were open to the public and functioned as workshops. One SSAB member described these meetings "as workshops in the sense that there was dialogue and education among those who attended the meetings. The SSAB also holds periodic retreats for its own members. In May 1999, the SSAB held a workshop on transportation for all of DOE's SSABs" (Telephone interview, November 18, 1998). Another SSAB member said that the SSAB held workshops on issues such as the On-Site Disposal Facility. An example of a workshop session was the *FUTURESITE* simulation game that the advisory board members played to determine an effective method of disposing of Fernald's wastes. Other SSAB workshops were conducted with FRESH to discuss issues such as government contracting and specific technologies being considered for Fernald's cleanup activities (Telephone interview, November 16, 1998). A third SSAB member commented that several community workshops were held when the advisory board first discussed whether Fernald's wastes should be buried on-site or off-site. Once the decision was made to build the on-site disposal facility, the SSAB held workshops on the proposed design of the on-site disposal facility (Telephone interview, November 18, 1998). In May 2000, the Fernald SSAB, FRESH, FLHP (Fernald Living History Project), and FHES held a public meeting to allow members of the public to give their opinions on what should happen to the Fernald site once the cleanup activities are completed. Another public meeting was held in September 2000 by these groups to allow the public to give additional comments on what should be done with Fernald after its cleanup activities are finished.

The SSAB does not hold public hearings as such. It does, however, provide the public an opportunity to make comments and ask questions at the end of its meetings. The SSAB members attend public hearings that are held by DOE on issues relating to Fernald. The SSAB often makes comments on these issues during the DOE hearings.

Reports

In November 1994, the Fernald SSAB published its *Interim Report.* This report recommended that all high-level radioactive and hazardous wastes be removed from the site. The *Interim Report* also recommended that the Fernald site *not* be used for recreational or agricultural purposes. During 1994, approximately 250 acres located near the outer boundaries of the Fernald site were leased to two farmers for cattle grazing. This lease was to expire in 1996. The report said that the Fernald site might be suited for commercial or industrial uses. Dr. Constance Fox, a member of Physicians for Social Responsibility and an SSAB member, stated that, "the cattle may to us symbolize hypocrisy because, in the past, Fernald operators were saying that nothing was contaminated and studies later showed problems. They may also symbolize the canary in the coal mine—that things are safe" (Reeves, November 13, 1994: B1). Guy Guckenberger, another SSAB member, stated that he "wanted grazing to be an option after cleanup because radiation would be reduced to levels low enough not to harm cow's meat or milk" (Reeves, November 13, 1994: B11). John Applegate, the SSAB chairperson, said that livestock would not be able to use the land during the cleanup activities because some areas would have to be dug up and replaced with uncontaminated soil. However, Lisa Crawford, president of FRESH and an SSAB member, stated that "it doesn't look good to have cows grazing on a hazardous waste site. It won't be taken down to background [radiation levels]. There's still a risk" (Reeves, November 13, 1994: B11). The *Interim Report* recommended that the site be used for commercial or industrial purposes to create jobs and maintain the area's tax base.

In July 1995, the Fernald SSAB published a report titled *Fernald Citizens Task Force: Recommendations on Remediation Levels, Waste Disposition, Priorities, and Future Use*. This report marked the accomplishment of the major part of the SSAB's short-term mission. As charged by its charter, the board in this report provided stakeholder advice and recommendations for waste disposal, environmental cleanup activities, and future uses for the Fernald site. As is true of the advice provided by any board chartered under the FACA, the report is *advisory*. While not legally binding, it is expected that the DOE and other federal agencies will weigh the SSAB recommendations heavily in making decisions about these critical issues. Moreover, the report provides a basis for an *on-going dialogue* among stakeholders and federal agencies—especially between Fernald stakeholders and the DOE. Finally, it is assumed that the failure of federal agencies to accommodate the SSAB's report would likely cause a breakdown in the public participation process so painstakingly created just four years earlier. This, in turn, likely would invite the return of protest, litigation, controversy, and gridlock. The Fernald SSAB recommended:

- Reducing the cleanup period at Fernald from 25 years to approximately 10 years.
- The most highly contaminated radioactive and hazardous wastes should be buried *off-site* at other facilities.
- An *on-site disposal facility* constructed on the Fernald site to bury only low-level wastes from the Fernald site.
- Residential and agricultural uses for the Fernald site *should be avoided* once the cleanup activities are completed.

DOE originally estimated that it would take the agency approximately 25 years to clean up the Fernald site. In June 1996, DOE gave tentative approval to a plan to accelerate the cleanup activities at Fernald and to complete the cleanup activities in 10 years instead of 25 years. The ten-year environmental cleanup period for Fernald was scheduled to begin during the federal fiscal year 1996 and end during the federal fiscal year 2005. Under the ten-year plan, DOE began the cleanup work at Fernald during the year 1996 and hoped to finish by the year 2006. However, once the cleanup activities began, DOE estimated that the cleanup activities might be completed in 2010. An Environmental Management Ten-year Plan was devised by DOE and FERMCO during the budget negotiations with Congress for the federal fiscal year 1996. DOE's Ohio Field Office in Miamisburg, Ohio, developed the Fernald ten-year plan for cleaning up the site. DOE estimates that the ten-year plan will save billions of dollars in environmental cleanup costs. The SSAB, EPA, and Ohio EPA provided support and assistance in developing DOE's ten-year plan for Fernald. These three organizations sent letters to DOE headquarters stating that they supported the DOE Ohio Field Office's revised ten-year plan for environmental cleanup at Fernald. FRESH, a neighborhood environmental group that monitors DOE's activities at Fernald, encouraged persons to write letters to members of Congress urging congressional support of Fernald's ten-year plan. DOE has ordered all of its regional offices and field offices to develop environmental management ten-year plans for completing the environmental cleanups at each of DOE's facilities.

A second recommendation is for the disposal of contaminated wastes from the Fernald site. The SSAB recommends that high-level contaminated waste be transported from the Fernald site. The high-level waste is to be buried permanently or placed in long-term storage at DOE's Nevada Test Site facility. Some of Fernald's waste is to be permanently buried or placed in long-term storage at the commercially owned and operated Envirocare hazardous waste disposal site located near Clive, Utah. This facility receives more than 95 % of the government's low-level nuclear wastes. On June 30, 1998, DOE announced that it awarded a $66 million, three-year contract to Envirocare of Utah, Incorporated. This contract allows DOE to bury low-level wastes at Envirocare's Clive, Utah, facility. Under federally imposed deadlines, DOE was to begin transporting the radioactive wastes from Fernald by March 1, 1999. If everything goes according to schedule, DOE hopes to complete the Fernald cleanup in 2006 (Melcer, May 31, 1998: A7). DOE has options to extend the contract if it wishes to do so (U.S. DOE, Fernald Report, July 1998: 3).

DOE also ships some of Fernald's waste to DOE's Oak Ridge Reservation site and burns the waste in a TSCA (Toxic Substances Control Act of 1976) hazardous waste incinerator located at the K-25 Oak Ridge Gaseous Diffusion Plant. The K-25 incinerator began operating in 1989 and receives hazardous wastes from many of DOE's nuclear facilities.

A third recommendation from the SSAB was that low-level contaminated waste be buried at the Fernald site. A disposal cell would be designed and constructed at the Fernald site to store the facility's low-level wastes. This low-level waste disposal facility would be called the On-Site Disposal Facility (OSDF). An On-Site Disposal Facility for storing low-level wastes at the site is being designed and will eventually be constructed in the OU2 area of Fernald.

The SSAB recommended that DOE construct a buffer zone with a minimum of at least 300 feet to separate the OSDF from other parts of the Fernald site that would be used for other purposes. The property may be used for other activities after the environmental cleanup activities are completed. In May 1997, DOE awarded Petro Environmental Technologies, Incorporated (PETI) a contract to begin the first phase of the OSDF's construction. PETI, Incorporated is an environmental engineering company that has its corporate headquarters based in Cincinnati. During July 1997, PETI began constructing the OSDF.

An Advanced Waste Water Treatment Plant (AWWTP) has been constructed in the OU5 area of the Fernald site. This plant was constructed to treat water contaminated with hazardous waste and radioactive wastes from the Fernald site. DOE plans an expansion project for this plant facility to increase its treatment capacity.

Several factors influenced the SSAB to recommend burying low-level waste at the Fernald site. One factor was the creation of a board game that was developed to help SSAB members and members of the public understand the complex technical information regarding Fernald's environmental problems. The name of the board game was *FUTURESITE*, which was developed by John Applegate and Douglas Sarno. The object of the game was to move piles of environmental waste, to try different means of disposing the waste, and to remain within a budget while disposing of the wastes. The *FUTURESITE* game board consisted of a map of the Fernald facility that was divided into a grid of 63 squares. On each square, colored chips represented the volume of waste material at particular locations at Fernald. Chips are color-coded to represent the degree of contaminated soil and wastes that had to be removed to achieve a given future use of the property within that square. Chips were stacked according to the level of contamination, with chips representing the most heavily contaminated material on top. All of the chips that were removed from the board required disposal; and, since the chips represented radioactive material, only two choices were available: on-site disposal and off-site disposal. The board game provided worksheets to help people determine the costs of various options, the number of truckloads needed for off-site disposal, and the number of acres needed for the on-site disposal of Fernald's wastes (Applegate and Sarno, July 1996: 12).

The *FUTURESITE* game is a graphic representation of the Fernald site that clarified the configuration of the site, and helped improve SSAB members' understanding of the cleanup options. The board game also illustrated trade-offs between such factors such as risk, cost, waste disposal, and transportation danger. After playing the board game, the SSAB members had a better understanding of Fernald's environmental problems and of the options available for disposing of the wastes (Applegate and Sarno, July 1996: 12). Playing the board game persuaded the majority of the SSAB members to recommend building the On-Site Disposal Facility.

A second factor that influenced the SSAB to bury some of the wastes at Fernald was that there were only two facilities available to handle large amounts of low-level radioactive waste from Fernald. These facilities are DOE's Nevada Test Site in Nevada, and the Envirocare facility in Utah. Both of these facilities face significant political pressures not to accept large amounts of low-level radioactive wastes from other states. The Envirocare facility has a limited capacity for burying large amounts of additional radioactive wastes. Moreover, political opposition to receiving high-level radioactive waste from Fernald already exists. For example, Nevada officials filed a lawsuit against DOE to prevent high-level hazardous and radioactive wastes from being transported from Fernald to the Nevada Test Site. The Nevada officials lost the lawsuit and DOE continued transporting the wastes to Nevada.

On May 22, 1997, a shipping container holding low-level radioactive waste burst open inside one of the buildings at the Fernald site. The burst container released radiation that did not escape the building. Hazardous waste disposal emergency crews were alerted and arrived at the building. The waste container was to be shipped to the Nevada Test Site for burial. DOE officials believe that a chemical reaction of an unknown source occurred among the wastes and caused the container to burst open. As a result of the incident, the mayor of Las Vegas, two Nevada congressmen, and the executive director of a Nevada nuclear waste agency called the incident a potentially serious problem (Bonfield, June 12, 1997: C9). These individuals wanted all truck shipments of waste from Fernald to the Nevada Test Site halted until an investigation of the incident is completed. There is concern because the route taken by the trucks passes through cities such as St. Louis, Missouri; Evansville, Indiana; Amarillo, Texas; Flagstaff, Arizona; and Las Vegas, Nevada (Bonfield, June 12, 1997: C9). The route taken by the trucks also passes close to hotels that are located in the downtown area of Las Vegas. Workers at Fernald have stopped shipping the particular waste that caused the chemical reaction. Fernald, however continued to send other high-level and low-level radioactive wastes to Nevada after the incident.

In December 1997, a second incident occurred involving trucks carrying wastes from the Fernald site to DOE's facility in Nevada. While stopped in Kingman, Arizona, a truck driver who was transporting wastes from Fernald noticed that several containers that held low-level wastes leaked while being transported from Fernald to the Nevada Test Site. This incident also resulted in criticism from Nevada politicians who opposed the shipments of radioactive wastes into Nevada. A DOE official said that the agency had halted additional waste shipments from Fernald to the Nevada Test Site until an investigation was completed. Wastes have been transported from Fernald to the Nevada Test Site since 1985.

Since the Kingman incident, DOE has suspended all shipments of wastes from Fernald to the Nevada Test Site. DOE said that it planned to evaluate its responses and policies regarding the Kingman incident and examine the types of waste containers that leaked during the incident. The agency is considering designing new containers or purchasing different types of waste containers to resume transporting wastes to the Nevada Test Site.

A second example of political opposition to receiving wastes from Fernald arose in Oak Ridge, Tennessee. Since 1986, DOE has been sending some wastes from Fernald to Oak Ridge's K-25 TSCA incinerator. Certain workers at the K-25 plant contend that they suffer a range of health problems caused by the emissions originating from the radioactive wastes and hazardous wastes that are burned at the K-25 incinerator. Many K-25 workers, local residents, and state legislators opposed DOE's policy of transporting radioactive and hazardous wastes from its other facilities to be burned in the K-25 incinerator. In 1987, EPA granted DOE a ten-year permit to burn hazardous waste and radioactive wastes at the K-25 TSCA incinerator.

In February 1997, *The Nashville Tennessean,* a Nashville newspaper, wrote a series of articles mentioning that the K-25 incinerator accepted hazardous wastes from other DOE facilities. The articles also stated that many K-25 workers had complained of health problems since the incinerator began burning wastes. The publishing of the articles caused widespread public reaction, and created political pressure on state legislators and state officials to respond to the K-25 workers' concerns. State officials believed that DOE should not send hazardous wastes from other states into Tennessee unless this policy was approved by state officials. However, DOE officials believed that the agency had the legal right to ship radioactive and hazardous wastes to any of its facilities, without the approval of state governments (Paine, February 12, 1997: 1A).

In June 1997, as a result of public pressure, Tennessee governor Don Sundquist appointed a panel of experts to review the possibility of renewing the permit for the K-25 incinerator and to address the health and safety concerns of DOE workers at Oak Ridge's K-25 plant. In 1987, the state of Tennessee issued DOE a solid waste permit to burn and handle hazardous wastes at the K-25 incinerator. The permit came up for renewal in September 1997. The incinerator has been operating since 1989. The governor created the panel in response to the complaints of the K-25 workers and the opposition to renewing the permit for the incinerator. In June and July 1997, the panel held public hearings in Oak Ridge, Tennessee. The public hearings were sponsored by the Tennessee Department of Environment and Conservation, which is the state of Tennessee's environmental agency. At the hearings, several K-25 workers stated that they suffered from symptoms such as headaches, fatigue, and memory loss and believed that the wastes burning in the incinerator caused these symptoms (Munger, June 27, 1997: A1). Many K-25 workers, local residents, and state legislators did not want the permit renewed.

In November 1997, the panel appointed by Governor Sundquist finished its report on the K-25 incinerator. The panel concluded that the K-25 incinerator was "operating well within its permissible limits and found no direct link between incinerator operations and the illnesses of the K-25 workers. The panel also recommended that the incinerator continue operating and that more medical care be given to workers and residents who believed that their illnesses are caused by toxic exposures at the Oak Ridge Reservation" (Munger, November 27, 1997: A17). The panel concluded, "none of the incinerator emissions exceeded permissible levels and only one of the measured air pollutant concentrations exceeded standards for a short time, and occurred during a construction project" (Munger, November 27, 1997: A17).

A third factor that led to the SSAB's recommendations was the concern that if a decision was made to send all of Fernald's wastes and contaminated materials to off-site facilities, the Fernald facility would face the possibility of political reprisals from other states. These states may face political pressure from their residents and legislators not to accept wastes from Fernald and other facilities. These political reprisals would result in Fernald being unable to transport any of its wastes to off-site facilities. Political opposition to accepting Fernald's wastes has already emerged in Nevada and Oak Ridge, Tennessee.

A fourth factor that led to the SSAB's recommendations was that, according to the SSAB, the cost of disposing all wastes in off-site facilities was three times the cost of on-site disposal (Fernald Citizens Task Force, July 1995: 40). The SSAB felt that under present and foreseeable budget conditions, a decision to transport all wastes from Fernald would significantly delay the completion of all cleanup activities and prevent any cleanup progress from occurring. The SSAB is concerned that the DOE's budgets reductions since the end of the Cold War may eventually hinder DOE's ability to successfully complete the environmental cleanup activities at its facilities. DOE said that the technology does not exist to return Fernald to the condition it was in before the DOE facility was built. In December 1996, John Bradburne, president of Fernald's current contractor FDF, said that:

> Restoration to a completely uncontaminated state would require surface soil excavation for 5 miles surrounding the site, which the Fernald SSAB rejected because of the high cost. The Fernald SSAB's recommendation on cleanup levels reduces the overall cleanup cost by $1.3 billion, while cleaning up the site so it can be used for certain industrial, not residential purposes. (Bradburne, December 9, 1996: E-24 and E-25)

Bradburne also said that the Fernald SSAB agreed with federal officials who felt that a disposal facility needed to be constructed on the Fernald site to store low-level wastes. The construction of such a facility would significantly reduce cleanup costs: "The Fernald SSAB also concurred with existing DOE and EPA decisions to dispose of the most highly contaminated wastes off-site and recommended construction of an on-site disposal facility (OSDF) to accept slightly contaminated materials from the Fernald site only. This strategy reduces the overall cleanup cost by an additional $850 million for a total cost savings of $2.1 billion" (Bradburne, December 9, 1996: E-24 and E-25).

The Fernald SSAB's decision to bury low-level waste on the Fernald site was controversial. Many persons vocally opposed the decision to bury any contaminated waste on the Fernald site. The SSAB met with members of the community, provided extensive publicity to announce its meetings, and held a special workshop to present the information that influenced the SSAB's decision. Thirteen SSAB members voted to allow the burial of low-level waste at the Fernald site. However, one SSAB member did not support the decision to place a disposal facility for low-level wastes at Fernald. SSAB member Darryl Huff opposed the decision for several reasons. First, placing a disposal facility at the Fernald site would limit the amount of land available for redevelopment. Second, local communities do not wish to be stigmatized for having waste disposal facilities located within their respective communities. Third, facilities located in the western region of the United States are more geologically suited for the long-term storage of radioactive and hazardous wastes than the Fernald site. Fourth, Fernald's contamination problems did not emerge because of local concerns and would not result in sufficient benefits for the community that would justify the construction and the long-term impact of a waste disposal facility at the site.

SSAB member Lisa Crawford said that, "she accepted the Ohio EPA's assurances that Fernald will not become a disposal site for nuclear wastes from other DOE sites. The on-site waste cell is quicker. It's cheaper and it's safer. We have to look at the financial issues because there's not a pot of gold at the end of the rainbow" (Feiertag, August 3, 1995: A5). There was additional opposition from some residents in communities located near Fernald. As one DOE official described the situation:

> Some opposition arose from local officials in Ross Township. Part of Fernald lies within the township. Some local officials and residents resented DOE's decision to construct the OSDF because the township had no representation on the Fernald SSAB from 1993 until 1998. DOE and FDF held monthly meetings with officials to discuss the OSDF, and asked township officials to consider recommending that one of their officials join the Fernald SSAB. (Personal interview, Harrison, Ohio, July 15, 1998)

The meetings also helped to resolve differences between DOE and the township officials. Eventually, in January 1998, a newly elected Ross Township Trustee, Ray Wurzelbacher, was selected to become a member of the SSAB.

The SSAB decided to focus its recommendations for the *future* use of the Fernald site on creating an understanding on how the site could be used after the environmental cleanup activities were completed. The SSAB decided not to identify specific land use plans for the Fernald site. The SSAB believed that specific uses for the site should be determined when the environmental cleanup activities were nearly complete and decided by the persons most affected by the land use. The SSAB recommended that the Fernald site not be used for residential and agricultural development and believed that productive uses for a remedied Fernald site included recreational use and industrial development.

During March 1996, the Fernald SSAB presented its *final* general land use recommendations to DOE. The SSAB recommended that DOE not use the Fernald site for agriculture or residential land use once the cleanup activities were completed. The SSAB also recommended that DOE enhance Fernald's existing natural resources and endangered species habitats. Finally, the SSAB recommended that DOE involve local stakeholders in the agency's final land use decisions (U.S. DOE, Fact Sheet: Request for Input on Final Land Use of the Fernald Site, September 1998: 1).

Other Groups Concerned with Fernald's Cleanup Activities

Residents who live near nuclear facilities have been long concerned about possible contamination problems. In 1984, the Fernald Residents for Environmental Safety and Health (FRESH) was established. FRESH is a community watchdog group consisting of residents who live near the Fernald facility. This group was established after Lisa Crawford, a local resident, discovered that her well water was contaminated with radioactive and hazardous waste from the Fernald facility. Crawford joined with several local residents to express their disgust at the environmental contamination threats that occurred within the community. FRESH initiated the lawsuit against DOE in 1985, complaining that DOE had contaminated the local underground well water supply by burying hazardous and radioactive waste at the facility, and the waste seeped into the underground well water supply. The group still exists and continues to monitor DOE's environmental activities. FRESH currently plays an active role in the Fernald cleanup process by educating the greater community on environmental issues, influencing important decision makers, and taking part in the national debate on environmental cleanup and nuclear waste issues.

In August 1996, the Fernald Community Reuse Organization (FCRO) was established. The FCRO is a community group composed of 19 Fernald area citizens and FEMP employees. The FCRO addresses economic development opportunities that will occur at the Fernald site once the Fernald environmental cleanup activities are completed. The FCRO advises DOE on socioeconomic issues that will emerge from the resulting employee layoffs and Fernald's eventual closure once the cleanup activities are completed. This group will also advise DOE on community planning and economic development issues for the communities located near Fernald. The purpose of the FCRO is to seek a consensus among stakeholders who are interested in or affected by these environmental and socioeconomic issues. After a consensus is reached, the FCRO develops recommendations for the Fernald site and gives these recommendations to DOE. DOE intends to consider carefully the FCRO's recommendations as part of the agency's decision making process, and ensure that the FCRO receives adequate support and resources. The FCRO planned to build upon the recommendations made in the SSAB's July 1995 report.

On April 30, 1997, DOE awarded a one-year, $150,100 grant to the FCRO to provide financial support for functions that would help the FCRO become more established within the local community. These functions included the retention of professional consulting services to help the FCRO become more organized, plan economic development strategies, plan strategies for public involvement, develop performance measures, and establish an office within the community. The grant was effective from May 1, 1997, until April 30, 1998. In May 1997, the FCRO became a nonprofit corporation based within the state of Ohio. The establishment of the FCRO as a nonprofit corporation was a requirement for receiving the grant from DOE (U.S. DOE, Fernald Report, May 1997: 3).

In 1993, DOE's Environmental Management 's (EM) Office of Science and Technology (OST) established the Community Leaders Network (CLN). The CLN is a network of persons associated with facilities that are part of the DOE complex. CLN members help OST by providing stakeholder viewpoints on, and reviews of, technology development issues and initiatives. CLN also helps other EM offices in their activities involving stakeholders. CLN members include representatives from site-specific advisory boards, state and federal regulatory agencies, organized labor, local citizens' groups, elected local officials, and Native American tribes. CLN members participate in budget reviews, priority setting, technology demonstrations, and technology conferences (Ohio Environmental Protection Agency, 1996: 23).

In 1996, the Centers for Disease Control and Prevention (CDC) established a Fernald Health Effects Subcommittee (FHES) at Fernald. This group was comprised of persons who were concerned with the effects of radioactive wastes and hazardous wastes on the health of residents who live near DOE's Fernald facility. SSAB members, state environmental officials, members of neighborhood groups, state health officials, physicians, and state emergency management officials comprised the membership of the Fernald Health Effects Committee. These stakeholders provided advice to the CDC and the Agency for Toxic Substances and Disease Registry (ATSDR) on what sorts of studies were needed to measure the health damage caused by radioactive and toxic chemical pollution from Fernald.

In 1997, DOE created the Fernald Living History Project (FLHP). The FLHP is a group comprised of the University of Cincinnati's Center for Environmental Communications Studies, Miami (Ohio) University's Institute for Environmental Sciences, volunteer advisors in the Fernald community, and DOE-Fernald. DOE, the community volunteers, and the universities are working together in a joint effort to preserve and record the histories and perspectives of how Fernald's role in producing nuclear weapons and components for the Cold War affected the lives of local residents, and current and former Fernald workers. The FLHP's work includes collecting historical artifacts, interviewing subjects, and the development of educational exhibits and other materials form the artifacts (FRESH News, March 2000: 4).

Various members of the SSAB belong to each of these groups. DOE has established Health Effect Committees, CRO groups, and CLN groups at each of its facilities where DOE has established SSABs. Members of neighborhood groups who are concerned with DOE's activities at the agency's facilities also belong to these groups. One reason that DOE established these groups is to increase stakeholder involvement in DOE's public policy activities. A second reason for the establishment of these groups is that DOE is attempting to reestablish public trust and confidence in the agency.

Environmental Cleanup Activities at Fernald

After DOE ceased production at Fernald in July 1989, many cleanup activities began. Some of the equipment and buildings at the Fernald site have been dismantled and transported to waste disposal sites. Trucks transport the radioactive and hazardous wastes for burial at DOE's Nevada Test Site. In March 1999, DOE planned to begin transporting low-level wastes by rail to the commercially owned and operated Envirocare hazardous waste burial site in Clive, Utah. DOE has transported radioactive waste from Fernald to the Nevada Test Site since 1987. DOE also sends some of Fernald's radioactive and hazardous wastes to be incinerated at the DOE Oak Ridge Reservation's K-25 TSCA hazardous waste incinerator in Oak Ridge, Tennessee. DOE has also sold some of the enriched uranium at Fernald to the private sector.

A public water supply system was installed in the area for residents living near the Fernald site who previously obtained their water from underground wells. In 1985, the media revealed that radioactive and hazardous wastes buried at Fernald had seeped into the groundwater and the underground well water and contaminated the water supply for many local residents. "Approximately $6 million was contributed by DOE for this construction project. The total cost of the public water supply construction project was approximately $10 million. The construction project was coordinated by DOE-FEMP (Fernald Environmental Management Project), the Hamilton County (Ohio) Department of Public Works, and the Cincinnati Water Works public utility" (FRESH News, May 1997: 2). DOE provided bottled water for residents who lived south of the Fernald site until the public drinking water system was installed. A water reservoir was constructed in the area and is part of the public water supply project. Residents who lived within a specific area near Fernald were eligible to have DOE pay the costs of connecting their homes to the public water supply system. In 1996, the public water supply system began operating within the residential areas near the Fernald facility. In June 1997, nearly all the residents in the affected areas had sewer systems that were connected to the public water supply system. Many residents who lived in the Crosby Township, a municipality located near the Fernald facility, "had received free service connection to the public water supply system" (FRESH News, May 1997: 2). Local residents, the Ohio EPA, and EPA provided input into the construction project and were also kept informed of the project's progress.

In November 1997, the installation of the public water system was completed for the residents who lived near the Fernald site and previously obtained their water from wells. The name for the public water system installation project was the Crosby Township Public Water Supply Project. During the construction of the public water system, construction workers discovered ancient Native American remains on the Fernald site.

Fernald's Radium and the Treatment of Cancer Patients

On May 11, 1995, Dr. David Scheinberg, a cancer specialist at the Memorial Sloan Kettering Cancer Center in New York City, met with DOE and FERMCO officials to discuss the benefits of encapsulating the radium at Fernald to produce isotopes for cancer treatment. The radium, which is an extremely rare substance, was mixed with other radioactive wastes in two of the K-65 silos located at Fernald. Small quantities of gold, silver, palladium, and other precious metals were also discovered mixed in with the radioactive wastes found in the silos (Gallagher, July 16, 1995: A1). Researchers wanted the radium and other precious metals to be extracted from the radioactive wastes stored in the silos. Representatives from Battelle Pacific Northwest Laboratory, the National Institute of Health, the Oak Ridge National Laboratory, and other medical institutions were also present at this meeting. This meeting was unannounced and was not open to the public, but was videotaped by FERMCO. John Applegate, the SSAB chairperson, was surprised to hear the news about the May 11 meeting and the discussions by the cancer researchers. Applegate said that the SSAB had worked closely with DOE and EPA on establishing Fernald's cleanup schedule. Applegate stated that, "I wasn't aware that there was this degree of interest in this issue. There are many questions that still have to be answered. Before I could be persuaded, I would have to be assured that this extraction could be done quickly and safely. Personally, I would hate to see the removal of the silos' radioactive material delayed further" (Gallagher, July 2, 1995: A16). Applegate said that since he was now aware of the medical community's interest in the radium, he would present the issue for consideration at the SSAB's upcoming July 8, 1995, meeting.

In July 1995, medical researchers announced that they also wanted to preserve the radium stored in the K-65 silos by using a vitrification pilot plant currently being constructed at Fernald to encapsulate the radium into glass-like beads to make it easier to bury the radium at a disposal site. The researchers believed that the encapsulated radium could be used to make isotopes for treating some types of cancer.

The radium stored in two of the K-65 silos was the largest stockpile of radium in the world. It was estimated that 4,500 grams of radium was present in approximately 20 million pounds of mixed radioactive wastes stored inside the silos. The radium was mixed with other radioactive substances, and it would become necessary to find a process for extracting the radium from the other radioactive wastes. Supplies of radium were present at other sites, but not in quantities sufficient to use for cancer treatment. There are concerns regarding whether the radium can be safely encapsulated and if this procedure could become cost effective. Presently, no technology exists for extracting the radium from the vitrified material. It would cost millions of dollars to develop the technology for removing radium from the vitrified material.

Some scientists stated that similar extraction processes have been used to obtain materials such as plutonium, americium, and curium from vitrified material under theoretical conditions. These scientists believed that the technology existed to also extract the radium from vitrified materials. A scientist stated that at DOE's Savannah River Plant facility in South Carolina, substances such as americium and curium were being placed into vitrified material to make these items safer to handle (Gallagher, July 27, 1995: B6). The vitrified material is later dissolved and these substances are retrieved for later use. The scientists want a similar procedure used to extract radium from vitrified materials. Tests would have to be done to determine if these procedures could be used for extracting radium.

Nevertheless, some researchers said that the radium could be extracted from Fernald's nuclear wastes without delaying the cleanup activities at the site. Dr. Manoranjan Misra, a chemical engineer at the University of Nevada-Reno and an expert in nuclear waste extraction, recommended a process to remove the radium from the wastes. Misra said that the radium could be extracted before the wastes are vitrified. Misra stated that it was less expensive to extract the radium from the wastes than to wait until the wastes were vitrified. He said that the problem with DOE and FERMCO's proposal to remove the radium from vitrified material was that this process had never been done before. Misra said that removing radium from vitrified material could take several years and cost several million dollars to do studies and conduct research to make sure that their process works (Associated Press, August 28, 1995: A10).

Medical researchers are currently working on developing a technique that would attach isotopes developed from radium to an antibody. The antibody would be injected into a patient where it would look for cancer cells, radiate the cells, and destroy them. Since the isotope would have a short half-life, the isotope would be radioactive in a person's body for only a short period of time. This cancer-treating technique is currently in the early stages of development. Presently, man-made isotopes are currently available and are also capable of treating some types of cancer. There are successful cases involving the use of radium to treat certain types of cancer. For example, radium-based isotopes were used successfully in treating animals and test tubes that possessed myeloid leukemia. During the fall of 1995, Dr. Scheinberg was to head the "first-ever, limited, first-phase study in which 12 to 20 persons suffering from myeloid leukemia would receive intravenous doses of radium-based isotopes" (Gallagher, August 9, 1995: A6).

Fernald SSAB chairperson John Applegate said that members met with FERMCO and DOE officials during July 1995 to discuss the possibility of delaying Fernald's cleanup activities to extract the radium, gold, and other precious metals from the radioactive wastes in the silos. Applegate stated that at the July 1995 meeting: "A number of concerns were raised about slowing things down and whether this was economically desirable. We wanted to know if there were any additional hazards to add to the cleanup process. The task force took no formal action on this issue. No medical researchers, scientists, or physicists had tried to discuss the issue or lobby for temporary halting of the cleanup" (Gallagher, July 16, 1995: A17). Applegate also said that, "*DOE and FERMCO made it very clear to us that they planned to proceed with the cleanup*" (Gallagher, July 16, 1995: A17).

Nevertheless, some local officials said that they supported efforts to extract the radium from the nuclear wastes at Fernald. Ross Township Trustees Donald Thiem, Thomas Willsey, David Young, and Ross Township Clerk Judy Huffman signed a letter urging DOE to pursue efforts to extract the radium from Fernald's nuclear wastes and use the radium for cancer research and treating cancer. The letter said although the officials wanted the Fernald site cleaned up quickly, the opportunity to extract the radium for cancer research and cancer treatment should not be lost. The letter claimed that the majority of Fernald-area residents also agreed with this viewpoint (Feiertag, August 24, 1995: A3). Irene Lewis, Butler County Emergency Management Agency director, also recommended that the radium be extracted from Fernald's nuclear wastes and research (Nichols, September 11, 1995: A3). Several elected officials from Butler County also endorsed the concept of extracting radium from the wastes at Fernald. The endorsement came because of a resolution passed unanimously by the executive board of the Butler County Emergency Management Agency (Feiertag, September 24, 1995: A1).

A spokesperson for FERMCO said that the contractor was not aware of any lobbying effort to stop Fernald's cleanup activities so the radium from the silos could be extracted. FERMCO spoke with several companies that had expressed an interest in obtaining the radium if technology were developed to extract the radium and if a market existed for the radium. FERMCO also received inquiries about the possibility of getting some radium samples for research purposes. The spokesperson stated that these were the only inquires that the contractor received about the radium.

In August 1995, the medical centers and cancer researchers wanted DOE and FERMCO to delay the cleanup activities at Fernald, extract the radium, and transport the radium to the researchers so that it could be used to treat cancer patients. However, FERMCO, DOE, and some members of the SSAB opposed the delay of the cleanup activities at Fernald. SSAB member Lisa Crawford stated that she wondered why the cancer researchers did not approach DOE, FERMCO, and the SSAB about using the radium at an earlier time before the SSAB released its July 1995 report. Crawford also stated that the cancer researchers should have contacted the SSAB in 1993 before the present cleanup recommendations and plans were created. The cancer researchers and medical centers made their request during the same time that the SSAB released its cleanup recommendations in its July 1995 report. DOE had announced and had just begun its ten-year plan for cleaning up Fernald. SSAB member Lisa Crawford said that the representatives of the medical centers and cancer researchers had met with EPA and DOE officials in closed meetings, and had never consulted with members of the SSAB. Crawford said that she was unhappy that the representatives of the cancer researchers and medical centers did not hold public hearings so that local residents, SSAB members, and other stakeholders could express their opinions and concerns regarding the use of Fernald's radium for cancer research. DOE later held public hearings on the subject of delaying the Fernald cleanup activities to extract the radium for use in cancer treatment.

DOE and FERMCO decided that removing the radium would delay the Fernald cleanup schedule. Many local residents had lived for several years near a Fernald site contaminated with radioactive and hazardous wastes. These residents feared that the radioactive and hazardous substances were potential threats to their health and did not want the cleanup activities delayed. The residents believed that cleanup delay was inevitable if DOE and FERMCO began removing the radium for use in cancer treatment. Delays of the cleanup schedule would also cost DOE and FERMCO in terms of time and money.

SSAB Chairperson John Applegate said that he understood why the researchers requested the radium for use in treating cancer patients; however, he did not want the Fernald cleanup schedule to be postponed. SSAB members, DOE, FERMCO, and other stakeholders were concerned because the existing technology for using radium-based isotopes in cancer treatment was in the experimental stages, and radium had not yet proven to be an effectively successful method of treating cancer. The radium stored in the K-65 silos was one of the most radioactive substances at Fernald. DOE and FERMCO affirmed that its top priority should be to remove the radium as soon as possible. There was the possibility that the process for removing the radium from other radioactive wastes at Fernald could be hazardous to the health of Fernald workers and local residents. This process could leave persons exposed to dangerous levels of radioactive material, such as radium. The technology for removing the radium from other radioactive substances did not yet exist, would cost millions of dollars to develop, and might take several years to develop.

Finally, federal environmental laws and court decisions to remediate the Fernald site legally bound DOE to clean up the Fernald site. DOE signed a Consent Degree with the state of Ohio in 1988. Fernald became a Superfund site in 1989, and DOE signed to a consent agreement with EPA in 1990. Both the Consent Degree and the consent agreement are legally binding and involve the completion of cleanup schedules. In order to make significant changes to the Fernald cleanup schedule, DOE would need the consent of the EPA, the state of Ohio, Fernald residents, and SSAB members. Because of these reasons, DOE and FERMCO decided not to extract and process the radium for cancer treatment, but to maintain Fernald's cleanup schedule and remove the radium for waste disposal.

In July 1997, the SSAB originally known as the Fernald Citizens Task Force changed its name to the Fernald Citizens Advisory Board. This was to accommodate those members who wanted the name to more accurately reflect the organization's role, which was to advise DOE and the environmental cleanup activities at Fernald.

An Expose of FERMCO's Environmental Cleanup Activities

In February 1996, the *Cincinnati Enquirer* completed a six-month investigation of the environmental cleanup activities of FERMCO and FDF at the Fernald site. *Enquirer* news reporters Mike Gallagher and Tim Bonfield published a series of reports alleging that, while managing the cleanup activities at Fernald, FERMCO personnel committed unethical and illegal actions, such as overbilling for travel allowances, safety violations, overcharging for work, and falsifying performance and inspection reports. It was also alleged that there was a lack of effective oversight of FERMCO's activities by DOE. For example, according to the reporters, FERMCO employees and the workers of other companies performing environmental cleanup work at Fernald often signed fictitious travel reports or overcharged travel expenses and sent the reports to DOE. Because FERMCO was a DOE contractor, DOE would reimburse FERMCO and Fluor Daniel for the travel expenses of the employees who conducted Fernald's cleanup activities. When sending the travel reports to DOE, FERMCO and other companies were not required to submit receipts and documents that verified the travel activities that were stated in their reports. From 1993 until 1996, FERMCO and the other companies cleaning up the Fernald site were paid $15 million by DOE for travel reimbursement expenses. The U.S. government, according to the press, eventually determined that FERMCO and the other companies:

> Improperly charged $1.6 million for travel expenses between September 1992 and September 1994. Between September 1992 and September 1993, the companies overcharged DOE by more than $1.2 million. From 1993 through 1994, the companies overcharged the agency by $400,000. FERMCO and Fluor Daniel were billing—and receiving an average of more than $417,000 per month for travel expenses according to the financial records of DOE, FERMCO, and Fluor Daniel. (Gallagher, February 11, 1996: A7)

The *Enquirer* also reported that FERMCO sent reports to DOE certifying that environmental cleanup work was continuing according to schedule or was already complete. In many cases, however, this proved false: the cleanup work actually was behind schedule or incomplete. DOE had, in consequence, paid FERMCO millions of dollars for performing environmental cleanup work that was not due to FERMCO (Gallagher, February 11, 1996: A1, A6).

In addition to billing problems, the newspaper expose claimed major health and safety problems. The *Enquirer* stated that many of FERMCO's workers had been exposed to radiation. These incidents occurred because of poor management and safety violations by FERMCO. These incidents also happened because FERMCO sometimes used employees as radioactive and hazardous waste inspectors even though many of these workers often had little or no training for the job of inspecting radioactive or hazardous waste. FERMCO workers stated that, in many cases, the safety training they received was inadequate or nonexistent. FERMCO also failed to conduct some inspections required by DOE, and failed to maintain inspection records of the handling, storage, and maintenance of radioactive and hazardous wastes at Fernald. The newspaper's investigation discovered that several inspection logs and other documents were missing. These actions were a violation of the Ohio EPA and the U.S. EPA's rules. FERMCO officials admitted to these activities after being confronted by Ohio EPA and U.S. EPA officials.

The *Enquirer* alleged that FERMCO pressured workers to make false statements about safety conditions at the Fernald site. Officials of the Fernald Atomic Trades and Labor Council (FATLC) claimed that FERMCO attempted to get them to write their signatures on a letter that stated that there were few significant safety problems at the Fernald facility. Gene Branham, the vice president of FATLC, stated that safety problems were allowed to go unresolved because "everyone, including DOE and FERMCO, is so concerned about getting Fernald's nuclear waste cleaned up as quickly as possible that they are willing to ignore—or just don't care about all of the safety and management violations that are going on" (Gallagher, May 5, 1996: A10).

The *Enquirer* expose identified significant problems with waste storage on site. It accused FERMCO of allowing drums filled with radioactive and hazardous wastes to leak during weekends. The drums were placed in storage areas to await shipment from Fernald to burial sites at the Nevada Test Site and the Envirocare site in Utah. When FERMCO began its work at Fernald, the company required its employees to work on weekends to repair leaky drums before shipping the drums from Fernald to permanent waste storage facilities. In recent years, however, employees were sent home during weekends because FERMCO did not wish to pay them overtime. FERMCO employees reported that they would leave Fernald on weekends and return to work on Mondays to find that several drums had leaked radioactive and hazardous wastes (Gallagher, March 5, 1996: A1).

The *Enquirer* also alleged that FERMCO did not adequately design and operate a containment system. A containment system surrounds tanks that hold radioactive or hazardous wastes. The containment system is designed to hold and contain the contents of the tanks. It was claimed that a containment system built by FERMCO was improperly designed and did not perform adequately. FERMCO also failed to adequately test the containment system before putting the system into operational use (Gallagher, March 5, 1996: A1).

According to the *Enquirer,* the problems at Fernald remained unnoticed or unresolved because of lax oversight by DOE and FERMCO. FERMCO made performance, safety, and financial audits, and conducted reviews of the cleanup activities. DOE, in its defense, stated that it had a staff of only 56 persons at the agency's Fernald Area Office to oversee the Fernald site. The agency mentioned that budget limitations had kept DOE from assigning more individuals to oversee cleanup activities at the Fernald site. FERMCO, in response to this charge, stated that it had only 12 persons assigned to perform oversight activities on the Fernald site (Gallagher, February 14, 1996: A4).

The *Enquirer* reported that a vitrification pilot plant under construction at the OU4 area of the Fernald site was improperly designed. A vitrification pilot plant is a facility that encapsulates radioactive material into glass-like blocks or pellets to make it less hazardous to humans and easier to bury or store. The vitrification pilot plant would be used to encapsulate the radium currently stored in the K-65 silos. The encapsulated radium would be transported to the Nevada Test Site for disposal. The inadequate design of the vitrification plant would prevent the facility from working properly, and structural problems have resulted from the plant's design. Construction problems, testing problems, and cost overruns also affected the vitrification pilot plant. FERMCO continued to construct the plant without making any adjustments to the original design, without making any structural repairs, or reinforcing the plant facility. FERMCO blamed one of its subcontractors for the inadequate work done in the pilot plant's construction (Gallagher, March 25, 1996: A1). FERMCO later admitted that it had issued false statements about the subcontractor. In March 1996, a DOE investigative team investigated the pilot vitrification project and discovered that the project had several problems. These discoveries confirmed the findings reported by the *Enquirer*. The DOE investigative team suggested that the agency should discontinue the vitrification pilot project and explore other methods for cleaning up the Fernald site (Gallagher, March 25, 1996: A1). In July 1996, DOE fined the contractor $810,000 because of a failure to alleviate the problems associated with the vitrification project. During July 1996, the subcontractor accused of performing shoddy work on the pilot vitrification plant filed a $15 million defamation lawsuit against FERMCO and FDF (Gallagher, July 26, 1996: C4).

Continuing problems at the vitrification pilot plant lent credibility to the *Enquirer*'s expose. On December 26, 1996, a Fernald worker noticed that a stream of molten glass was emerging from underneath the melter inside the vitrification pilot plant. The glass had originated from a small hole in the melter. The melter inside the pilot plant was undergoing test operations with nonradioactive material when the incident occurred. Some of the molten glass leaked into the floor, causing a small fire. Emergency personnel at Fernald extinguished the fire. In February 1997, DOE was fined $4 million because of the continuing problems with the pilot vitrification project (Gallagher, February 1, 1997: C1).

In July 1997, DOE released a report on the vitrification plant incident. The report stated that FDF officials ignored the warnings of its own engineers when they reported test results indicating that the components in a vitrification melter might not work properly. The melter parts, indeed, *did* fail during the December 26, 1996, incident. An FDF executive associated with the vitrification project later stated that FDF officials were deliberately negligent and ignored the concerns of the engineers. They were motivated by an overwhelming desire to keep the vitrification plant project on schedule. The FDF executive, who wished to remain anonymous, contended that FDF officials deliberately omitted the engineers' concerns from a company report that would have alerted DOE to the melter's problems. The DOE report stated that FDF's actions contributed to the vitrification pilot plant melter incident (Gallagher, July 17, 1997: A1).

FDF originally was awarded the Fernald contract in December 1992. During the period from December 1992 to February 1997, FDF was fined more than $30 million by DOE for various cleanup, safety, design, construction, and off-site shipment problems. During a six-month review from October 1, 1995, until March 31, 1996, DOE assessed fines of $5 million against FDF for poor performance of its duties at Fernald (Gallagher, February 1, 1997: C1).

During May 1996, FDF was fined by DOE for $135,000 because FDF failed to correct estimates of subcontracting costs on a building demolition project that were millions of dollars higher than the actual costs (Gallagher, May 2, 1996: A1). FERMCO failed to correct the estimates of subcontracting costs in 1993-1994 reports that the firm sent to DOE. In addition to failing to correct the subcontracting cost estimates, FERMCO also made other mistakes: "FERMCO failed to change the figures in the 1993-94 reports to DOE, which resulted in erroneous cost and schedule data for the demolition project to be sent to the agency. As a result, FERMCO benefited financially because DOE used the false data as part of a formula to determine the amount of a performance fee or penalty that FERMCO should receive for the demolition project" (Gallagher, May 2, 1996: A1, A4).

A Financial Review Team from DOE's Ohio Field Office discovered that DOE overpaid FERMCO by $135,000 in award fees for the April 1994 to September 1994 performance period. The overpayment occurred because FERMCO incorrectly received a "satisfactory" rating for the cost and schedule variances for the performance period (Gallagher, May 2, 1996: A4). These findings were provided on April 1, 1996, report. This report confirmed the *Enquirer*'s findings. The *Enquirer* reported that FERMCO had originally estimated that it would cost $5.5 million to demolish the plant building. The *Enquirer* also reported that FERMCO did not reduce the estimate when the contractor discovered that the actual cost for demolishing the building would only be about $1.8 million. The Financial Review Team's report stated that DOE's Fernald personnel did not adequately perform its oversight duties because the staff allowed FERMCO to wait 17 months before ordering FERMCO to formally change the estimated subcontractor costs for the demolition project to the actual costs for the project. The Financial Review Team also recommended that FERMCO be penalized $135,000 because this was the exact amount that DOE had overpaid to the contractor (Gallagher, May 2, 1996: A4).

During September 1996, DOE ordered FDF to refund $768,000 to the agency. An audit conducted by DOE's inspector general's office discovered that during 1992 and 1993, FDF improperly charged DOE for $768,000. The audit revealed that FDF violated government accounting rules and engaged in inadequate bookkeeping practices. The DOE audit also discovered additional violations such as improperly reimbursing employees for travel expenses and paying invoices without verifying the prices or the rates paid by employees (Gallagher, September 14, 1996: B1, B9).

The *Enquirer*'s allegations prompted Senator John Glenn (D-Ohio), Senator Mike DeWine (R-Ohio), Congressman Steve Chabot (R-Ohio), Congressman Robert Portman (R-Ohio), and Congressman John Boehner (R-Ohio) to demand a government investigation of FERMCO's cleanup activities at Fernald. Chabot, Portman, and Boehner are congressional representatives from the Cincinnati area. Also, FERMCO was under investigation by several government agencies including the U.S. General Accounting Office (GAO), DOE's Office of Inspector General, and auditors from DOE's Ohio Field Office (Gallagher, February 15, 1996: C1).

The reaction of SSAB members to all of this disturbing news was measured and temperate. Lisa Crawford, president of FRESH and an SSAB member, stated that "she wanted to see more substantiation of the reported problems before commenting" (Gallagher, February 15, 1996: C7). John Applegate, the SSAB chairperson, stated that "FERMCO has been a model of openness and candor in their dealings with us. I really can't say enough about how committed FERMCO has been at involving the public in the project" (Gallagher, February 15, 1996: C7).

During August 1996, DOE awarded Fluor Daniel, Incorporated, a $4.8 billion, five-year contract to oversee the environmental cleanup activities at DOE's Hanford Reservation site near Richland, Washington (Westneat, August 7, 1996: A1). The Hanford site is much larger than the Fernald site. The Fernald site covers 1,050 acres, while the Hanford Reservation site covers 360,000 acres. After receiving the cleanup contract, FDL attempted to construct a vitrification pilot plant at Hanford. This project, however, was suspended after newspapers in Washington state reported the problems with FDF's Fernald vitrification plant that were exposed in such detail by the *Enquirer*. In September 1996, FERMCO (Fernald Environmental Management Corporation) changed its name to Fluor Daniel, Fernald (FDF).

In March 1997, the GAO released its report on FDF's administration of the Fernald site cleanup activities after an eleven-month investigation (U.S. GAO, March 1997). The GAO found that the Fernald cleanup activities had wasted millions of dollars through mismanagement by FDF compounded by inadequate management and a lack of oversight by DOE. GAO took DOE officials to task for failing to monitor FDF's safety and health programs and procedures. FDF failed, according to GAO auditors, to comply with required procedures for maintaining the contractor's financial and performance systems. The weaknesses in oversight activities at Fernald resulted in increased costs, projects falling behind schedule, and safety and health risks to workers at the site. GAO reported finding a lack of safety procedures and training for Fernald workers. Continuing weaknesses in DOE's oversight of FDF's cleanup activities limited the agency's ability to ensure that FDF was following safety and health requirements. FDF's practices for maintaining the contractor's financial and performance systems at the Fernald site made it difficult for FDF and DOE to maintain effective control over the contractor's financial costs and cleanup activities.

The GAO report considered the most seriously mishandled project at Fernald to be the pilot vitrification plant. "Originally estimated at $14.1 million, the pilot vitrification plant's cost by 1997 was found to be more than $56 million over budget and over 19 months behind schedule" (Gallagher and Bonfield, March 19, 1997: A6). The GAO report stated "despite the numerous problems at the Fernald site; investigators did not uncover any criminal wrongdoing or any willful pattern of fraud and deception on the part of Fluor Daniel Fernald" (Gallagher and Bonfield, March 19, 1997: A6).

The GAO auditors summarized FDF's problems as "underestimating the job that the contractor was hired to do at Fernald; giving overly optimistic predictions of how rapidly the contractor could recover from delays; and performing design work and construction work at the same time" (Gallagher and Bonfield, March 19, 1997: A6). The GAO report made recommendations for improving the cleanup project at Fernald. One recommendation was to make improvements to the Fernald contract. DOE's five-year contract with FDF was scheduled to expire on November 30, 1997. This approaching contract expiration would provide an opportunity for DOE to test the implementation of contract reforms that the agency had made in its contracts with companies to operate and clean up its facilities. The GAO report suggested that DOE could improve its contracts by amending them to "demonstrate the effectiveness of these incentive mechanisms, contract performance criteria and measures, its commitment to a policy of full and open competition, and the effects of its training of DOE personnel in performance-based contracting" (U.S. GAO, March 1997: 14).

A second recommendation was that DOE's Fernald Area Office should strengthen its oversight of FDF to correct the problems identified by the GAO auditors. This strengthened oversight would need to attend to weak project management, performance system weaknesses, financial system weaknesses, and Fernald's troubled safety and health programs. The GAO report allowed that DOE's Fernald Area Office had made some progress in improving its oversight of health and safety of workers at Fernald.

On March 18, 1997, Glenn, DeWine, Portman, and Boehner issued a press release that mentioned their comments on the GAO report. The press release stated that FDF and DOE were responsible for wasting millions of dollars at Fernald over the previous two years, mainly as a result of the problems associated with the vitrification pilot plant. It was difficult to determine the amount of money that had been wasted during the cleanup efforts at Fernald because FDF failed to maintain adequate financial and performance systems. The press release also said that, "the GAO's investigation, however, did not uncover any criminal wrongdoing or a willful pattern of fraud and deception on the part of the contractor. While some problems remain with DOE's safety oversight, GAO was not able to prove most of the allegations concerning serious safety and contamination problems" (Congress of the United States, March 18, 1997: 1). They further stated: "We should not lose sight of the fact that Fernald's accelerated plan is saving taxpayers billions of dollars when compared with earlier plans. Five or the six major site activities are on or ahead of schedule and within budget. We pledge to do all we can to make sure this accelerated plan is implemented, keeping the safety and health of the workers and the community as the top priority" (2). In their press release, Glenn, DeWine, Portman, and Boehner also commented that: "Nonetheless, we are concerned that management problems by both DOE and the contractor could put into jeopardy any continued, steady funding for Fernald and the accelerated plan. To ensure that these problems are resolved, we request that the DOE Fernald Area Office make quarterly reports to the Secretary of Energy" (2).

Two days after the GAO released its report on Fernald, DOE announced that FDF would be removed as the administrator of the vitrification project and that a new contractor would supervise the project. DOE's search for a new contractor for the vitrification project would begin immediately. DOE also announced that it would review FDF's overall performance on the Fernald cleanup contract that was awarded to FDF in December 1992. FDF's cleanup contract expired in November 1997 and was subject to renewal. DOE's contract with FDF was up for a one-to-three-year renewal in November 1997.

During April 1997, DOE's independent review team finished its study of the vitrification plant project and released a report. The review team recommended that the vitrification project be taken away from FDF and given to another contractor. This recommendation was similar to recommendations made in the GAO report. The review team also recommended that the radium wastes at Fernald should be disposed of through vitrification, even though finishing the vitrification plant project would cost additional millions of dollars and take several years longer to complete than originally anticipated. The review team voted 6 to 5 to recommend building a vitrification plant to process the radium wastes in Fernald's silos 1 and 2. The team also recommended that the less hazardous waste in Fernald's silo 3 be encased in concrete. However, the five dissenting members of the review team did not believe that vitrification would ever become successful because there were either too few companies or no companies that had the experience or qualifications to manage the vitrification plant project. The dissenting members of the review team stated that, to their knowledge, no companies "had ever successfully melted lead glass in commercial quantities while using sulfate-containing raw materials" (Bonfield, April 29, 1997: A4). The dissenters believed that the waste in all of Fernald's silos should be encased in concrete. This process would be cheaper and faster than vitrification and less likely to cause a catastrophic accident.

FDF originally estimated that it would take the contractor 10 years to clean up the Fernald site. However, DOE changed that estimate to 12 to 15 years. The explanation given for this announcement was that DOE had reduced its environmental cleanup budget by $10 million per year, making it more difficult for FDF to meet the original cleanup goal of 10 years. For the past few years, Congress has reduced its budget appropriations to DOE, making less money available for the agency's environmental cleanup programs at its facilities. DeWine, Glenn, Portman, Chabot, and Boehner said that FDF's contract should not be renewed or extended unless the major problems at Fernald were resolved.

The GAO stated that the problems at Fernald also existed at other DOE sites. DOE agreed with the GAO that DOE's problems at Fernald were similar to problems at DOE's other facilities. The GAO's findings confirmed the allegations previously reported by the *Enquirer* in February 1996.

The SSAB responded publicly to the GAO's report on FDF's cleanup activities. Lisa Crawford, the president of FRESH and an SSAB member, said that the GAO report should influence DOE and FDF to correct the problems that have occurred at Fernald. Crawford believed that FDF's contract should not be renewed unless FDF significantly changed its business practices at the Fernald site. Crawford said that "DOE will have to take a very strong look at renewal of their contract. Fluor Daniel will have to demonstrate some very good effort before we [FRESH] will support their rehiring" (Gallagher and Bonfield, March

20, 1997: A12). Crawford stated that the project involving the pilot vitrification plant "should be taken away from Fluor Daniel because of FDF's poor work performance record on the plant project. DOE officials, SSAB members, and other Fernald stakeholders needed to hold discussions and brainstorming sessions to determine which company would be awarded the contract for the plant project" (A12).

John Applegate, the chairperson of the SSAB, placed the *Enquirer* expose and subsequent GAO and DOE investigations in context when he said that: "Many of the financial questions and oversight concerns mentioned in the GAO report are not the direct concerns of the Fernald SSAB. The Fernald SSAB is more concerned about whether the controversy over the GAO report's findings would slow down Fernald's cleanup project" (A12). Applegate also mentioned the Fernald SSAB's concerns regarding the cleanup project when he stated that: "The Fernald SSAB is most concerned about plans for cleaning up the K-65 silos containing the waste to be vitrified. DOE and the stakeholders consider these wastes to comprise the most significant health risks at Fernald" (A12).

Three days before the GAO released its report on the Fernald cleanup activities, the SSAB held its monthly meeting and "recommended that vitrification should be pursued vigorously. *The GAO report on the problems at Fernald did not change this viewpoint.* However, the SSAB also called for the development of an alternative plan for removing the waste from the K-65 silos in case vitrification did not work" (A12). Applegate stated that he "did not believe that the problems described in the GAO report justified entirely removing FDF from the Fernald cleanup project when FDF's contract expired in November 1997" (A12).

During May 1997, the *Enquirer* obtained an unreleased report written by the U.S. Army Corps of Engineers that discussed cleanup activities at Fernald. The report recommended that solidification (concrete encasement) was the most effective method of removing the wastes that were stored in the silos. In October 1996, DOE commissioned the Army Corps of Engineers to examine the cleanup activities at DOE's nuclear facilities and to recommend improvements. The Army Corps of Engineers determined that:

> The decision to vitrify the waste was correct and was based on the disposal criteria and cost data available at that time (1994). But, based on current knowledge and experience with vitrification and solidification methods, solidification becomes a more favorable stabilization method than vitrification. Cost and schedule estimates provided to the independent review team by FDF were "pre-conceptual and conservative," and thus were not reliable. (Gallagher, May 16, 1997: A9)

In June 1997, DOE officials predicted that if Congress appropriated $6 billion a year to DOE, the agency could clean up most of the radioactive wastes located at most of its nuclear facilities by the year 2006. Regardless of how much money Congress appropriates, the cleanup activities at the Fernald facility will not be completed by the year 2006. Under DOE's most recently recommended plan, the treatment of the radioactive material in the K-65 silos will not begin until the year 2006. On June 12, 1997, "a DOE official presented a plan that called for 'substantially' completing the nuclear cleanup efforts at seven DOE facilities in Ohio, the Rocky Flats facility near Denver, and the Nevada Test Site by the year 2006. However, if Congress limits DOE's funding to $5.5 billion, the DOE official stated that these deadlines would not be met" (Bonfield, June 14, 1997: B7).

A spokesperson from DOE's Ohio Field Office stated that if the agency received full funding for its cleanup programs, DOE's current plans "called for the removal of all of the nuclear materials from Fernald by the year 1999, and the completion of the ground water treatment by the year 2005. DOE based these assumptions on data from the year 1995 and were no longer valid" (B7). The biggest change in DOE's plans was that the pilot vitrification plant failed to test whether the radium-laced radioactive waste in Fernald's silos could be melted into glass-like beads before shipping the waste to a disposal facility. After the *Enquirer's* February 1996 investigation, DOE officials admitted that the vitrification plant project had fallen significantly behind schedule.

DOE officials still support the plan to vitrify the silos' wastes, but plan to award the vitrification job to another contractor. In April 1997, an independent review team reported that the earliest year that vitrification could begin was in 2006, with the completion occurring in 2010. However, if the waste is encased in cement, the project could begin in 2003 and be completed by 2008.

A DOE spokesperson stated that the Fernald site has made significant progress toward the complete cleanup of the facility. DOE and FDF have destroyed plant buildings, excavated soil, and shipped other stored wastes to disposal facilities. The silos are the only area at Fernald where significant cleanup progress has not been made. The shipment of Fernald's stored wastes might be completed by the year 1999. The treatment of groundwater is progressing ahead of schedule for an estimated completion date of 2015. However, the completion of the groundwater treatment might not meet a 2005 deadline that DOE presented to members of Congress.

During July 1997, DOE penalized FDF for a record $6.6 million for allowing several problems to remain unresolved. These problems included poor performance, the troubled vitrification plant project, injuries to workers, and the failures of other safety programs. The $6.6 million penalty represented "more than 58% of the performance-based fee that FDF was eligible to receive during its last performance review period, which lasted from October 1, 1996, until March 31, 1997. Every six months, FDF was eligible to earn $10.8 million in a performance fee that is based on a point system tied to FDF's successes or failures in the cleanup activities" (Gallagher, July 8, 1997: A1). The performance fee was FDF's profit for managing the Fernald site for DOE. Since DOE awarded FDF the $2.2 million contract in December 1992, FDF has been "penalized more than $36 million by DOE for problems involving cleanup, design, safety, construction, and the shipment of wastes to off-site facilities. During FDF's previous six-month review period, which lasted from April 1, 1996, until September 30, 1996, DOE penalized FDF $4 million for poor performance at the Fernald site" (Gallagher, July 8, 1997: A1). DOE released a report describing the problems that led to the penalties against FDF. The problems included the following:

> Several incidents such as the inadvertent removal of a lid from a pressurized drum; an employee being struck during a scrap metal removal process; problems with the safe operations of electrical power sources; failure to implement a mandatory safety program; failure to meet mandatory EPA and DOE completion dates for things such a cleanup project deadlines; and failure to complete testing of the pilot vitrification project. (Gallagher, July 8, 1997: A6)

Among the more serious findings discovered by DOE were problems with FDF's Nuclear Criticality Safety performance by FDF's line managers: "During DOE's review of FDF's handling of Fernald's nuclear waste stockpile, DOE found that FDF's on-site management demonstrated a lack of knowledge and appreciation for the established safety of the site, which was indicated by the surpassing of the authorization limit for storage of nuclear materials at a Fernald warehouse" (A6).

During July 1997, the Fernald Citizens Task Force changed its name to the Fernald Citizens Advisory Board. This was more than a *cosmetic* change. The members changed the organizational name to identify more closely with and to align itself with the other SSABs. The members of the group felt that the term "Task Force" implied that the group was only a temporary organization. The members believed that the new name indicated that the advisory board was a long-term and continuous organization.

DOE originally estimated that it would take ten years to clean up the Fernald site. DOE's ten-year plan for Fernald originally projected those cleanup activities at the Fernald site would be completed in Fiscal Year 2005. In June 1997, as a result of budget cuts, DOE revised the ten-year plan for the FEMP, estimating that it would take twelve to fifteen years to clean up the Fernald site. The agency estimated that the environmental cleanup activities at Fernald will be completed in Fiscal Year 2008 (U.S. DOE, Narratives, June 1997: I.1-22).

In October 1997, DOE announced that it would extend FDF's contract for two additional years. This was done, according to DOE "because FDF has accelerated site cleanup, reduced waste inventories, and improved programs for public involvement" (Associated Press, October 1, 1997: B5). The contract extension was from December 1, 1997, until November 30, 1999. DOE allowed that FDF was to improve its safety and health program if the contractor hoped to receive a third year on the extension. The agency declared that FDF had to improve its management of nuclear material and its development of an assessment program (B5).[2]

In December 1997, DOE officials announced that a British company, British Nuclear Fuels Limited's (BNFL) Uranium Asset Management subsidiary, purchased 2.1 million pounds of enriched uranium from the Fernald site. BNFL decontaminates, enriches, and sells uranium as commercial nuclear reactor fuel to produce electricity in Great Britain. BNFL received its first shipment of Fernald's uranium on November 3, 1997. DOE's contract with BNFL required that all shipments of uranium from Fernald be completed by December 31, 1998. The British company had other business relationships with DOE. BNFL was a cleanup contractor at DOE's Savannah River Plant, Oak Ridge Reservation, Rocky Flats, and the Hanford Reservation facilities (Associated Press, December 22, 1997: B6).

Recent Developments at Fernald: 1998-2000

The SSAB and FDF continue to work at developing an effective long-term relationship. Thus, for example, since the creation of the Fernald SSAB, DOE has issued the advisory board members badges so that they can visit the Fernald site anytime. The advisory board members know several DOE and FDF officials at Fernald and remain in frequent contact with them. DOE and FDF members now contact SSAB members as soon as incidents occur at the site. For example, DOE officials once called SSAB member and FRESH president Lisa Crawford at 4:00 a.m. to tell her that an incident had occurred at Fernald. DOE contacted Crawford so that she would already know about the incident and would not hear about the incident for the first time when it was reported by the news media (Personal interview, Harrison, Ohio, July 14, 1998).

In June 1998, DOE awarded contracts to four companies to develop new technologies and methods for transporting radioactive wastes from Fernald's K-65 silos to the Nevada Test Site. The contracts were awarded to Toledo-based EnVitco for $2 million; Collegeville, Pennsylvania-based Vortec Corporation for $1.34 million; Monroeville, Pennsylvania-based Industrial Technologies Corporation for $305,000; and Columbia, South Carolina-based Chem-Nuclear for $576,000. These companies are to develop technologies that will enable DOE to transport wastes from Fernald to the Nevada Test Site. DOE awarded the contracts because of a December 15, 1997, incident in which radioactive wastes leaked from a container while inside a truck transporting wastes from Fernald to the Nevada Test Site (Melcer, June 9, 1998: A1).

Vitrification and chemical stabilization are two of the technologies being considered for processing Fernald's wastes. Chemical stabilization involves mixing the wastes with concrete and molding the concrete into blocks before transferring the material to waste disposal facilities. The EnVitco and Vortec companies will try developing vitrification while Chem-Nuclear and Industrial Technologies will try developing chemical stabilization as a method for disposing the wastes at Fernald. In spite of DOE's problems with vitrification, it is still considering vitrification for disposing of Fernald's wastes. Because of EPA-imposed deadlines, the agency must select a specific technology to develop a disposal method. DOE was to subject the technology decision to the scrutiny of public hearings and solicit bids on the project (A4).

In July 1998, DOE, FDF, and the CSX Railroad completed the construction of a rail yard at the Fernald site. The Army donated two locomotives to DOE. DOE purchased 50 gondola railroad cars to transport wastes from Fernald. The railroad cars were expected to arrive at Fernald (U.S. Department of Energy, August 10, 1998: 2). Beginning in March 1999, DOE planned to use trains to transport wastes from Fernald to the Envirocare facility in Utah. DOE planned to transport some of its wastes by rail because of the container leak incident that occurred in Kingman, Arizona. Since the Kingman incident, DOE suspended all Fernald waste shipments to the Nevada Test Site and began reevaluating its safety procedures. Agency officials from the Nevada Test Site visited Fernald in July 1998 to inspect the site and determine if Fernald could resume its waste shipments to the Nevada facility. Final approval must also come from DOE officials in Washington, DC (Melcer, July 30, 1998: B2).

During July 1998, DOE and FDF completed construction on several extraction wells at the Fernald site. These extraction wells began pumping contaminated groundwater from the Great Miami Aquifer to the Advanced Wastewater Treatment Facility. The contaminated groundwater will be treated at the facility and then be discharged into the Great Miami River. DOE and FDF also plan to initiate other aquifer restoration projects at the Fernald site to help treat the contaminated groundwater. Once the other restoration projects are initiated, some of the treated water will be injected back into the aquifer (U.S. Department of Energy, August 1998: 9).

In September 1998, DOE inspectors from the Nevada Test Site said that Fernald was not quite ready to resume shipments of low-level radioactive wastes to the Nevada facility. The inspectors said that Fernald had corrected several problems that contributed to the Kingman incident. One problem that Fernald still needed to work on was to keep better records and have more inspections on Fernald's scales, torque wrenches, and other equipment. Fernald personnel used the wrenches to seal containers of low-level radioactive waste before it was shipped, and the scales ensured that the containers were packed to the correct weight. A random inspection of the equipment by Nevada Test Site inspectors revealed that FDF and DOE officials could not always verify when some of the equipment was calibrated, or when the next calibration was due. Mike Noland, the Nevada Test Site inspection team leader, said that some of the records were loosely kept by DOE and FDF personnel (Melcer, September 3, 1998: B1).

DOE requested that waste container manufacturing companies try designing waste containers that are stronger than the one that leaked in Kingman, Arizona. DOE and FDF planned to solidify the hazardous and radioactive wastes that were contained in Fernald's waste pits and the K-65 silos. DOE and FDF must solidify these wastes to meet Envirocare's waste standards before transporting the wastes from Fernald. Once solidified, DOE would transport the wastes by rail from Fernald to the Envirocare facility (Melcer, June 9, 1998: A4).

During September 1998, DOE released a report that recommended converting the Fernald site into a wildlife refuge once the cleanup activities were completed. Officials from DOE, Ohio EPA, the U.S. Fish and Wildlife Service, and the U.S. Department of the Interior drafted this report. The report also proposed developing the site for industrial purposes or keeping it a controlled-access area with no development until after the restoration activities were completed. These alternatives were developed in consultation with several Fernald stakeholder groups including the Fernald SSAB; FRESH; the FCRO; the Fernald Health Effects Subcommittee; the Fernald Living History Project; the trustees of Ross, Crosby, and Morgan townships; and the Butler County Planning Commission. DOE officials stated that restoring the Fernald site's natural habitat as a wildlife area is consistent with public opinion and promised that the agency would meet all regulatory requirements to restore the area. Under the plan, 884 acres of the 1,050-acre site would be rehabilitated through a series of projects designed around a cleanup of the area's topsoil. Features proposed included an upland forest, a riparian forest, a tall grass prairie, 15 acres of wetlands, and an open water area. Hiking trails, bicycle paths, and wildlife viewing areas may be added later. Some portions of the Fernald site would not be included in the natural restoration. These areas include a 23-acre section in the northwestern corner where the OSDF is located and a 20-acre portion of the southwestern corner that may be developed for commercial and industrial purposes (Jonson, September 23, 1998: A1, A2). In 2000, DOE and the Fernald stakeholder groups were still discussing what to do with the Fernald site once the cleanup activities were completed.

In April 1999, the Fernald SSAB, FRESH, FLHP, and the FCRO held the first of a series of public meetings known as the Future of Fernald Workshops. At the Future of Fernald Workshop meetings, people expressed their opinions and participated in discussions on what uses they would like to see for the Fernald site and what uses they would oppose for the site, once the cleanup activities were completed. A second Future of Fernald Workshop was held in May 2000. A Fernald SSAB member said "that approximately 150 people attended the May 2000 meeting" (Telephone interview, July 15, 2000). Possible uses for the site expressed at the May 2000 meeting included a Cold War museum that would describe the role that Fernald played in the production of nuclear weapons during the Cold War and a Native American museum that described the history of Native Americans who first inhabited the area. DOE and FDF discovered Native American remains at Fernald when installing sewer pipes to connect local residents to the local sewer system. Other suggested uses included bike trails and walking trails, detailed descriptions and displays of Fernald's cleanup activities, and environmental research facilities. A third Future of Fernald Workshop public meeting was held in September 2000.

At the September 2000 meeting, citizens suggested that the following actions be taken regarding the site's future use: Allocation of property for the reburial of Native American remains; the establishment of an on-site educational facility that described the history of Fernald from the earliest known Native American settlers through present-day Fernald's use, that explained the site's role in the production of nuclear materials during the Cold War, that assessed Fernald's impact on local residents and site workers, and that gave descriptions of cleanup and restoration efforts at the site (Goetz, November 4, 2000: B2).

In all of the Future of Fernald Workshops held so far, the following possible future uses for the Fernald site were suggested: (1) The idea of a public park with bike trails and walking trails was discussed, even though a low-level On-Site Disposal Facility (OSDF) is located on the site; (2) 90 percent of the Fernald site is to be restored to a natural state with wetlands, woods, and prairies; deep excavation holes that were left as contaminated soils were removed from these areas will likely become lakes; and (3) plans include using 100 acres of the site as a reburial ground for Native American remains and the construction of a Native American museum to house historical records (Melcer, April 22, 1999: B3).

In May 1999, the Fernald SSAB hosted a Transportation Workshop conference for all of the SSABs. The conference participants discussed issues concerning the transportation of low-level waste shipments from their respective DOE facilities to the waste disposal facilities at the Nevada Test Site.

Also during 1999, Fluor Daniel changed its name to Fluor Corporation and organized itself into four divisions: Fluor Daniel; Fluor Global Services;

Fluor Construction International, Incorporated; and Fluor Signature Services. Fluor Daniel, Fernald changed its name to Fluor Fernald. Fluor Fernald became a unit of Fluor Global Services.

On November 17, 1999, DOE's Ohio Field Office and Fernald Area Office received the Organization of the Year award from the International Association of Public Participation at the organization's annual conference in Banff, Alberta, Canada. This award recognized the offices for their work in "developing a citizen advisory board dedicated to involving the public in the decision making process for the cleanup activities at Fernald. The Association's judges cited DOE's success in overcoming significant citizen distrust to achieve a complex consensus decision in a very difficult arena. Additionally, the judges also were impressed by DOE's efforts to maintain an enduring and meaningful relationship with the public at Fernald" (U.S. DOE, Fernald Report, January 2000: 11). The award was formally presented to the Fernald site in January 2000.

Radioactive waste shipments to the Nevada Test Site resumed in January 2000. The shipments were halted in December 1997 after a low-level radioactive waste shipment container leaked near Kingman, Arizona while being shipped from Fernald to Nevada. To remedy the problem, FDF planned to use new "M100" metal containers specifically designed for cross-country radioactive shipments. Before actual use, the containers would be subjected to rigorous on-site testing (Melcer, December 31, 1998: B1).

Also, during January 2000, the Fernald SSAB recommended that the radioactive wastes now being held in the K-65 silos be combined with concrete to form solid bricks so that the wastes can be transported to the NTS facility. The process is known as chemical stabilization. The advisory board felt that using chemical stabilization would be safer and easier than using vitrification as a method of transporting and disposing of the wastes. Vitrification is a process that involves melting the wastes into glasslike pellets, which are then transported to a waste disposal facility for burial. Vitrification was tried in 1996, but was abandoned after a meltdown occurred. DOE also approved the use of chemical stabilization over vitrification. But some Fernald SSAB members felt that vitrification was a more effective means of disposing of wastes. They noted that the chemical bricks would require three times as many cross-country truck shipments than the compact glass pellets—which would increase the risk of a traffic accident (Melcer, January 16, 2000: B4). An environmental engineer who is familiar with the Fernald SSAB said that: "the Fernald SSAB felt that chemical stabilization is a proven and more reliable process than vitrification. Vitrification is also a more expensive procedure. This is why the advisory board recommended to DOE that the wastes should undergo chemical stabilization instead of vitrification" (Personal interview, Oak Ridge, Tennessee, June 13, 2000).

In the meantime, radioactive waste shipments to the Nevada Test Site resumed with limited quantities of wastes being shipped in the "M100" metal containers. that were specifically designed for cross-country radioactive shipments. Several of these containers were already in use at Fernald. This time, the type of wastes being shipped changed. From now on, only solid material would be shipped (Melcer, December 31, 1998: B1).

As of August 2000, DOE and FDF estimated that Fernald's cleanup activities would be completed in 2008 or 2010, instead of in 2006 or 2007. The revised completion date resulted from factors such as budget shortfalls from Congress and changes in the estimated completion time of cleanup projects such as the waste pits and the construction of new waste silos to replace the existing K-65 silos. A DOE official said that "during the year 2000, Congress had allocated $290 million for Fernald's cleanup budget while DOE originally requested $320 million" (Telephone interview, July 17, 2000). Such budget shortfalls have a significant impact on Fernald's cleanup projects and have led to changes in the estimated completion dates for cleanup activities.

In November 2000, DOE announced that it had signed a new closure contract with FDF, which allows the contractor to continue working at a DOE site until all of the cleanup activities are finished. This means that FDF will continue as DOE's primary contractor at Fernald until FDF's cleanup work is completed.[3] FDF's contract was set to expire on November 30, 2000. The closure contract offered FDF a $53 million bonus if it finished the cleanup work by the end of 2006. However, the FDF president said that the accomplishment of the 2006 goal was unlikely. DOE and FDF estimated that Fernald's cleanup activities would be completed by 2010 (Bonfield, November 22, 2000: B2). When asked to comment on the closure contract and predict when the cleanup might be finished, one DOE official said that "cleanup progress and the final year for cleanup activities will depend on funding from Congress" (Telephone interview, December 15, 2000). Another DOE official said that "DOE awarded FDF a closure contract and FDF will remain Fernald's contractor until the cleanup work is finished. FDF will receive a financial bonus if it finishes all of the work by the year 2006. FDF hopes to finish the cleanup by 2010" (Telephone interview, December 21, 2000).

One of Fernald's cleanup problems includes disposing of the wastes held at the site's aging K-65 silos. These silos contain Fernald's most radioactive wastes and have held these wastes beyond the period that the silos were originally designed to hold them. During 2000, contractors began construction work on what is known as Plan B. Plan B involves constructing new steel tanks and moving the wastes from the K-65 silos into these new tanks. DOE stated that the removal of the K-65 wastes might begin during 2002. Once the wastes are removed from the new tanks, the wastes must be encased in concrete blocks and transported to disposal sites. The new tank construction, waste removal, encasing, and disposal of these wastes will take a period of several years to complete (Bonfield, November 22, 2000: B2).

In August 2001, a DOE official said, "The fiscal year 2002 budget had not been finalized by Congress or signed by the president. The George Walker Bush administration requested $290 million for Fernald in the 2002 budget. Recent congressional actions indicate that Fernald could receive an increase of as much as $30 million, depending on the actions of the conference committees and the willingness of the administration to approve the increase" (Telephone interview, August 17, 2001).

Also during August 2001, the CDC disbanded the Fernald Health Effects Subcommittee (FHES) although several committee members said that many health questions remained unanswered. These questions included adverse health effects and birth defects among Fernald-area residents and Fernald's workers. Mike Donnelly, a CDC official, said, "We are not suggesting that we are going away, but the purpose of the Federal Advisory Commission Act was for the government to gain outside advice from experts. The need for advice from this committee has ended—because our work is done" (Bonfield, August 23, 2001: B3). The CDC promised that the health concerns of the Fernald community would continue to receive attention from federal health agencies (B3).

Conclusion

The creation, operation, and activities of the Fernald SSAB are described in this chapter. To summarize: the DOE, EPA, and the Ohio EPA hired a convener to select the members of the SSAB. The SSAB's mission was to determine what activities that Fernald would be used for after the cleanup activities were completed; how would the wastes be disposed of; what risk levels of waste exposure are acceptable once the cleanup activities are finished; and what actions should be taken to conduct the cleanup activities. The SSAB holds regular meetings and allows the public to make comments during these meetings. The advisory board released reports that describe their recommendations for Fernald. The SSAB discusses issues, tries to reach a consensus, and then votes on these issues. The SSAB's decisions on these issues are decided by a majority vote.

The creation and the activities of the Fernald SSAB are an example of the Stakeholder Involvement Model discussed in Chapter 1. In the Stakeholder Involvement Model, the agency and the affected stakeholder groups discuss their interests and concerns about a particular public policy that affects the agency and the stakeholders. For example, during each stage of the Fernald environmental management and cleanup process, the SSAB and DOE discuss their interests and concerns. The SSAB provides *stakeholder representation* through its membership and, due to its members' overlapping organizational memberships in other citizen's organizations in the community and region, also integrates the board into a larger web of citizen participation mechanisms.

The SSAB and other affected stakeholder groups discuss their concerns and interests with DOE regarding the agency's policies that affect Fernald's cleanup activities. In the Traditional Regulatory Process Model, the agency and the affected stakeholder groups do not begin discussing their interests and concerns about a public policy until public hearings occur during the policy implementation stage.

The SSAB accomplished its *primary* short-term mission by issuing a report containing recommendations concerning environmental management, remediation, waste disposal, and future land use at Fernald. While federal agencies are not legally bound to accept and implement the advice offered by FACA committees, it is expected that the DOE, EPA, and state and local agencies will weigh the SSAB recommendations heavily in making future decisions. The report provides, as well, a basis for a *continuing dialogue* among stakeholders and federal agencies—especially between Fernald stakeholders and the DOE. Finally, the failure of federal agencies to accommodate the SSAB report would risk a breakdown in the public participation process and would likely return the process to the bad old days of protest, litigation, controversy, and gridlock. Indeed, the record shows that DOE has largely accommodated its decision making to the report; and work at Fernald consistent with the SSAB's recommendations is well underway.

The utility of the Stakeholder Involvement Model was further shown when numerous problems with the Fernald contractor's operations became the subject of an expose by the *Cincinnati Enquirer*. This expose triggered congressional, GAO, and internal DOE investigations which tended to confirm many, though not all, of the allegations made in the newspaper's extended series of stories. The more open and inclusive decision making process represented by the operation of the SSAB, however, absorbed the negative publicity. Further, DOE and the Fernald contractor found they could rely upon the SSAB to provide a balanced and credible perspective on the total Fernald operation that helped prevent a complete breakdown in public confidence and rancorous conflict over Fernald's future. What remains to be seen, however, is whether the SSAB's long-term mission of monitoring future operations can and will serve to avoid a repetition of the DOE and FDF management failures.

In the next chapter the focus is on evaluating in more detail the SSAB's contribution and performance as a stakeholder involvement mechanism. Special attention is paid to the evaluations of key actors in the process.

NOTES

1. The Fernald stakeholder organization, as will be seen, in its relatively brief history has operated under several different names. For clarity, the name *Site Specific Advisory Board* (SSAB) will be used for reference.

2. Organizational charts for the various incarnations of the SSAB committee system are provided in Figures 5 to 8.

3. On November 21, 2000, DOE awarded a new contract to FDF. This is a closure contract that allows FDF to continue working at Fernald until the cleanup activities are finished. The original contract extension began on December 1, 1997. DOE and FDF estimated that they might finish Fernald's cleanup activities in 2010.

4

The Effect of the Fernald SSAB: From Conflict to Cooperation

Introduction

The assessment of the impact and performance of Fernald SSAB on the environmental management and remediation at DOE's Fernald facility continues in this chapter. Attention is paid to the effect media coverage, public attention, recent DOE budget cuts, and community reaction have had on the Fernald SSAB and its role in the cleanup program. The accomplishments, strengths, and weaknesses of the Fernald SSAB also are discussed.

Media Coverage

How much media attention has been paid to the operation of the SSAB and its contribution to the Fernald environmental management and remediation program? Media coverage proved *limited* but *favorable*. During the span of its work, few editorials appeared either in the *Cincinnati Post* or the *Cincinnati Enquirer* about the SSAB. An important exception was an editorial printed in the *Cincinnati Post* which praised the Fernald SSAB's work and agreed with the recommendations offered in the July 1995 SSAB report. The editorial said that the Fernald SSAB's work was "a tedious and unpaid job, done mostly at nights and on weekends, and it seldom garnered much in the way of headlines. Nevertheless, the SSAB has done important work, and its members deserve credit for their role in bringing the cleanup at Fernald as far along as it is today" (White, August 12, 1995: 8A). The editorial mentioned that the SSAB did not demand that the Fernald site be returned to the condition that existed before the facility was built. The Task Force members did not conclude that the site should be permanently closed and declared off limits to all individuals. The editorial stated that, "the Task Force [SSAB] seeks a sensible middle ground aimed at protecting human health, preventing further environmental harm and doing remediation where it is cost effective" (White, August 12, 1995: 8A). The editorial also said that the Fernald SSAB concluded that:

> It is neither feasible nor necessary to haul every speck of contaminated soil to a federal disposal site. It suggested, that the most heavily contaminated soil be hauled away, and the least contaminated soil should remain in place and the remaining contaminated soil be treated and permanently stored on site in an engineered structure designed to prevent contaminants from escaping into the atmosphere and leaking into the Great Miami Aquifer. (White, August 12, 1995: 8A)

While gratifying to SSAB members who had labored long and hard to forge a report consonant with stakeholder and community interests, this media praise must especially have pleased the DOE and FDF. After years of bad press engendered by closed decision making and reflective of stakeholder suspicion, opposition, and hostility, the *Post* editorial was an important indicator that stakeholder involvement would win community acquiescence. But, the editorial sent the DOE an important additional message as well. After endorsing the SSAB's recommendations, it noted that all that really was needed for implementation was for the agency to press Congress for sufficient funds to support the program. That is to say, for the *Post*, it was a given that the agency would accommodate the SSAB and not treat its report as *merely* advisory. In any event, the SSAB report and its endorsement by a major local newspaper provided a solid basis for public acceptance of future agency decision making.

The existence of the SSAB sometimes allowed for improved media coverage of DOE operations, even in the midst of otherwise highly negative and potentially damaging stories. Thus, SSAB Chairperson John Applegate consistently was quoted in the press as supporting the DOE's *good faith* efforts to improve the Fernald program. When the *Enquirer* began its reports alleging mismanagement by Fernald's contractor, for example, Applegate said that the contractor had gone out of its way to be open and candid with the SSAB and the public. Applegate also said that the contractor was committed to involving the public in the cleanup project activities. These statements of support continued even after the GAO released its critical report on Fernald. The SSAB had held its monthly meeting only a few days before the GAO released its report. During the meeting, the SSAB stated that it supported the construction of the vitrification pilot plant and the use of vitrification to dispose of the radium at Fernald. This statement of support was given in spite of the allegations of mismanagement and safety violations that were mentioned in the *Enquirer's* news reports.

In contrast to the SSAB chairperson, FRESH president and SSAB member Lisa Crawford sometimes was more critical of Fluor Daniel and DOE. When the SSAB released its *Interim Report* in November 1994, Crawford said that she did not think that it was prudent to allow cows to graze in the area immediately outside the plant site while cleanup activities were occurring. When the *Enquirer* began its series of reports on the contractor's mismanagement of Fernald's cleanup activities, Crawford said that she would withhold her comments until she saw more substantiation of the *Enquirer's* allegations. However, Applegate said that the contractor had been open and candid when dealing with the SSAB. After the GAO released its report on Fernald and criticized FDF's handling of the pilot vitrification plant, Crawford said that FDF needed to significantly improve its managerial performance and work performance on the site. Crawford also said that a new contractor should be found to administer the pilot vitrification project.

Several of the newspapers in the smaller cities located near Fernald often published articles and editorials about the activities at Fernald. These newspapers included *The Hamilton Journal-News, The Harrison Press,* and the *Middletown Journal.* The *Hamilton Journal-News* is published in Hamilton, Ohio; the *Harrison Press* is published in Harrison, Ohio; and the *Middletown Journal* is published in Middletown, Ohio. Each of these newspapers published many articles and editorials regarding the activities occurring at the Fernald site, especially during the years from 1993 until 1995.

The stories that attracted media attention included reports on the following Fernald activities: remediation; labor disputes; lawsuits; cost overruns; layoffs; alleged safety violations; newspaper investigations; and government investigations—but they did not find fault with the SSAB. These articles often contained quotes by SSAB members John Applegate and Lisa Crawford, who were asked by reporters to comment about the activities at issue. However, *there were few articles and editorials written about the activities of the Fernald SSAB itself.* All of these newspapers published the announcements of upcoming SSAB meetings and the recommendations and findings of the SSAB reports. The release of the SSAB's July 1995 recommendations report did not receive extensive media coverage from the *Post,* the *Enquirer,* and the *Hamilton Journal-News.* One article each appeared in the *Post,* the *Enquirer,* and the *Hamilton Journal-News* describing the SSAB's July 1995 recommendations report. The SSAB report was actually completed near the end of July, and was announced to the public on August 1, 1995. An article in the *Hamilton Journal-News* reported that some local officials in Ross Township objected to DOE's plan to bury low-level waste at the Fernald site. Ross Township is located near the Fernald site. The town officials were concerned that if the wastes were buried at the site, the waste burial facility would become a health hazard for nearby residents.

During August 1995, the *Post,* the *Enquirer,* and the *Hamilton Journal-News* published several articles about the efforts of some cancer researchers that tried either to postpone Fernald's cleanup efforts or find a way to extract the radium from the K-65 silos. The cancer researchers wanted the opportunity to retrieve the radium and use it for cancer treatment. DOE, FDF, local residents, and the SSAB were reluctant to comply with the request because it had not been unequivocally proven that the radium from Fernald would be effective in treating cancer, and because to comply with the request would significantly extend Fernald's cleanup schedule.

A possible reason why the release of the July 1995 report received little media coverage is that the local residents may have felt that DOE and the SSAB significantly involved local stakeholders in the public meetings and in the policy process. Perhaps the local residents felt that they were adequately informed of all of the activities that would occur at Fernald and felt that they were adequately included in the policy making process. Historically, community outrage against closed agency decision making has been triggered most often by DOE announcements regarding local storage of radioactive, hazardous, or toxic wastes. This, however, did not occur in the Fernald case.

When a senior DOE official was asked to comment on the SSAB's response and the local community's reaction to DOE's plan to build an on-site disposal facility at Fernald, the official responded: "The Fernald SSAB represented the community. FRESH, a local environmental group, also approved of the plan. There was little opposition to the plan to build an on-site disposal facility at Fernald. There was no problem at all with the community. *The Fernald SSAB has done an excellent job of representing the community* (Personal interview, Knoxville, Tennessee, March 30, 1998). An environmental engineer who works closely with SSABs and DOE contractors, recalled that:

> There was some opposition from local residents to DOE's plan to construct the On-Site Disposal Facility at Fernald. The local newspapers apparently felt that the controversy over the medical community's desire to use Fernald's radium for treating cancer patients would capture the attention of readers more readily than stories about local opposition to Fernald's OSDF facility. (Personal interview, Oak Ridge, Tennessee, May 28, 1998)

When asked about the community reaction to the proposed OSDF facility, an EPA official said that: "There was no outcry against the OSDF because DOE held many public hearings with all of its stakeholders and went to great lengths to explain why the agency felt it was necessary to construct the OSDF facility at Fernald. The Fernald SSAB concurred with DOE on the OSDF project and worked with the agency" (Telephone interview, May 15, 1998). An Agency for Toxic Substances and Diseases Registry official commented that: "There was no outcry from the local community regarding DOE's plans to build the OSDF. The Fernald SSAB concurred with DOE on the project. The OSDF project represented a balanced approach to resolving Fernald's waste disposal problems" (Telephone interview, May 5, 1998).

As remembered by a DOE official close to the SSAB and familiar with public reaction to its report, there was *some* opposition to the recommendation to construct the OSDF. The DOE official recalls: "There was some opposition to the construction of the OSDF. This opposition was from some developers who wanted to develop land overlooking the Fernald site once DOE finished its cleanup activities. These developers wanted to build upscale housing near the Fernald site" (Telephone interview, July 30, 1998). Reflecting on community reaction to the on-site disposal decision and the surprisingly little opposition it engendered, an SSAB member commented that:

> Several people from Ross Township opposed the OSDF project. Township officials held a meeting to discuss the project and about 100 people came to the meeting who opposed it. The opposition was ineffective in stopping the OSDF. These opposition leaders had little previous involvement with the Fernald site and had opposed the project for economic reasons. They were unsuccessful because they did not have an alternative plan to the OSDF. (Personal interview, Cincinnati, Ohio, July 16, 1998)

Nearly all of the key actors interviewed agreed that there was a paucity of opposition to the OSDF project. Thus, the decision to dispose of waste on-site, which customarily brings extensive media coverage of agency decision making (usually in a highly negative light), in the Fernald case, engendered virtually *none*. In the end, the SSAB and its report recommending on-site disposal defused the issue and thus, as one key actor observed, "the radium issue was more newsworthy than the Fernald SSAB's July 1995 recommendations report" (Personal interview, Oak Ridge, Tennessee, May 28, 1998).

Key actors were asked if the Fernald SSAB's activities ever received any media coverage. These people were also asked if the media coverage received by the SSAB was generally positive, negative, or a combination of both. The consensus was that the SSAB's activities, in and of themselves, received very little media coverage. It was generally agreed that whenever the SSAB's activities did receive media coverage, the media coverage was generally positive. One SSAB member said that: "The Fernald SSAB activities received some media coverage particularly in July 1995 when the advisory board published its report. The *Post, Enquirer,* and *Journal-News* each wrote editorials about the July 1995 report" (Personal interview, Harrison, Ohio, July 13, 1998).

Not all the interviewees, however, agreed that the media coverage of the SSAB was always positive. Another SSAB member commented that: "The *Enquirer* had very poor coverage of Fernald's activities, especially during 1997 when Mike Gallagher and Tim Bonfield wrote articles alleging that safety violations and mismanagement at Fernald were frequent. The smaller community newspapers did a better and more accurate job of reporting on what went on at Fernald" (Personal interview, Harrison, Ohio, July 13, 1998).

A local DOE official recalled that, occasionally, one or two reporters *might* have attended an SSAB meeting, but otherwise coverage was virtually nonexistent. SSAB members confirmed this. Several SSAB members and DOE officials who worked with the board observed that the reporters responsible for the Fernald expose in the *Cincinnati Enquirer* never attended any SSAB meetings. They were also quick to point out that these reporters did not bother to interview any SSAB members other than John Applegate and Lisa Crawford.

Several subjects were asked if the Fernald SSAB received positive media coverage during the period of 1998 to 2000. An FDF official commented that "since the *Enquirer's* 1997 investigation of alleged mismanagement at Fernald, coverage by the *Enquirer* has decreased since 1997. From 1998 to 2000, media coverage regarding Fernald has been generally positive" (Telephone interview, July 26, 2000). A Fernald SSAB member said, that, "for the past two years, a reporter from the *Hamilton Journal-News* frequently attends the SSAB meetings and writes good articles about the meetings and doesn't sensationalize the news. The SSAB receives good coverage from the *Hamilton Journal-News"* (Telephone interview, July 26, 2000). Another SSAB member stated that "no TV reporters attend the meetings unless there's a big issue involved" (Telephone interview, July 14, 2000).

Public Attendance at Fernald SSAB Meetings

Has the SSAB attracted sufficient public interest and concern as to generate a high level of public attendance at its meetings and workshops? Those interviewed were asked about public attendance at the SSAB's meetings. Several persons said that many people attended the meetings from September 1993 until July 1995. After the SSAB released its July 1995 report, however, public attendance dropped off considerably. One SSAB member, for example, recalled that: "About 40 to 50 people attend the Fernald SSAB's meetings now. From September 1993 until July 1995, about 200 to 300 people attended Fernald SSAB meetings. Attendance at meetings dropped off considerably after we released our July 1995 report" (Personal interview, Harrison, Ohio, July 13, 1998).

According to those DOE officials who worked with the SSAB, *very few people ever attended the Fernald SSAB meetings* including the period from September 1993 until July 1995. One DOE official commented that "very few members of the public attended the Fernald SSAB meetings" (Personal interview, Harrison, Ohio, July 15, 1998). One FDF official commented that: "Presently, an average of about 20 to 40 people attend Fernald SSAB meetings. The residents have become complacent since July 1995. They know that cleanup activities are underway at Fernald and that Fernald will eventually close" (Personal interview, Harrison, Ohio, July 14, 1998).

Many of the persons interviewed seem to think that since there are presently no controversial issues being confronted by the SSAB, there is little reason for citizens to attend the advisory board's meetings. One Fernald SSAB member said that:

> Few people attend the SSAB meetings. The major decisions have already been made. The public is pretty confident in the SSAB's work and in their ability to represent the community. Attendance increases only when some kind of crisis exists. DOE holds public meetings once a month where the agency reports on the progress of Fernald's cleanup activities. Many people now attend the DOE meetings instead of the SSAB meetings. (Telephone interview, July 21, 2000)

Another SSAB member commented that "the regular bimonthly SSAB meetings are held on Saturday mornings and, since no crisis currently exists in the community, few people attend the meetings" (Telephone interview, July 24, 2000). In May 2000, the Fernald SSAB, FRESH, FLHP, and FHES jointly held a public meeting where members of the public were allowed to give their opinions on how the Fernald site should be used once the cleanup activities were completed. Several SSAB members said that about 100 people attended this meeting.

From September 1993 until July 1995, the SSAB was trying to decide which would be the most feasible method of disposing of Fernald's wastes. The

SSAB published its recommendations in its July 1995 report and the interviewees felt that many members of the public believed that the cleanup issues had been resolved in the 1995 report. Since the release of the 1995 report, DOE and FDF have been conducting cleanup activities at Fernald and no new controversial issues have emerged that have influenced large numbers of persons to attend the SSAB meetings.

DOE Budget Cuts and Fernald's Cleanup Program

Since the end of the Cold War in 1989, the election of Bill Clinton in 1992, and the Republican takeover of both houses of Congress in 1994, DOE's budget has been significantly reduced. Have budget cuts affected the work of the SSAB and the Fernald environmental management and remediation program? Key actors were asked if these budget cuts adversely affected Fernald's cleanup program. From the early 1990s until Fiscal Year 2001, Fernald had little trouble receiving the money it had requested for its cleanup programs. One SSAB member said that: "DOE and other federal agencies have maintained Fernald's cleanup program as a high priority. The goal was to have Fernald cleaned up by either 2005 or 2006. The budget has been sufficient to meet Fernald's cleanup goals" (Telephone interview, August 7, 1998). Another SSAB member commented that:

> The Fernald SSAB watches the yearly budget cycles very closely and fights hard to keep funding for Fernald. We also keep in close contact with our elected officials and people in D.C. to ensure that our budget is adequate. The budget reductions have not had an adverse impact on Fernald's cleanup program. We get the biggest bang for our buck and do things as quickly, cheaply, and more cost effectively. (Telephone interview, July 26, 1998)

FDF officials agree with this perspective. An FDF official said that: "Fernald and Rocky Flats are part of what is called a defense closure fund. They are part of the defense closure fund since these two facilities are so far along on their way to meeting their cleanup goals. As a result, we do not anticipate any budget cuts for at least the next two years at Fernald" (Telephone interview, September 10, 1998). A local reporter said that, "DOE budget cuts haven't affected the Fernald cleanup efforts. The cleanup activities at Fernald are a big priority for DOE" (Telephone interview, July 31, 1998).

State officials concerned with the Fernald cleanup, however, see it differently. In the words of one Ohio state environmental official: "DOE budget cuts have had a negative impact on Fernald's cleanup program. DOE's expertise is in weapons building. Now DOE is told to do more with less money" (Telephone interview, August 10, 1998). With this notable exception, however, virtually all of the key actors interviewed *agreed* that, whatever the impact elsewhere, the budget cuts the DOE had sustained since 1989 had not negatively impacted the Fernald environmental management and restoration program significantly. This was, according to one DOE official, due to the fact that "Fernald's cleanup program receives high priority from DOE. Ohio's two senators and congressional representatives from the Cincinnati area are very supportive of Cincinnati's program and see to it that Fernald receives the money it needs for its cleanup program" (Personal interview, Harrison, Ohio, July 15,

1998). An environmental engineer familiar with the Fernald program noted that, "DOE's cleanup budget has increased since the late 1980s" (Personal interview, Oak Ridge, Tennessee, May 28, 1998). It appears as if, at the very least, the SSAB is satisfied that the Fernald site continues to receive enough money to support an effective environmental management and remediation program. A major aspect of the SSAB's mission, of course, continues to be to monitor and advise the DOE on budget priorities for the program.

However, during the year 2000 (Fiscal Year 2001), Fernald was not likely to receive all of the budget outlays it had requested for its cleanup programs. An environmental engineer familiar with the Fernald SSAB said that, "There is a problem this year. Fernald had requested about $320 million for its cleanup programs but expects only to receive $290 million from Congress for the Fiscal Year 2001" (Personal interview, Oak Ridge, Tennessee, June 11, 2000). A DOE official agreed and said, "Fernald had requested about $320 million from Congress for the 2001 fiscal year. The House of Representatives has approved $290 million for Fernald's cleanup activities. The Senate still needs to decide how much money to appropriate for Fernald's budget" (Telephone interview, July 17, 2000).

During August 2001, a DOE official said, "The George Walker Bush administration requested $290 million for Fernald in the fiscal year 2002 budget. Recent congressional actions indicate that Fernald could receive an increase of as much as $30 million, depending on the actions of the conference committees and the willingness of the administration to approve the increase" (Telephone interview, August 17, 2001).

Community Reaction to the Fernald SSAB

How have the communities surrounding Fernald, especially various organized groups, reacted to the operation of the SSAB? According to several key actors, there was no real opposition to the SSAB. A survey of the newspapers in the Fernald region between 1993 and 1998 confirms this. The study found no stories indicating the presence of any specific community activists, environmental activists, or organizations questioning the SSAB's activities. A local reporter commented that: "The Fernald SSAB has no formal opposition from any particular organization or persons. This is because of public participation. The people who want to get involved do get involved. People get to voice their opinions. Some members of the Fernald SSAB may not agree with the Fernald SSAB's official positions, but they get to voice their opinions" (Telephone interview, July 30, 1998).

When asked about the existence of community opposition to the SSAB, another local reporter stated that: "The Fernald SSAB has few critics. The Fernald SSAB and FRESH are now part of the system. They use their own jargon when conducting their meetings. As a result, the public may feel intimidated when attending these meetings" (Telephone interview, July 31, 1998).

Newspaper coverage since the creation of the SSAB reinforces the impression that the SSAB has no organized opposition and, indeed, few vocal critics. Newspaper reporters who covered environmental affairs for their respective papers were asked if there were any activists or organizations that opposed the advisory board. It was assumed that if there were any community activists, environmental activists, or any organizations that opposed the actions of the SSAB, these reporters would be the first persons to know. Where there is protest, there is a *story*. The impression that one gets is that the public is generally satisfied with the SSAB's actions, otherwise opposition groups and activists would emerge to speak out against the SSAB.

The Fernald SSAB's Accomplishments

Perhaps the best indicator of the success of the SSAB at Fernald as an exercise in stakeholder involvement is its recognition by the Clinton administration as an illustration of what empowering communities through citizen participation can accomplish. The National Performance Review led by former Vice-President Al Gore issued a progress report in October 1997. This presidential report, *Putting Customers First '97: Standards for Serving the American People,* highlighted those agencies and programs around the country that best exemplified the administration's reinvention of government at the national level. The Fernald SSAB was prominently featured. According to the report:

> The Fernald SSAB saved more than $2 billion on an environmental restoration project that DOE and its contractor began at the Fernald site. Partnering with customers can have big payoffs. DOE set up a citizen advisory board at its Fernald facility to help with an environmental restoration project. Local citizens offered reasonable solutions that the community could live with that helped save a bundle on the project, too. (8)

This is great praise indeed from an administration led by a vice president who consistently has been among DOE's most severe critics.

SSAB Strengths

Given that the Clinton administration considered the Fernald SSAB one of its major successes, what did key actors see as the strengths of the SSAB? The answers varied to some degree, but six factors were consistently cited as strengths of the SSAB:

1. Strong and consistent board focus on the most important issues;
2. Membership stability and leadership;
3. Excellent technical support from an independent consultant;
4. An effective working relationship with DOE and FDF;
5. Board member dedication and commitment; and
6. Diversity among members in background, experience, and viewpoints.

Among key actors, several strengths were consistently emphasized. The first of these strengths was the SSAB's focus. Thus, when asked to comment on the SSAB's strengths, an environmental engineer familiar with the operation of federal SSABs said that, "The Fernald SSAB is a *focused* SSAB. It has strong leadership, focuses on the important issues, has staff support, and a stability of membership and leadership" (Personal interview, Tennessee, May 28, 1998). Or, in the words of one SSAB member: "The Fernald SSAB's strengths are that it is focused. [It] focuses on important issues regarding Fernald's cleanup activities" (Personal interview, Harrison, Ohio, July 15, 1998).

Membership stability and strong leadership was the second commonly identified strength of the SSAB. Membership stability is considered an important feature of any successful SSAB. In the words of one environmental scholar who often consults with local, state, and federal agencies on citizen participation issues: "Continuity is needed on an advisory board for it to become effective" (Personal interview, Knoxville, Tennessee, June 28, 1996). At Fernald, in the words of a board member, success was linked to "stability of membership and leadership" (Personal interview, Harrison, Ohio, July 15, 1998).

The leadership factor was paramount. Virtually all key actors interviewed agreed that the leadership of SSAB chairperson John Applegate made the advisory board an effective group. According to an FDF official: "Applegate was a consensus builder and was not dictatorial. He was able to keep the Fernald SSAB focused. Some SSABs spend their time talking about the same issues. Applegate also had political savvy and helped the Fernald SSAB focus on 'fightable' battles. He was able to sense the political climate when focusing on Fernald SSAB issues" (Personal interview, Harrison, Ohio, July 15, 1998). An Ohio state environmental official said that: "John Applegate became educated on issues relating to Fernald. He also consulted with members of the public, DOE, and other agency regulators to make informed decisions. He didn't want to be rushed into making a decision" (Telephone interview, August 10, 1998).

Other board members, most notably Lisa Crawford, contributed to the leadership factor. Key actors commonly praised the leadership of Crawford as a factor in SSAB strength. Clearly, the SSAB benefited from Crawford's background, experience, and proven leadership skills as an environmental activist and organizer. Recall that since 1984, Crawford has been active in mobilizing local citizens over health, safety, and environmental issues at Fernald. As an SSAB member, and in her capacity as president of the major grassroots environmental watchdog group in the Fernald area, Crawford made numerous public appearances, gave frequent interviews, and testified in congressional hearings about the FEMP and the role of the SSAB. Crawford also remained in close contact with local, state, and federal officials and the Ohio congressional delegation. Thus, as one SSAB member put it, "Lisa Crawford has been a great leader for the Fernald SSAB" (Personal interview, Harrison, Ohio, July 13, 1998).

The SSAB hired a technical consultant who could independently verify the technical information provided by DOE and FDF. The technical consultant also advised the board on scientific and technical matters. This was a third major SSAB strength about which all key actors tended to agree. The contribution of technical consultant Douglas Sarno, and DOE's cooperation with him, was a major SSAB asset. In the words of an SSAB member:

"DOE gave Doug Sarno direct access to their officials. Sarno dealt directly with DOE's program people. These people were very helpful and gave Sarno plenty of information and assistance. He also had extensive contact with DOE scientists and engineers" (Personal interview, Cincinnati, Ohio, July 16, 1998). Having this independent consultant was a very important factor strengthening the SSAB's capacity for dealing with scientific and technical issues. As one FDF official saw it: "Since Doug Sarno is the Fernald SSAB's technical consultant, he is an independent entity and is not associated with DOE. The Fernald SSAB can ask Doug any technical questions that they are not familiar with. He gives them information and can present technical information in such a way that is understandable to the average person" (Personal interview, Harrison, Ohio, July 15, 1998).

The *effective working relationship* forged over time among SSAB members and DOE and FDF officials was a fourth major strength about which key actors tended to agree. This relationship was rooted in *trust*. As one SSAB member described it: "DOE officials such as Ken Morgan and J. Phillip Hamric have a sincere desire to make the Fernald SSAB work. They gave the Fernald SSAB information whenever it was requested and never tried to hide anything from the advisory board. The Fernald SSAB and regulatory officials frequently contact each other, often on a weekly basis" (Telephone interview, August 8, 1998).

The dedication and commitment of all the SSAB members was the fifth major strength cited by many key actors. As expressed by one board member: "The Fernald SSAB are dedicated individuals who became very knowledgeable about issues concerning Fernald. They took a great deal of time to learn about the technical issues that impact the cleanup problems at Fernald" (Personal interview, Harrison, Ohio, July 13, 1998).

Because most of the SSAB members held full-time jobs, meetings were held at night. Some of the members lived considerable distances from the Fernald site. Thus, SSAB service exacted a considerable price in time and energy—with little or no compensation beyond the satisfaction of public service. For example, as described by an SSAB member: "Fernald SSAB members John Applegate and Guy Guckenberger did not live near the Fernald site. Both of them lived on the other side of Hamilton County from the Fernald site, yet they respected the people who lived near the site. John Applegate never missed a meeting during the five years that he was the Fernald SSAB chairperson" (Personal interview, Harrison, Ohio, July 15, 1998).

This kind of dedication promoted an atmosphere of cooperation and mutual respect. Although they all came from different backgrounds, they respected each other's viewpoints, and had taken the time to learn about the technical information and other types of information that impact Fernald's environmental problems.

Finally, the *diversity of membership* backgrounds, experiences, and viewpoints proved an important strength. Local residents, attorneys, Fernald workers, local officials, environmental activists, physicians, scientists, labor union officials, business people, and college professors came together to forge an effective, consensual decision making body. An SSAB member said that, "one of the strengths of the advisory board was that it had outstanding people from a wide variety of backgrounds—including professors, lawyers, county commissioners, and its own technical consultant" (Personal interview, Harrison, Ohio, July 15, 1998). Another SSAB member mentioned that some of the board members had technical backgrounds, while other board members did not. Some SSAB members had been involved with issues concerning Fernald for several years before joining the advisory board. Nevertheless, regardless of the members' different backgrounds, the SSAB was able to make decisions by reaching a consensus on issues regarding Fernald's cleanup problems.

SSAB Weaknesses

What weaknesses did key actors discern in the operation and performance of the Fernald SSAB? Many of the persons associated with the SSAB when asked this question claimed that they could not think of *any* weaknesses. One possible explanation for this viewpoint is that, so far, the Fernald SSAB has been the most successful of DOE's SSABs. Fernald has been held up as an example noted for effective public participation. So far, other SSABs have not had the successes or good working relationships with DOE and contract officials that the Fernald SSAB has had with DOE and FDF officials at Fernald. One Fernald SSAB member said that "Fernald is now ahead of the curve instead of behind the curve" (Telephone interview, July 24, 2000) when it comes to effectiveness as an SSAB. Another SSAB member commented that "at many of DOE's other sites, many people see the SSABs as a DOE front and the SSABs do not want to have anything do with DOE" (Telephone interview, July 14, 2000).

Other persons, however, were able to identify some defects in the SSAB. For example, one person associated with the SSAB felt the right balance had not been struck in stakeholder representation:

> Some groups are not represented on the Fernald SSAB. The Butler County government does not have any representatives on the Fernald SSAB. Some local government representatives were asked to join the Fernald SSAB but they declined. The Fernald workers from Kentucky and Indiana are not represented as stakeholders on the Fernald SSAB. The workers complain more about Fernald's activities and the residents seem less committed to monitoring Fernald's cleanup program. (Personal interview, Harrison, Ohio, July 13, 1998)

This person also felt that some groups were *overrepresented* on the Fernald SSAB: "FRESH is 'over represented' with two members on the board, while environmental groups such as the Sierra Club, the National Audubon Society, and members of environmental advisory committees are not represented on the Fernald SSAB" (Personal interview, Harrison, Ohio, July 13, 1998).

Another person associated with the Fernald SSAB felt that "the Fernald SSAB had a tendency to rely too much on DOE and the board's facilitator, Doug Sarno, for information concerning site and complex activities" (Telephone interview, July 17, 2000). Other weaknesses mentioned by persons associated with the SSAB were that "the Fernald SSAB does not have enough people who have a technical background" (Telephone interview, July 7, 2000) and that: "The Fernald SSAB has no teeth when it comes to making recommendations. DOE can accept or reject the Fernald SSAB's recommendations. DOE does not compensate the members for their work on the advisory board, considering how much time the members spent working on the Fernald SSAB" (Telephone interview, July 25, 2000).

Further weaknesses cited by local reporters were the SSAB's limited ability to provide *timely* information to the public and to engage in effective pubic outreach. As expressed by one reporter: "The challenges for the Fernald SSAB are keeping people informed about cleanup activities and getting information from DOE and FDF promptly. Occasionally, it takes a while for information to get from DOE and FDF to the Fernald SSAB" (Telephone interview, July 29, 1998). A second journalist commented that: "The Fernald SSAB needs more outreach into the community. People don't attend the Fernald SSAB meetings unless there's a crisis or something bad happens" (Telephone interview, July 31, 1998). A Fernald SSAB member also agreed with this viewpoint: "Sometimes DOE doesn't give the advisory board information in a timely manner. DOE doesn't always respond quickly to requests for information. Sometimes there are communication breakdowns between a DOE site and a DOE field office, and between the DOE field office and DOE headquarters" (Telephone interview, July 26, 2000).

Key actors typically expressed the view that current SSAB operations did not have any serious weaknesses, but worried about the future. Thus, an SSAB member, when queried about weaknesses, allowed that *remaining appropriately inclusive and the maintenance of stable membership over time might well prove serious problems*: "One of the challenges of the Fernald SSAB is to maintain stable membership. Another challenge is to reach out to the local community. For a significant time, local officials from Ross Township were not represented on the Fernald SSAB" (Personal interview, Cincinnati, Ohio, July 16, 1998).

A related concern arose when the well-regarded chairperson, John Applegate, resigned from the SSAB in July 1998. Several board members and agency officials admitted serious concern for future leadership without Applegate. Another SSAB member was concerned that a future weakness would be an inability to find qualified and dedicated citizens to serve on the board: "It is difficult to find people to serve on the SSAB. The advisory board's activities take up a great deal of time. Sometimes, the Fernald SSAB takes on too much work. A great deal of involvement is needed to learn the technical information" (Personal interview, Harrison, Ohio, July 15, 1998).

Concern for the SSAB's future led one DOE official to worry that, "since the release of the July 1995 report, the Fernald SSAB's role has changed. The advisory board needs to decide if it is going to be an advisory group or an oversight group" (Personal interview, Harrison, Ohio, July 14, 1998). That is to say, there was the danger that the SSAB might become "complacent" with its achievements and, in the future, fail to maintain its focus. One official expressed it this way: "After giving DOE its cleanup recommendations . . . the Fernald SSAB may end up struggling for something to do" (Personal interview, Harrison, Ohio, July 14, 1998). An FDF official said that: There are seven or eight people who have been on the Fernald SSAB since it was founded in 1993. People start to get tired. DOE rules say that people can't stay on an SSAB forever. The people must be reappointed and their reappointments have to be justified. There are term limits for SSAB members. It'll be hard to lose eight or nine knowledgeable people out of a 14-member board" (Telephone interview, July 28, 2000). Another FDF official agreed with this viewpoint. "Sometimes you get tired after working on something for so long. It's hard to keep up the enthusiasm after seven years" (Telephone interview, July 26, 2000).

Conclusion

This chapter describes how the Fernald SSAB organized and operated as a stakeholder involvement organization. Its contribution to DOE's FEMP was delineated, and on-going problems were detailed. The chapter analyzes from the perspective of informed sources and key actors the emergence of the Fernald SSAB as a featured performer in the Clinton administration's effort to reinvent the federal government.

A close review of media coverage of the SSAB revealed limited and essentially uncritical treatment in the press. In the few instances of critical coverage, such as the sensationalistic *Cincinnati Enquirer* expose, fault was not laid at the door of the SSAB. All evidence indicates that the SSAB organized quietly and efficiently. It went about its business in a serious, professional, and consensual fashion. There simply was not the kind of controversy, drama, accusations, and failures that normally attract heavy press coverage. For similar reasons, the SSAB engendered no organized protests or opposition in its work. Given the history of the DOE's Fernald facility, this, in and of itself, must be counted as a major accomplishment.

It was found that the SSAB's performance can be attributed to six strengths: sustained focus; leadership and membership stability; excellent technical support; effective cooperation; member dedication and commitment; and membership diversity. While few major weaknesses in the existing SSAB were identified, some concerns were expressed regarding the timely dissemination of information to the public and the failure to spur more directly the involvement of the general public. A few key actors questioned the sufficiency of stakeholder representation. More importantly, key actors often worried about the SSAB's future ability to maintain its focus, leadership, and membership stability.

Chapter 5 discusses the results of a survey that DOE gave to its SSABs in 1997. The chapter also compares the responses of all the SSABs with the responses of the Fernald SSAB members.

5

The Results of a Survey Involving DOE's Site Specific Advisory Boards

Introduction

This chapter describes the results of a 1997 survey that DOE sent to several of its SSABs. These surveys were known as the SSAB Initiative Evaluations. In September 1997, DOE published the results of these surveys in a report titled, *Site-Specific Advisory Board Initiative, 1997 Evaluation Survey Results: Volume I, Summary Report* and *Site-Specific Advisory Board Initiative,1997 Evaluation Survey Results; Volume II, Individual Site Results.* During 1997, DOE sent surveys to SSABs at the following sites: Fernald, Hanford, Idaho, Los Alamos, Monticello, Nevada Test Site, Pantex, Rocky Flats, Sandia, Savannah River, Paducah, and Oak Ridge (U.S. Department of Energy, September 1997, Volume I: iii).

Objectives and Goals

The primary objectives of the SSAB Initiative Evaluations were to:

I. Gain clarity and agreement regarding the goals of the SSAB Initiative, as defined by SSAB and DOE representatives.

II. Identify and evaluate the important factors affecting the effectiveness of the Initiative and accurately gauge the SSAB Initiative survey's success.

III. Monitor trends and progress in attaining SSAB goals. (iii)

DOE's report addressed the third objective: monitoring trends and progress in attaining SSAB goals. For the SSAB Initiative survey, the level of success or effectiveness was defined by using the following criteria:

- Effective, or successful: 66 % or more positive or favorable results.
- Area for improvement: 50 % to 65 % positive or favorable results.
- Area for concern: fewer than 50 % positive or favorable responses.

The larger the proportion of goal or objective items that had 66 % or more positive responses, the more successful the SSAB Initiative survey was in achieving the overall goal of objective (iii). The SSAB Initiative survey was developed by a committee of SSAB representatives who were managed by DOE's Office of Intergovernmental and Public Accountability. Technical support was provided by researchers from the Pacific Northwest National Laboratory (PNNL). The committee assembled a list of expectations for the SSAB Initiative survey. A set of mutually agreed-upon goals and a general approach for the evaluation were developed from the initial list of expectations, which drew upon findings in the literature and recommendations from a panel of experts in public involvement and evaluation (iv).

During 1997, two surveys were developed—a long survey and a short survey. In the long survey, members of all of the SSABs were asked to evaluate the effectiveness of their respective advisory boards and indicate the strengths and weaknesses of the SSAB program. In 1997, the long survey was mailed to all of the SSAB members, ex-officio members (i.e., DOE representatives and participating regulators), and DOE area/field staff members closely associated with the SSAB program. The response rate for the 1997 long survey was 61 % (v). The short survey was mailed to a sample of members of the public and to DOE Headquarters staff members that were involved with the SSAB program. This chapter discusses the results of the 1997 long survey because it was the most recent survey mailed to the SSAB members. The short survey was not mailed to SSAB members.

Questions asked in the 1997 SSAB Initiative Evaluation survey were structured to provide evaluative information about the respondents' perceptions of the following subject areas:

- SSAB Initiative performance relative to the set of agreed upon goals.
- SSAB processes and outcomes.
- The role of DOE and the regulators.
- The effectiveness of the SSABs as a group.
- The overall value of the SSAB program. (iv)

DOE stated that the purpose of its SSAB program was to involve stakeholders more directly in the agency's cleanup decisions. During the period of the 1997 survey, SSABs were operating at twelve major DOE sites. All of the respondents who participated in the 1997 surveys answered questions involving six goals established by DOE for its SSAB program and also answered open-ended questions about the SSAB program. Along with the answers to the open-ended questions, the six goals were:

Goal 1: Establish processes and procedures to provide an effective forum of exchange of information and viewpoints regarding DOE issues.

Goal 2: Facilitate interaction and exchange of information and viewpoints regarding DOE site issues.

Goal 3: Provide useful advice and recommendations to DOE.

Goal 4: Improve DOE's (and where applicable, the regulators') site decisions and decision making process.

Goal 5: Lead to more acceptable actions.

Goal 6: Contribute trust and confidence in DOE. (iv-vii)

The survey was structured to provide information about the respondents' perceptions of the following:

- The SSAB program's overall performance relative to the SSAB program's agreed-upon goals.
- SSAB processes and outcomes.
- The roles of DOE, state, and federal regulators in the SSAB program.
- The effectiveness of the respondent's own SSAB.
- The overall value of DOE's SSAB program. (iv)

The respondents to the long version of the SSAB survey were similar in their demographic background and other characteristics. The respondents were highly educated (over half held advanced degrees), predominantly white (85 %), and male (67 %). A total of 252 respondents completed the long survey in 1997 (iv-v). The survey results varied for the individual SSABs. These differences were apparent in how well the SSABs functioned as groups, in their relationships with DOE, in their mutual (DOE/SSAB) support, and in their perceptions about progress at respective DOE sites (viii).

Survey Results

There are six tables on the following pages that have questions corresponding to each of the six goals. In the six tables listed, all of the percentages have been rounded off to the nearest percent. The survey responses of all the SSABs combined are compared to the survey responses of the Fernald SSAB members. The tables also show the differences between the combined SSAB responses and the Fernald SSAB responses for each of the questions. Average responses for all the SSABs and the Fernald SSAB are compared at the bottom of each table.

Table 5.1 Goal 1: Evaluation: All Sites v. Fernald

	All	Fernald	Difference
1. The board has established processes and procedures for the effective exchange of of information.	82%	100%	+18%
2. The board has agreed-upon procedures to operate the board.	90%	95%	+5%
3. The board has adequate support to allow it to focus on substantive issues.	60%	80%	+20%
4. The board provides sufficient time for the discussion of issues.	63%	80%	+17%
5. The board has effective leadership.	68%	95%	+27%
6. DOE requests board advice far enough ahead of decision deadlines.	22%	35%	+13%
7. DOE handles board administrative issues promptly.	49%	80%	+31%
8. The SSAB staff provide satisfactory support.	75%	95%	+20%
9. The facilitator for the board has helped the board function effectively.	68%	95%	+27%
AVERAGE	64%	84%	+20%

Sources: *U.S. DOE, September1997, Volume I: B-49; Volume II: B-15.*

The survey respondents for all of the SSABs felt that Goal 1 was being successfully met, and responses indicated effectiveness on five of the nine items that defined Goal 1. *Overall, the favorable responses averaged* 64 %. One area of concern was the low percentages of respondents (22 %) for question 6, who felt that DOE requested advice before project deadlines (v). In contrast, the Fernald SSAB members gave consistently more favorable responses to all of the questions that defined Goal 1. The Fernald SSAB gave favorable response rates (66 % or higher) on all of the items of Goal 1 except for item 6. The Fernald SSAB listed item 6 as an area of concern (50 % or lower). Only 35 % of Fernald SSAB members agreed with the statement that DOE requested advice far enough ahead of decision deadlines, while only 22 % of all of the SSAB survey respondents agreed (B-19).

Table 5.2 Goal 2: Evaluation: All Sites v. Fernald

	All	Fernald	Difference
1. The SSAB facilitates effective exchange of viewpoints on site issues.	76%	95%	+19%
2. The SSAB contributes to board members understanding of the basis for key site decisions.	82%	95%	+13%
3. The SSAB contributes to DOE and the regulators understanding of the public's viewpoints on key site decisions.	76%	90%	+14%
4. The SSAB contributes to a constructive working relationship among the participants.	71%	95%	+24%
5. The SSAB strives for consensus.	75%	100%	+25%
6. The SSAB gives fair consideration to dissenting opinions.	72%	95%	+13%
7. The board has made the effort needed to learn about site issues.	86%	95%	+9%
8. The board invites expert advice into its discussion on key policy issues.	76%	85%	+9%
9. The board responds to public inquiries and comments about its decisions.	60%	90%	+30%
10. The board solicits feedback from the community on its work.	52%	80%	+28%
11. DOE makes information on key site issues readily available to the board.	73%	85%	+12%
12. The regulators make important contributions to the board's work.	67%	85%	+18%
13. The SSAB creates a climate supportive of differing viewpoints.	72%	100%	+28%
AVERAGE	72%	92%	+20%

Sources: *U.S. DOE, September 1997, Volume I*: B50; *Volume II*: B-19, B-20.

The respondents of the combined SSABs felt that the SSABs were successfully meeting Goal 2. The percentage of favorable responses for all thirteen items that defined Goal 2 was the highest for all of the aggregated scores. The favorable responses averaged 72 % and the responses on 11 of the items indicated success in meeting the goal (i.e., greater than 66 %) (v). Over 80 % of the respondents thought the SSABs contributed to board members understanding of the basis for site decisions, and 76 % of the respondents believed that the SSAB contributed to DOE and the regulators' understanding of public viewpoints (vi). Fernald SSAB members gave even higher favorable responses to the items listed in Goal 2. The Fernald SSAB's favorable response rates varied from 80 % to 100 % for all of the items included in Goal 2. However, there were some significant differences for two of the items in Goal 2. On item 9, only 60 % (area of improvement, from 50 % to 65 %) of the SSAB respondents believed that their respective boards responded to public inquiries and comments about its decisions. Ninety percent of Fernald SSAB respondents felt that the Fernald SSAB did respond to public inquiries and comments about its decisions. There was a 30 % difference between the positive responses of all of the SSABs and the Fernald SSAB for item 9. On item 10, only 52 % of the combined SSAB respondents felt that their respective boards solicited feedback from the community on its work. The SSABs believed that this was an area that needed improvement (i.e., ranging from 50 % to 65 %). In contrast, 80 % of the Fernald SSAB respondents felt that the Fernald SSAB solicited feedback from the community on its work. A 28 % difference existed between the positive response rates of the combined SSABs and the Fernald SSAB for item 10.

The response rates for the combined SSABs and the Fernald SSAB were the most similar for items 7 and 8. On item 7, 86 % of the respondents for all the SSABs felt that the board had made an effort to learn about site issues, while 95 % of the Fernald SSAB respondents agreed with this statement. For item 8, 76 % of the respondents for all of the SSABs agreed that the board invited expert advice into its discussion on key policy issues, while 85 % of the Fernald SSAB respondents agreed with this statement.

Table 5.3 Goal 3: Evaluation Overall v. Fernald

	All	Fernald	Difference
1. The board provides useful advice to DOE (and regulators, when appropriate).	70%	95%	+25%
2. The SSAB reaches agreement about prioritization of key site issues for which advice is sought.	51%	90%	+39%
3. The board helps define site problems.	72%	95%	+23%
4. The board addresses issues in a timely manner.	53%	90%	+37%
5. The board reaches consensus on key site issues.	62%	90%	+28%
6. The board provides informed advice to DOE (and regulators, when appropriate).	72%	95%	+23%
7. The board provides advice that reflects the viewpoints and priorities of the community.	58%	80%	+22%
AVERAGE	62%	91%	+29%

Sources: *U.S. DOE, September 1997, Volume I*: B-52; *Volume II*: B-21.

Survey respondents indicated that the SSABs successfully met a majority of the items in Goal 3. The favorable responses averaged 62 % for the seven items that defined Goal 3. Respondents felt that three of the seven goals were being met (i.e., 66 % or more positive or favorable results). These included item 1 with a 70 % favorable response rate, item 3 with a 72 % favorable rate, and item 6 with a 72 % favorable rate (vi). Fernald SSAB respondents gave favorable ratings to all of the questions in Goal 3. There were two items that the SSAB respondents felt were areas for improvement (response rate between 50 % and 65 %). For item 2, only 51 % of the respondents from the combined SSABs believed that the SSAB reached agreement about prioritization for which advice was sought. But 90 % of the Fernald SSAB respondents agreed that the SSAB reached agreement about prioritization when advice was sought. For item 4, 53 % of the SSAB respondents felt that their respective boards addressed issues in a timely manner. The SSAB respondents felt that item 4 was an area for improvement. Ninety percent of Fernald SSAB respondents believed that their SSAB addressed issues in a timely manner.

Table 5.4 Goal 4: Evaluation Overall v. Fernald

	All	Fernald	Difference
1. The SSAB has improved DOE's site decisions.	53%	95%	+42%
2. The board understands the decision making process at (a particular) site.	57%	80%	+23%
3. DOE discusses with the board important policies that affect site decisions.	73%	80%	+7%
4. DOE has explained to the board its site decision making process.	57%	75%	+18%
5. DOE shows how board advice is reflected in site decisions.	43%	75%	+32%
6. The decision making process used by DOE at (a particular) site is effective in furthering site cleanup.	57%	60%	+3%
AVERAGE	57%	78%	+21%

Sources: *U.S. DOE, September 1997, Volume I*: B-53; *Volume II*: B-22.

The survey results indicated for the responses concerning the items in Goal 4 that the SSABs thought there was room for improvement (50 % to 65 % favorable response rate). An area of concern (favorable response rate below 50 %) was issue 5. Only 43 % of the SSAB respondents agreed that DOE shows how the board advice is reflected in site decisions. However, 75 % of the Fernald SSAB members agreed with the statement that DOE shows how an individual SSAB's advice is reflected in site decisions (vi). Also, 95 % of the Fernald SSAB members felt that the SSAB has improved DOE's site decisions, while only 53 % of all of the SSAB respondents agreed with this statement.

Table 5.5 Goal 5: Evaluation Overall v. Fernald

	All	Fernald	Difference
1. The SSAB leads to more acceptable site actions.	57%	95%	+38%
2. The Board supports the recommendations it gives DOE.	80%	95%	+15%
3. The Board supports DOE's site actions. actions.	33%	45%	+12%
4. DOE pays attention to the Board's advice on key site issues.	48%	90%	+42%
5. There is support in the community for DOE's site decisions that have SSAB input.	48%	84%	+36%
6. Progress is being made on key site issues. site issues.	68%	95%	+27%
AVERAGE	56%	84%	+28%

Sources: *U.S. DOE, September 1997, Volume I:* B-54; *Volume II:* B-23.

For all of the SSABs, favorable responses averaged only 56 % for all of the issues in Goal 5 (vi). There were several areas of concern (favorable response rate below 50 %) for Goal 5. For example, issue 3 stated that the board supports DOE's site actions. Only 33 % percent of all the SSAB respondents agreed with this statement, while only 43 % of Fernald SSAB members responded favorably to this statement. Other areas of concern included issue 4 and issue 5. Only 48 % of all the SSAB respondents agreed with the statement in issue 4; in contrast, 90 percent of Fernald SSAB members agreed with the statement the DOE pays attention to the SSAB's advice on key site issues. For issue 5, only 48 % of all the SSAB respondents believed that there was support for DOE's site decisions that had SSAB input. In contrast, 84 % of Fernald SSAB members felt there was support for DOE's site decisions that received input from SSABs.

Table 5.6 Goal 6: Evaluation Overall v. Fernald

	All	Fernald	Difference
1. The SSAB contributes to trust and confidence in DOE.	47%	75%	+28%
2. Relationships between DOE and the public have improved since the formation of the SSAB.	58%	85%	+27%
3. DOE is committed to cleaning up the (name of the site) site.	65%	84%	+19%
AVERAGE	57%	81%	+24%

Sources: *U.S. DOE, September 1997, Volume I:* B-54; *Volume II:* B-23.

For the SSABs, the favorable responses averaged 57 % in 1997 for the three items that defined Goal 6. None of these items received ratings that indicated success. Items 2 and 3 were areas for improvement (a favorable response rate between 50 % and 65 %). Item 1 was an area of concern (i.e., a favorable response below 50 %) for the SSABs with a favorable response rate of 47 %. In contrast, the Fernald SSAB members gave favorable responses of effective or successful (66 % or higher) for all three items listed under Goal 6.

Conclusion

The survey results for the Fernald SSAB were very positive. Responses on the 1997 survey showed that the SSAB Initiative was viewed as successful in almost all areas of the survey: levels of success (66 % or more favorable responses) were shown on more than 85 % of the individual items included in the survey. *Fernald SSAB respondents believed that all six of DOE's SSAB goals were effectively achieved; the SSAB program was functioning effectively; the public was aware of the SSAB's role; Fernald SSAB members felt positive about their SSAB experience; and believed that their individual SSABs were a good use of funds.* The Fernald SSAB was substantially more positive about all aspects of the SSAB Initiative program than were all of the other SSABs combined in 1997. However, Fernald SSAB members noted a few areas of concern (levels of agreement below 50 %): DOE timeliness when requesting advice; FCAB support for DOE site actions; and DOE HQ's guidance and consideration of SSAB advice. On these items, Fernald respondents nevertheless remained less negative than respondents from all other SSAB sites combined, (U.S. DOE, Volume II: B-1).

Chapter 6 makes an overall evaluation of the performance of the Fernald SSAB as a case study of the U.S. DOE's effort to implement the Stakeholder Involvement Model. The next chapter also places the Fernald case in its larger context, draws conclusions, and offers the implications of this research.

6

The Eternal Quest for Public Participation: Assessing the Fernald SSAB Experience

Introduction

In this chapter, the operation and performance of the Fernald SSAB are placed in a larger context. First, the Fernald case is summarized and the most important findings are reviewed. The larger experience of the DOE with its Stakeholder Involvement Model is discussed, and its relative strengths and weaknesses are compared to the Fernald case. Finally, conclusions based on the findings and the implications of these conclusions are presented.

Study Summary

This study explored the establishment of a citizen advisory board by DOE at its Fernald facility in Fernald, Ohio. DOE created these advisory boards in response to lawsuits; declining public trust and confidence; polluting the ground, air, and water at its sites; and criticism about the agency's failure to disclose its activities. The U.S. Department of Energy's experience was presented as an example of policy gridlock and implementation failure. It provides an example of how the citizen participation movement, energized and revitalized by the rise of environmentalism, brought closed decision making of technocratic agencies such as the DOE to accept a Stakeholder Involvement Model.

The DOE experience in its Fernald, Ohio, facility was presented as a single case study. The purpose was to allow a preliminary assessment of how and to what effect federal agencies were implementing the Stakeholder Involvement Model. The DOE adoption of the Stakeholder Involvement Model at Fernald was found to be effective. A third-party convener chosen by EPA, DOE, the Ohio EPA, selected the original members of the Fernald SSAB. In a most expeditious fashion, the advisory board organized itself into committees, held meetings and workshops, reached consensus on all critical issues, and accomplished on time its primary mission. With the publication of comprehensive recommendations for the environmental management, remediation, and future use of the Fernald site, the SSAB met its short-term responsibilities. The study found that this report provided a basis for a continuing dialogue among stakeholders and federal agencies concerned with the Fernald facility—especially between Fernald stakeholders and the DOE.

In assessing the Fernald SSAB's performance the study found many strengths and some weaknesses. Informed sources and key actors identified six particular strengths: *sustained focus; leadership and membership stability; excellent technical support; effective cooperation; member dedication and commitment; and membership diversity.* Evidence was found of problems regarding the timely dissemination of information and concerning failure more directly to spur the greater involvement of the general public. Also, some key actors questioned the sufficiency of stakeholder representation. More importantly, key actors often worried about the SSAB's future ability to maintain its focus, leadership, and membership stability. Whatever the strengths and weaknesses of the Fernald SSAB, however, its overall success was such that the Clinton administration considered it a major example of how federal agencies could be reinvented to produce a government that works better and costs less (National Performance Review, October 1997).

Public involvement strategies, such as the Stakeholder Involvement Model, are promoted as a means to enhance the effectiveness of public agencies and the decisions they make. Among the many gains expected according to its promoters are:

1. Decision quality may improve as citizens and citizen groups add to the information available for making decisions. That information might prevent repetitions of many ill-advised public decisions.

2. With citizens involved in making decisions, acceptance of decisions may increase, enhancing the likelihood of successful implementation.

3. If citizens assist in service delivery, services may become more effective and more efficient.

4. As involvement increases citizen understanding of government operations, criticism of government agencies may lessen. (Thomas, 1995: 180)

The findings in the Fernald case indicate that, at least in the critical first stages of the environmental management and restoration program, the SSAB program made a significant contribution to realizing these gains for the U.S. Department of Energy—especially in comparison to what had transpired *before* the agency adopted the Stakeholder Involvement Model. According to John C. Thomas (1995), "the most important rewards of public involvement, however, may come in terms of democratic values" (1995: 181). In this, he echoes a fundamental belief of the citizen participation movement as a long-term political phenomenon:

> We live in an era when the democratic values of accountability and legitimacy are routinely described as compromised or endangered with the connections between citizens and their governments are said to be badly attenuated. Public involvement should enhance accountability by giving citizens new channels through which to communicate with government and to hold government accountable. Greater public involvement should also build the public acceptance of governmental decisions that underlies governmental legitimacy. (1995: 181)

The study found that the Fernald case produced a mixed result. The evidence clearly supports the conclusion that the SSAB enhanced DOE accountability and helped the agency build public acceptance of its FEMP decisions. The problem arises when one considers the very limited degree of public interest and participation that actually was engendered by SSAB operations. Despite newspaper notices and mass mailings, general public attention to the SSAB appears to have been minimal. Public attendance at SSAB meetings and workshops was limited even when it was engaging in its most important activities. It has fallen off even further since. If the Fernald SSAB case proves typical, this form of public participation runs no risk of confirming Samuel P. Huntington's (1975) fear of the "excess of democracy" that could threaten government effectiveness by overinvolving the public in governance (1975: 113).

The Fernald SSAB in Context

It is worth recalling that the DOE effort to employ the Stakeholder Involvement Model through citizen committees was not the first federal attempt to use advisory boards to promote more open agency decision making. Citizen advisory boards were first established in the 1960s as an important feature of President Lyndon Johnson's Great Society social programs. In the felicitous words of one of the architects of these programs, who later became one their most powerful critics, "Community action with citizen participation was a coherent and powerful idea working its way into national policy, albeit little noticed or understood at the time" (Moynihan, 1969: xvi). The problem was that this incarnation of citizen participation did not work well or as intended. But, the "coherent and powerful idea" did not disappear. It reemerged with the environmental movement and eventually engendered the Fernald SSAB. As one social scientist who often serves as a stakeholder involvement consultant to local, state, and federal agencies reviews the situation: "The National Environmental Policy Act required public participation programs for many federal projects that involved issues of environmental policy. This legislative act was significant because it made citizen participation more prevalent. The Fernald Citizens Advisory Board did not replace other types of citizen involvement" (Personal interview, Knoxville, Tennessee, June 28, 1996). Another social scientist who has extensively studied and consulted about citizen participation through stakeholder involvement commented that:

> The concept of stakeholder involvement in public policy decisions emerged in the late 1980s and early 1990s. There is a greater emphasis on the use of advisory committees. In the past, advisors consisted of "an elitist group of a few wise men." Now, there is a greater emphasis placed on determining that the members of advisory boards adequately reflect the demographics of the communities affected by the policies. (Personal interview, Oak Ridge, Tennessee, April 19, 1996)

Pressure on the DOE to adopt this particular model of pubic participation was especially pronounced because of its roots in the Atomic Energy Commission, a prototypical closed technocratic agency, and because of the potentiality for dire environmental, health, and safety conditions that may result from the nuclear weapons complex operations. Thus, according to this social scientist:

> In the past, the Atomic Energy Commission (AEC), DOE's predecessor, allowed only technical questions to be asked regarding environmental projects at the nuclear facilities. Questions about the environmental impact that environmental projects would have on stakeholders were not allowed. The technical questions regarding the environmental projects had to be approved in advance by the AEC. (Personal interview, Oak Ridge, Tennessee, April 19, 1996)

Finally, under unrelenting pressure from Congress, federal and state environmental agencies, and citizen protest and litigation, the DOE adapted the Stakeholder Involvement Model.

How does the Fernald SSAB experience compare with that of other DOE sites within the nuclear weapons complex? A comprehensive analysis is not possible, given the limits of this research. The study may, nonetheless, offer some preliminary information based on informed sources, key actors, and the public record to date. Prior to the DOE stakeholder involvement initiative, relations among the agency, its contractors, surrounding communities, environmental groups, and other federal and state agencies were consistently at an impasse. Thus, in the opinion of one informed observer, the mere adoption of the stakeholder model brought a significant improvement in its program: "The immediate result [of operationalizing the Stakeholder Involvement Model] was the opening of a three-way communication between the stakeholders, the government agencies, and the DOE SSABs. The SSABs also frequently communicate with each other" (Personal interview, Oak Ridge, Tennessee, April 19, 1996). In thinking about the Fernald SSAB in comparison with others within the nuclear weapons complex, this interviewee noted how much more progress had been made in Ohio. This was attributed in part to the more efficient fashion in which the board membership was identified and appointed. The respondent noted that Dr. Eula Bingham, the facilitator chosen by DOE, EPA, and the Ohio EPA, selected the members of the Fernald SSAB. Members of other SSABs were selected after completing questionnaires, filling out applications, and being interviewed for the positions (Personal interview, Oak Ridge, Tennessee, April 19, 1996).

In the considered view of another social scientist intimately familiar with DOE's program, several benefits occurred from the establishment of the SSABs. One benefit is that the advisory boards contain persons who are from technical and nontechnical backgrounds. As a result, DOE gets advice from a *diverse* group of stakeholders. The social scientist said that: "The advisory boards have people who are 'techies' and 'non-techies.' The 'non-techies' often ask the questions that ideally get asked. DOE gets good advice and gets to hear citizens' values and concerns. As a result, DOE can get durable and dependable decisions, and get a sense of community values from the SSABs" (Personal interview, Oak Ridge, Tennessee, May 28, 1996). This individual also said that some provisional trust has developed between the members of the advisory board and DOE officials. The agency's officials have to continually demonstrate that they are being responsive to the concerns of the advisory board members. The Fernald SSAB was the first SSAB that DOE established. As a result, the Fernald SSAB was considered further along in terms of experience and relationships with DOE, contractors, and state environmental regulators than the SSABs at other DOE sites. This resulted in a more effective environmental management and cleanup effort because it had produced:

> First, openness; second, responsiveness; third, one-on-one communication with members of the advisory board and agency officials; fourth, long-term interaction which allows personal relationships to develop between agency officials and advisory board members; and fifth, the Fernald SSAB has its own technical consultant to independently verify the information that DOE gives them. This characteristic gives the Fernald SSAB more credibility in the eyes of the public. (Personal interview, Oak Ridge, Tennessee, May 28, 1996)

It is generally accepted among informed sources and key actors that the overall DOE Stakeholder Involvement Model has opened access to the agency in an unprecedented way. A local reporter said: "The SSAB allows people to express views who previously did not have the opportunity to this. However, DOE allows this to occur only because the agency is required to do so. It is better to have the SSAB program in existence than to not have the program" (Personal interview, Oak Ridge, Tennessee, April 1, 1998). The experience at Fernald certainly confirms this. An environmental activist and long-time critic of the DOE's closed decision system said that DOE established its SSAB program with the declared goal of increasing citizen participation and stakeholder involvement in its decision making activities.

However, there remained significant skepticism among environmentalists because DOE still maintains powerful influence over the SSABs' agendas and activities. The environmental activist opined: "DOE has the authority to set the agenda, call the meetings, and tell its advisory boards what issues to focus on. The SSABs' procedures and environmental cleanup issues are governed by DOE's charter" (Personal interview, Oak Ridge, Tennessee, April 1, 1998). This, in the environmentalist's view, tends to limit SSAB effectiveness around the nuclear weapons complex. However, no evidence of this was found in the Fernald case. The activist granted that the expeditious fashion in which the Fernald SSAB had established its membership and conducted its business set it apart from the other SSABs around the country. But, whether this could be sustained at Fernald or anywhere else remained an important question. The activist was concerned that participation on an SSAB requires a significant amount of time and that many persons who might be qualified may be unable or unwilling to participate because of time constraints. This concern is consistent with the findings in the Fernald case. Key actors were clearly worried about what would happen in the future with respect to sustaining board membership and leadership.

It is, to be sure, difficult to compare the Fernald SSAB with SSABs at other DOE sites. Many other DOE's sites are considerably larger than Fernald and have even more serious contamination problems. An Ohio state environmental official summarized the situation: "Fernald is a site that will be closed by DOE once all of its cleanup activities are completed. As a result, there are no further issues for DOE at Fernald. Fernald is one of DOE's smaller facilities. Other sites have more complex issues to resolve. DOE sites such as Hanford, Oak Ridge, and the Savannah River plant are much larger sites with more serious contamination problems" (Telephone interview, August 10, 1998). This is further emphasized when an examination is made of the following review offered by a DOE official:

> Every SSAB is unique. The selection process, activities, working relationships with agency officials, and the number of advisory board members are different for each SSAB. Oak Ridge has waste contamination problems that are even worse than Fernald's, and the Nevada Test Site's contamination problems are even worse than Oak Ridge's. The Fernald work force lives in 18 to 27 different communities in Ohio, Indiana, and Kentucky. (Personal interview, Oak Ridge, Tennessee, May 14, 1998)

The investigation of the Fernald case confirms the accuracy of the DOE official's assessment—the site, surrounding community, and other important factors differ from characteristics found elsewhere in the complex. In the future, after extensive systematic, longitudinal, comparative studies, this might explain variation in SSAB performance. This remains to be seen. The Fernald SSAB record of accomplishment remains. This is true even if much of the credit may be due to inherent site advantages and good fortune. The DOE and the SSAB seem to have been effective in achieving their purposes at Fernald.

> Other SSABs lack adequate funding, have poor quality consultants, and have ineffective chairpersons. At sites such as the Hanford Reservation, the SSAB members live in different states and it costs a significant amount of money to hold a meeting. The Fernald SSAB is lucky; there are many DOE and FDF officials at Fernald who are very committed to seeing that the Fernald SSAB is effective. (Personal interview, Harrison, Ohio, July 13, 1998)

The interviewee also pointed out that, "While Fernald has a technical consultant working for them, other SSABs do not have *any* technical consultants working for them" (Personal interview, Harrison, Ohio, July 13, 1998). This invites the observation that other SSABs have much to learn from the Fernald experience—even given the obvious variation in local conditions.

The Strengths and Weaknesses of DOE's SSAB Program

Program Strengths: Key Actor Views

Key actors and informed sources were asked to assess the strengths of the DOE SSAB program. The program strengths consistently mentioned actually were variations on the same theme: *The DOE SSAB Program provided citizen access to, involvement in, and influence over critical agency decisions that affected their health and safety.* A Fernald SSAB member commented that: "The SSABs provide a need for citizen involvement that is important at the local level. At a national level, citizens are involved in a way that influences public policy without going through the political system or the courts. For example, issues in both Ohio and Nevada affect each other. The SSABs are a way for these people to communicate with each other on a national level" (Telephone interview, August 7, 1998). Another Fernald SSAB member said that: "One of the strengths of the SSABs is that these advisory boards give access to anyone at DOE. With the SSABs, the local communities are better able to make value judgments than DOE can on how the agency's cleanup activities will affect the communities, especially the risk levels" (Personal interview, Harrison, Ohio July 13, 1998). An FDF official stated that: "The SSABs allow people to play a role in creating the policies that affect them. DOE's involving of the community in the creation of policy makes the policy a better product. The satisfaction of the Fernald SSAB is very high. DOE listens to the Fernald SSAB" (Personal interview, Harrison, Ohio, July 14, 1998). When asked to comment on the strengths of the SSAB program, an environmental engineer said that:

> DOE was forced to pay attention to the concerns of stakeholders. In the past, DOE had been reactive in its approach to the public. The SSABs taught DOE how to be proactive and how to engage in public participation. For example, the holding of public meetings, the distribution of public materials, and how to deal with volatile individuals are methods that DOE now uses to increase levels of public participation. (Personal interview, Harrison, Ohio, July 13, 1998)

Thus, according to most interviewees, the most common strength of DOE's SSAB program was that these advisory boards allowed citizens to play a role in creating the environmental policies that affected them. Persons are more supportive of public policies that they helped to create. Citizens are less likely to issue criticism or file lawsuits against an agency if they play a role in creating and monitoring that agency's policies.

Program Weaknesses: Key Actor Views

Key actors and informed sources were asked to assess the weaknesses of DOE's SSAB program. The most common weaknesses identified were: *problems with getting information from DOE headquarters, the lack of an effective national network for information exchange among SSABs, and problems in recruiting and keeping members with the qualities required for a focused SSAB.*

DOE headquarters, apparently, has problems with how it handles requests for information from SSABs. A person who is associated with the Fernald SSAB and who is knowledgeable about those at other sites described the problem this way: "The response [to requests for information] from DOE's headquarters depends on the particular person who receives the request. Some DOE officials do not respond as quickly to the other SSABs as they do to the Fernald SSAB" (Telephone interview, August 7, 1998).

It appears as if the DOE has yet to create an effective national network for the effective and timely exchange of information among the SSABs. For example, in the words of an environmental engineer: "The SSAB chairpersons get together once a year at a conference where they usually discuss procedural matters. There are not good networks for the SSABs to get together and interact with each other. The SSABs are not being used as effectively by DOE as they could be. DOE is sometimes relegated to telling the SSABs which issues are important" (Personal interview, Oak Ridge, Tennessee, May 28, 1998). The lack of an effective network for information exchange leads an SSAB to excessive reliance on DOE for issue identification. This can also create problems in dealing with intersite issues such as waste disposal and transportation (Personal interview, Cincinnati, Ohio, July 16, 1998).

The maintenance and continuity of SSAB membership is a major problem. As one Fernald SSAB member put it: "It is also difficult to get replacements for SSAB members who resign. Serving on an SSAB takes a large amount of time" (Personal interview, Harrison, Ohio, July 15, 1998). This, of course, exacerbates the problem of maintaining a focused board—especially for the monitoring of long-term operations and problems for which the SSABs are responsible. As one informed source describes it: "One of the challenges for the SSABs is to maintain an interest in environmental issues at DOE sites. This interest must be maintained over a period of several years" (Personal interview, Cincinnati, Ohio, July 16, 1998).

In its most severe form, the problem of recruiting, developing, and keeping high-quality SSAB membership compromises the very purpose of the organization. In the words of an environmental activist:

> DOE's SSAB program is ineffective because the agency has to approve all the persons who become members of the SSABs. In some cases, when people first joined some of the SSABs, they received no training in how to analyze and evaluate the detailed technical information regarding the environmental problems at the DOE sites. SSAB members have varying backgrounds and experiences, and some SSAB members had little or no technical backgrounds. (Personal interview, Oak Ridge, Tennessee, April 1, 1998)

The activist also noted that "sometimes the training occurred several months or a few years after the persons became SSAB members" (Personal interview, Oak Ridge, Tennessee, April 1, 1998).

An environmental engineer commented that, "the problems involving environmental pollution are not technical, but are sociological in origin. There is too much focus on technical issues and too little focus on sociological issues" (Personal interview, Oak Ridge, Tennessee, May 28, 1998).

Fernald in Context

The DOE Stakeholder Involvement Initiative Program has worked well at Fernald. It has not worked well at other DOE sites. It is understood that local conditions vary, and one would not expect the same results throughout the nuclear weapons complex. Still, it appears that Fernald has far outpaced its sister facilities. Why has this occurred?

There are several reasons why the SSAB program has worked well at Fernald. First, there was the leadership of Fernald SSAB chairperson John Applegate. Many interviewees praised him as a consensus builder who was able to work effectively with other Fernald SSAB members, DOE officials, and FDF officials.

Second, the Fernald SSAB hired Douglas Sarno to become its technical consultant and to independently verify the technical information given to the advisory board by DOE and FDF. One interviewee said that Sarno could present technical information in a way that is understandable to nontechnical persons. Some SSABs do not have their own technical consultants.

Third, Fernald SSAB members have a good working relationship with DOE and FDF officials. There are several DOE and FDF officials who are dedicated to ensuring that Fernald's cleanup program continues to meet its goals and go out of their way to work with the Fernald SSAB in order to meet these goals. Several interviewees stated that this relationship does not always exist between other SSABs and DOE officials.

Fourth, the leadership of Fernald SSAB member and FRESH president Lisa Crawford greatly enhances the effectiveness of the Fernald SSAB. Crawford has been active in environmental affairs concerning Fernald since 1984. Crawford grants interviews to reporters and has testified at congressional hearings regarding Fernald's contamination problems. She also remains in close contact with Ohio congressional representatives and travels extensively to environmental conferences and DOE's SSAB conferences. Crawford is well informed on environmental matters and has a great deal of knowledge regarding the operations of regulatory agencies such as DOE and EPA.

Finally, the Fernald SSAB has a dedicated group of members. Fernald SSAB members come from a variety of backgrounds. Members include local officials, while others are academics, environmental activists, physicians, scientists, Fernald workers, businesspeople, schoolteachers, local residents, and labor union representatives from the Fernald site. Some members have technical backgrounds while other members do not. Nevertheless, Fernald SSAB members try to become knowledgeable about environmental cleanup activities at Fernald. Although they all have different backgrounds, the Fernald SSAB members all work well together. All of these factors have made the Fernald SSAB a successful citizen advisory group. Other SSABs have not been as effective and do not appear to possess all five of the factors previously mentioned. One characteristic mentioned repeatedly by interviewees was that some of the other SSABs do not enjoy harmonious working relationships with DOE officials and DOE's contract officials at other DOE sites.

An individual associated with the Fernald SSAB said that as a result of the factors previously mentioned, the stakeholder group produced:

- A balanced approach to remediation that takes into account both local and national concerns regarding cleanup and waste disposal activities.
- Cleanup recommendations by the Fernald SSAB that have saved over $2 billion in costs from previous estimates of cleanup costs.
- Recommendations that were unanimously accepted by DOE, EPA, and the Ohio EPA.
- A continuing voice of reason that facilitates progress in cleanup activities.
- The basis for excellent on-going working relationships between stakeholders and all levels of government. (Telephone interview, November 18, 1998)

Perhaps another reason why the Fernald SSAB has been successful is because Fernald is scheduled to close. Production activities at Fernald stopped in 1989, and the facility is scheduled to close once the cleanup activities are completed. DOE hopes to finish the cleanup activities by 2010. Since DOE plans to close Fernald in a few years, perhaps DOE and FDF officials do not feel threatened by the existence of the Fernald SSAB. The impending closure of Fernald and DOE's cleanup mandates may have given DOE and FDF officials little reason to oppose the Fernald SSAB, and prompted DOE and FDF officials to work with the Fernald SSAB to achieve Fernald's cleanup goals.

Conclusion

This study of the U.S. Department of Energy's Stakeholder Involvement Initiative has three major findings: First, the DOE was successful in establishing the Fernald Site Specific Advisory Board. Second, the SSAB organized and operated largely as designed as a stakeholder involvement organization; and in developing its comprehensive recommendations for environmental management, remediation, and future land use, it accomplished its primary mission. Third, the public record, DOE reports, and personal interviews with informed sources and key actors indicate that SSABs at other sites within the nuclear weapons complex have not had the success found at Fernald. What conclusions can be drawn from these findings?

First, *the Stakeholder Involvement Model does work, but it is not a guaranteed, easy, or cheap solution.* The time, energy, commitment, and resources required to create and maintain these organizations are substantial. Whether the results produced over time will justify the investment remains an open question. The simple truth is that the model is being employed to deal with problems that are among the most intractable problems confronting our society. Even when SSABs, such as that at Fernald, manage effectively to communicate stakeholder views to agency officials, mutually agreeable and effective policy decisions are by no means assured. As Rosemary O'Leary and associates (1999) have averred: "Two-way communications [between stakeholders and public managers] about environmental management issues is a difficult process. This is especially true when shared understandings about health, safety, or ecological risk do not exist" (1999: 163).

Second, the study concluded that certain conditions appear critical to successful application of the stakeholder involvement model on the scale required by most federal agencies. The Fernald case may prove unique as a success story within the larger DOE stakeholder involvement initiative because other sites do not currently have and may prove unable to develop the requisite conditions for success. The conditions for success at Fernald were:

1. An efficient and effective mechanism for board recruitment;
2. A limited set of critical issues so that board focus could develop;
3. A facility of manageable size, complexity, and operational scale;
4. The development of cooperative relationships among key actors and institutions: mutual respect and trust that were based on timely and affirmative agency responses to board concerns and recommendations;
5. The provision of effective technical support for the board: this means the board had access to the advice of technical consultants independent of the agency; and
6. Board leadership and membership that was dedicated and committed.

In conclusion, there is much more to learn. If the findings in the Fernald case are to be truly tested and the promise and performance of the Stakeholder Involvement Mode to be truly understood, then longitudinal comparative research is required. This research needs, over time, systematically to compare the SSABs at all DOE facilities. Also needed are comparable studies of the large-scale DOD stakeholder involvement programs. These must then be compared to the results of the DOE program. Other comparative work must be undertaken to compare the Stakeholder Involvement Model as it is applied across *policy domains and at different levels of government.*

Implications

What implications can be drawn from the conclusions in this study? First, the federal government is committed to the Stakeholder Involvement Model. Its application is well underway and is likely to continue well into the future. How well this innovation works will affect the body politic for a long time to come. Second, their timing, size, breadth, and nature make DOD's RAB programs and DOE's SSAB programs groundbreaking efforts. DOE is spending billions of dollars to manage, store, and remediate the pollution from radioactive and hazardous wastes from its facilities. Jacqueline Vaughn Switzer and Gary Bryner (1998) said that: "From 1990 to 1996, DOE spent almost $35 billion on its environmental management program, with another $6.5 billion expected in fiscal 1997. DOE has spent over two-thirds of its expenditures on six major sites: Hanford, Savannah River, Rocky Flats, Oak Ridge, Fernald, and the Idaho sites: Hanford, Savannah River, Rocky Flats, Oak Ridge, Fernald, and the Idaho National Engineering Lab" (1998: 105).

The billions of dollars invested by DOE give the agency a long-term incentive to maintain its SSAB program to help meet its cleanup goals and to increase public satisfaction with the agency through increased citizen participation efforts. DOE may believe that the alternatives to maintaining its SSAB program might include an increase in negative publicity, decreased public confidence in DOE, and an increase in the number of lawsuits filed against the agency. Actions such as an increase in lawsuits would greatly add to the expenses DOE faces besides its cleanup costs. The Fernald case suggests the agency's aspirations in avoiding these negative externalities are not ephemeral.

The Department of Defense has also established citizens' oversight boards at its facilities worldwide. Again, arising from the Keystone Committee reports, these Restoration Advisory Boards (RABs) are designed to give advice and help monitor future land use, environmental management, and remediation activities. Many of these facilities are scheduled to close and be converted to civilian use, and RABs will play an important role in this process.

Other federal agencies, indeed government at all levels, would do well to attend closely to the DOE and DOD's unfolding efforts to apply the Stakeholder Involvement Model. In this capacity, the DOD and DOE serve as laboratories within which a vast citizen participation experiment will continue for some time. From their experiences, there are many lessons to be learned. Thus, it appears that citizen participation programs such as DOE's SSAB program may become more common in the foreseeable future:

> There is a growing recognition by administrators that decision making without public participation is ineffective. In recent times, interest in public participation in administration decision making has increased as a result of a number of factors—including a citizenry with diminished trust in government is demanding more accountability from public officials. There is also a growing recognition by public administrators that decision making without public participation is ineffective. (King, Feltey, and Susel, 1998: 319)

Cheryl Simrell King, Kathryn M. Feltey, and Bridget O'Neill Susel also said that "under contemporary political and economic conditions, we can no longer afford to exclude the public in decision making" (1998: 319).

Third, the Stakeholder Involvement Model seems likely to improve somewhat, but it does not *solve* the conundrum of citizen participation in the modern democratic state. The adoption of a Stakeholder Involvement Model *can* promote progress on what otherwise appear to be intractable problems; deadlock can be broken in a process where institutions are infused with focused and institutionalized public participation. Robert Entman (1989) bemoans the decay of American politics and the emergence of "democracy without citizens." The Fernald case suggests that the possibility of "bureaucracy with citizens" is a significant but incremental contribution of a rejuvenation of republican democratic institutions. But the larger issue of promoting widespread direct popular engagement in government remains. The Stakeholder Involvement Model holds real promise for widening the *representational* base for agency decision making. Public attention to and engagement in the Fernald case proved limited and declined as time passed. That is to say, whatever its other virtues, the Stakeholder Involvement Model *in practice* is a significant but incremental improvement in citizen participation. It may contribute in some degree to slowing the "civic disengagement that weakens America" (National Commission on Civic Renewal, 1998); but it alone does not solve the problem. The goal of a highly participatory democratic polity continues to elude us.

Appendices

Appendix A

Chronology of Important Fernald Events

Date	Event
1951	Feed Materials Production Center begins operations
1985	National Lead of Ohio declines to renew contract & Westinghouse takes over as contractor
	Press reports buried hazardous & radioactive wastes have seeped into local water supply
	Local residents sue DOE for polluting their water supply
1986	Ohio EPA sues DOE for failing to comply with state environmental laws at Fernald
1989	DOE settles lawsuit by local citizens for $78 million
	Production ceases at Fernald
	EPA places Fernald on the *CERCLA National Priorities List*
1990	DOE sued by groups alleging unsafe working conditions produced cancer among workers
1992	U.S. Supreme Court decision in *Ohio v. DOE*
	Fluor Daniel becomes Fernald contractor; the FEMP is created
1993	Fernald Citizens Task Force is established
1994	DOE agrees to $15 million dollar settlement to end unsafe working conditions lawsuit
	SSAB issues its *Interim Report* on the FEMP
1995	SSAB issues its *Recommendations on Remediation Levels, Waste Disposition, Priorities, and Future Use* report on the FEMP
1996	*Cincinnati Enquirer* expose of past DOE & contractor problems
	DOE & GAO investigations launched due to press expose
1997	GAO issues report critical of DOE and FDF
1999	DOE extends FDF's contract to November 2000
2000	DOE awards FDF a 'closure contract' that allows FDF to continue working at Fernald until FDF's cleanup activities are completed.

Appendix B

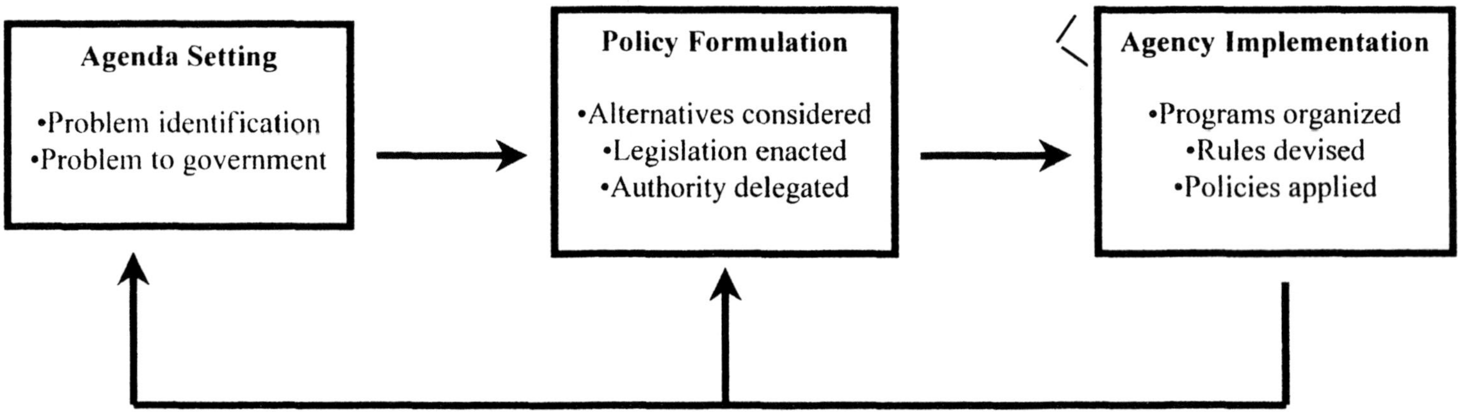

Figure 1 The Traditional Regulatory Process

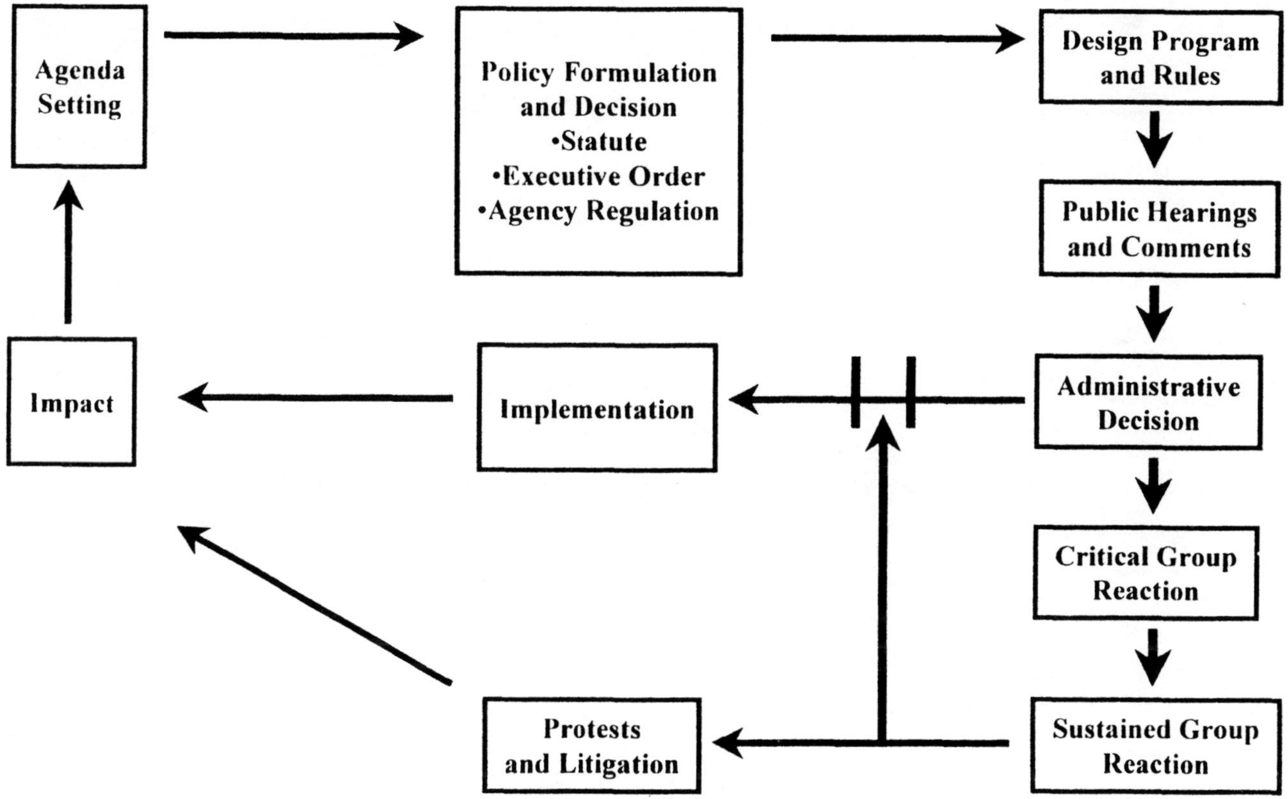

Figure 2 The Contemporary Regulatory Process
Source: Adapted from McCabe, Colglazier, and Fitzgerald, 1993.

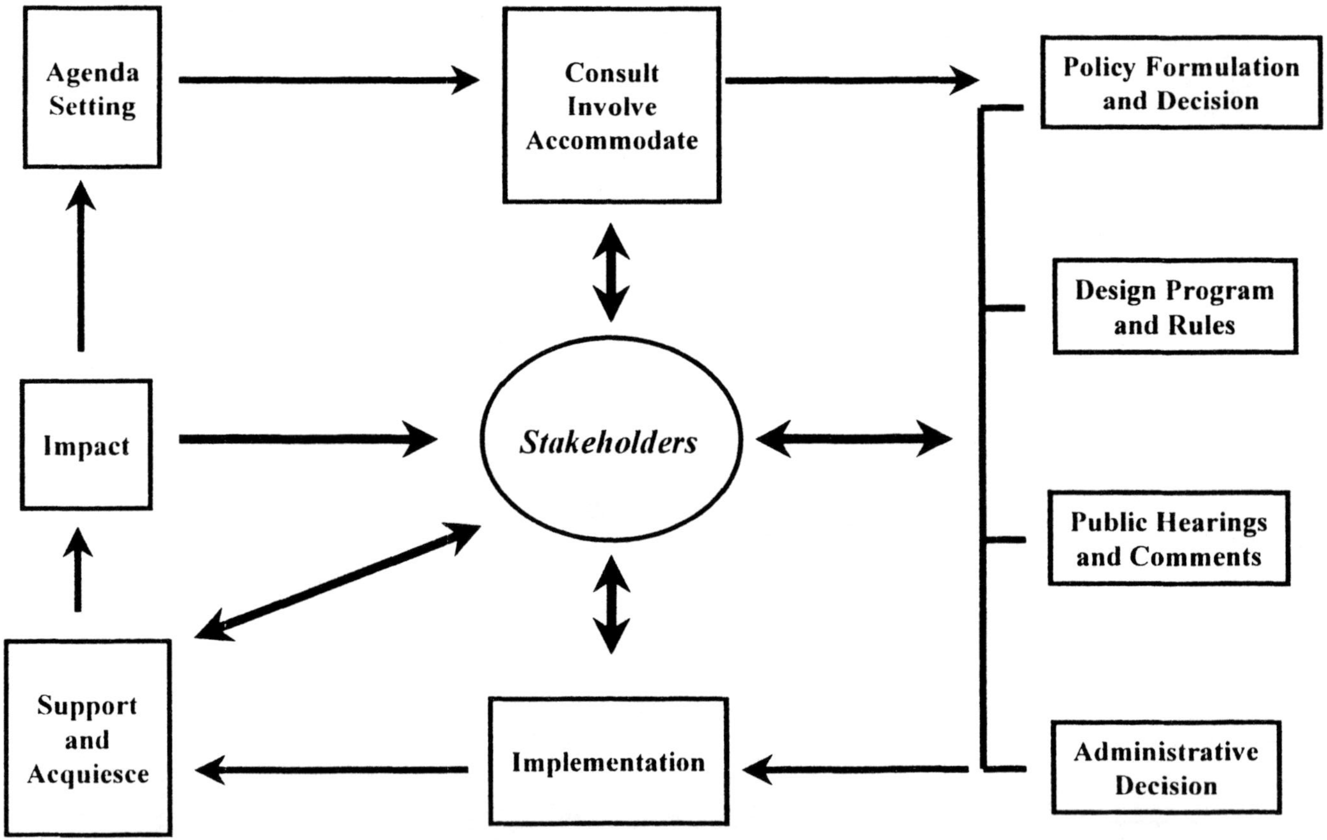

Figure 3 The Stakeholder Involvement Model
Source: Adapted from McCabe, Colglazier, and Fitzgerald, 1993.

Major Communities in Southwestern Ohio

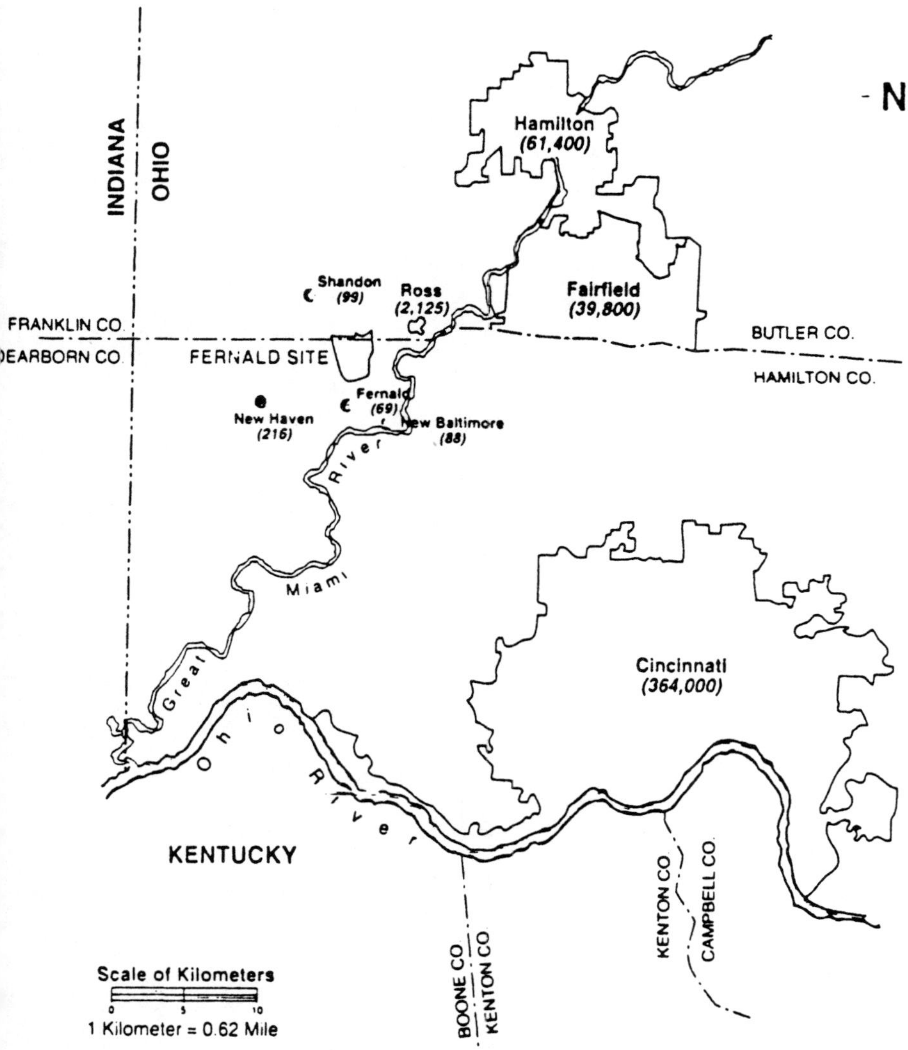

LEGEND

- Population in parenthesis estimated in 1989
- Population in parenthesis from 1990 U.S. Census Figures

Figure 4 Location of the Fernald Site in Ohio

Source: Fernald Environmental Restoration Management Corporation, June 1996, 22.

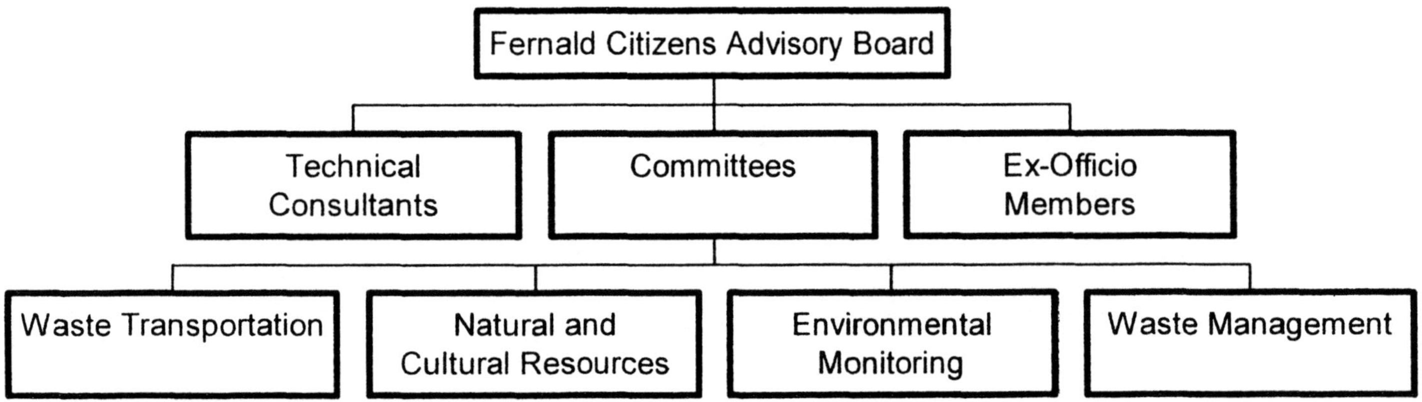

Figure 5 **Fernald Citizens Advisory Board, December 1995**

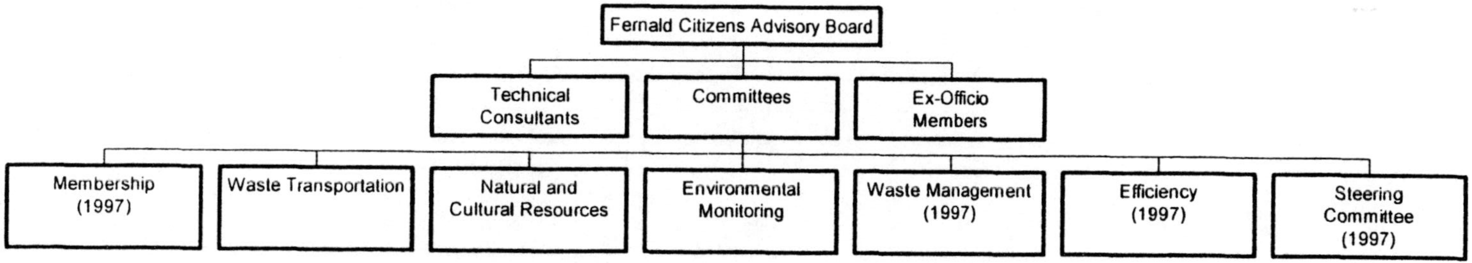

Figure 6 Fernald Citizens Advisory Board, January 1997

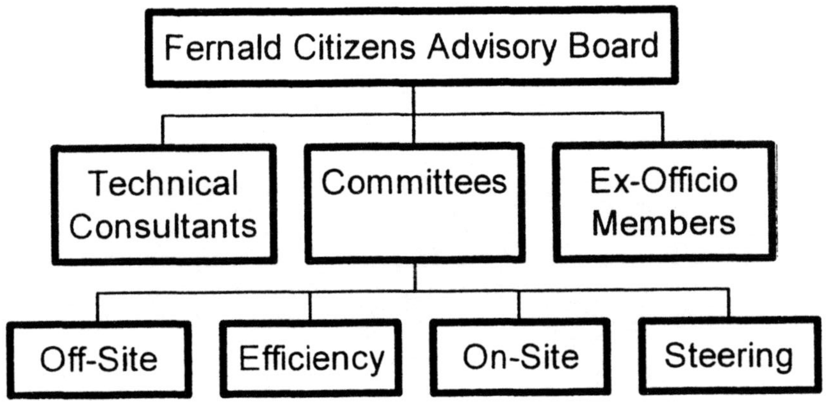

Figure 7 Fernald Citizens Advisory Board, January 1998

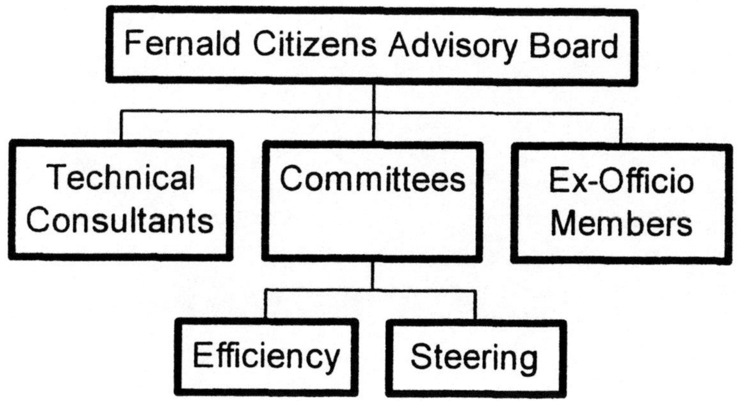

Figure 8 **Fernald Citizens Advisory Board, January 2000**

Appendix C

ADDITIONAL INTERVIEW INFORMATION

In 1998, interviews were sought with current and retired members of the Fernald Site Specific Advisory Board (SSAB). Two current board members began service in January 1998. Because they were so new to the board, interviews with them were not sought. Four current members of the SSAB and one former member granted interviews. One current member was unavailable for a personal interview, but agreed to grant a telephone interview at a later time. Three board members did not return telephone calls or e-mail messages, so interviews could not be arranged. One newspaper reporter did not return telephone calls or e-mail messages. Another newspaper reporter had to postpone an arranged interview. Another meeting with this reporter could not be scheduled. All four ex-officio members of the SSAB were interviewed—one by personal interview and three by telephone. The other persons interviewed were people knowledgeable about U.S. DOE weapons complex operations. These included newspaper reporters, consultants, state and local officials, and citizen activists.

In 2000, interviews were sought with all fourteen current members of the Fernald SSAB and one ex-officio member. Twelve board members and an ex-officio member granted telephone interviews. A thirteenth board member requested that the researcher fax him a list of the interview questions. The board member did not send back his responses to the questions. A fourteenth board member failed to return telephone calls or e-mail messages, so an interview could not be arranged. Other persons interviewed during 2000 also included persons knowledgeable about DOE operations. These included reporters, state and local officials, citizen activists, and consultants. In 2001, a DOE official was interviewed.

Each interview was conducted in a semi-structured fashion. Subjects initially were asked about DOE history in general and the Fernald site in particular. Specific questions about the organization, operation, and impact of the Fernald SSAB were asked. All of those interviewed then had the opportunity to offer additional observations and comments.

Bibliography

Abramson, Rudy. "Energy Dept. Agrees to Pollution Penalty." *The Los Angeles Times,* May 11, 1991, A19.

Aeppel, Timothy. "Cold War Legacy: Uranium Mill's Woes Highlight Huge Cost of Nuclear Cleanup." *The Wall Street Journal,* June 30, 1994, A1, A2 (E).

Aleshire, Robert A. 1970. "Planning and Citizen Participation: Costs, Benefits, and Approaches." *Urban Affairs Quarterly,* 5: 369-393.

Aman, Alfred C., Jr. 1992. *Administrative Law in a Global Era.* Ithaca, NY: Cornell University Press.

Applegate, John S. 1998. "Beyond the Usual Suspects: The Use of Citizens Advisory Boards in Environmental Decision Making." *Indiana Law Journal,* 73: 903-957.

Applegate, John S. and Douglas J. Sarno. 1997. "Citizens Get Involved in Cleaning Up Fernald." *Forum for Applied Research and Public Policy,* 11: 122-124.

Applegate, John S. and Douglas J. Sarno. July 1996. "Coping with Complex Facts and Multiple Parties in Public Disputes." *Consensus: Harvard-MIT Public Disputes Program,* 31: 1, 12.

Applegate, John S. and Douglas J. Sarno. 1997. "FUTURESITE: An Environmental Remediation Game-Simulation." *Simulation and Gaming,* 28: 13-27.

Applegate, John, Gary D. Stegner, Jack Hoopes, and Douglas J. Sarno. 1996. "The Fernald Citizens Task Force: Shifting the Focus." A paper presented at the Waste Management '96 Conference. Tucson, AZ.

Arnstein, Sherry R. 1969. "A Ladder of Citizen Participation." *American Institute of Planners Journal,* 35: 216-224.

Aron, Joan B. 1979. "Citizen Participation at Government Expense." *Public Administration Review,* 39: 477-485.

Associated Press. "British Firm Buying Some Fernald Uranium for Use: Purchase Price Kept Under Wrap." *The Cincinnati Enquirer,* December 22, 1997, B6.

Associated Press. "Experts: Getting Fernald Radium Won't Slow Cleanup." *The Hamilton Journal-News,* August 28, 1995, A10.

Associated Press. "Fluor Daniel Contract Extended at Fernald." *The Cincinnati Enquirer,* October 1, 1997, B5.

Associated Press. "Group Says Fernald Cleanup Shouldn't Stop." *The Hamilton Journal-News,* July 18, 1995, A3.

Associated Press. "Task Force Issues Advisory Report on Fernald Cleanup." *The Hamilton Journal-News,* July 30, 1995, A5.

The Associated Press News Service. "Report: Wastes Leak at Fernald." March 4, 1996, A1.

Barton, Paul. "Corps May Take Over Fernald Cleanup: Groups Oppose Moving Job Away from DOE." *The Cincinnati Enquirer,* May 12, 1998, B4.

Barton, Paul. "Fernald Cleanup Allocated $266.5M." *The Cincinnati Enquirer,* February 7, 1997, A6.

Barton, Paul. "Fernald Contractor Generous in Washington: But Politicians Say They Like Firm For Its Expertise, Not Money Gifts." *The Cincinnati Enquirer,* December 26, 1996, B5.

Barton, Paul. "Fernald Gets Another F." *The Cincinnati Enquirer,* October 24, 1997, A1.

Barton, Paul. "Senate Trims Funding for Nuclear-Cleanup Sites: Reduction Is Greater Than Voted by House." *The Cincinnati Enquirer,* October 1, 1993, C2.

Barton, Paul. "Technology Doesn't Exist for Fernald: Energy Chief Says Cleanup Won't Be Perfect." *The Cincinnati Enquirer,* August 8, 1993, B1.

Barton, Paul and Tim Bonfield. "Fernald Contractor Loses Big Job: Pilot Project Stripped from Fluor Daniel." *The Cincinnati Enquirer,* March 21, 1997, A1, A4.

Barazia, Virginia. "Slight Drop Proposed for Fernald Funding." *The Hamilton Journal-News,* February 7, 1997, A1.

Bender, Penny. "Lawmakers Want DOE Briefing on Incinerator." *The Nashville Tennessean,* February 13, 1997, 1A, 2A.

Benveniste, Guy. 1972. *The Politics of Expertise.* Berkeley, CA: The Glendessary Press.

Berry, Jeffrey M. 1981. "Beyond Citizen Participation: Effective Advocacy Before Administrative Agencies." *The Journal of Applied Behavioral Science,* 17: 463-477.

Berry, Jeffrey M. 1997. *The Interest Group Society, Third Edition.* New York: Longman.

Bibby, John F. 1996. *Politics, Parties, and Elections in America, Third Edition.* Chicago: Nelson-Hall.

Bolman, Lee G. and Terrence E. Deal. 1987. *Modern Approaches to Understanding and Managing Organizations.* San Francisco: Jossey-Bass.

Bond, David F. "Fernald Contract May Set Pattern for Energy Dept. Cleanup Management." *Aviation Week and Space Technology,* April 6, 1992, 136: 48-49.

Bonfield, Tim. "Action Sought on Radium: Fernald Neighbors Fear Clean-Up Delay." *The Cincinnati Enquirer,* August 13, 1995, B1, B11.

Bonfield, Tim. "Fernald Cancer Survey May Be Done: With Risk Factor Confirmed, Next Step Is to Determine Actual Cases." *The Cincinnati Enquirer,* July 12, 1997, B2.

Bonfield, Tim. "Fernald Clean-Up Won't Finish by Deadline." *The Cincinnati Enquirer,* June 14, 1997, B7.

Bonfield, Tim. "Fernald Event Riles Vegas: Nevada-Bound Cargo Burst at Loading Dock." *The Cincinnati Enquirer,* June 12, 1997, C1, C9.

Bonfield, Tim. "Fernald Finish Date Now 2010: Less Money, Cleanup Problems Lower Expectations." *The Cincinnati Enquirer*, November 22, 2000, B2.

Bonfield, Tim. "Fernald Study Group Ended Over Some Members' Protests." *The Cincinnati Enquirer*, August 23, 2001, B3.

Bonfield, Tim. "Fernald Truck Leaks in Arizona." *The Cincinnati Enquirer,* December 17, 1997, B1.

Bonfield, Tim. "Glass-Pellet Method Endorsed: But It Will Cost More." *The Cincinnati Enquirer,* April 29, 1997, A1, A4.

Bonfield, Tim. "Hope, Caution Ring Cancer Treatment: Tests Would Need Radium Buried at Fernald." *The Cincinnati Enquirer*, August 8, 1995, A1, A4.

Bonfield, Tim. "More Fernald Trucks Leak." *The Cincinnati Enquirer,* December 18, 1997, A1, A6.

Bonfield, Tim. "Study: Cancer Risks Higher Near Fernald." *The Cincinnati Enquirer,* August 23, 1996, A1, A8.

Bonfield, Tim. "Tristate's Nuclear Legacy: Greater Cincinnati Played a Key Role in the Dream and Nightmare of the Atomic Age." *The Cincinnati Enquirer,* April 6, 1995, A1.

Bonfield, Tim and Mike Gallagher. "Senators Call for Fernald Probe." *The Cincinnati Enquirer,* February 15, 1996, C1, C7.

Boyer, Mike. "Three-Hundred at Fernald to Be Fired." *The Cincinnati Enquirer,* August 5, 1993, A1.

Bradburne, John. "Innovative Management Techniques Accelerate Cleanup at DOE's Fernald Site." *Engineering News Record* (*ENR*), December 9, 1996, 237: E-24 to E-26.

Brownell, Blaine A. and Warren E. Stickle. 1973. *Bosses and Reformers: Urban Politics in America, 1880-1920.* Boston: Houghton Mifflin.

Cable, Sherry and Charles Cable. 1995. *Environmental Problems, Grassroots Solutions: The Politics of Grassroots Environmental Conflict.* New York: St. Martin's Press.

Callow, Alexander B., Jr. 1976. *The City Boss in America: An Interpretive Reader.* New York: Oxford University Press.

Chandler, Ralph Clark. 1987. *A Centennial History of the American Administrative State.* New York: The Free Press.

The Cincinnati Enquirer. "History of Fernald." August 23, 1996, A1.

The Cincinnati Post. "Don't Short-Change Fernald." July 18, 1995, 10A.

Coates, Joseph F. 1975. "Why Public Participation Is Essential in Technology Assessment." *Public Administration Review,* 35: 67-69.

Congressional Informational Service, Annual 1992: Legislative Histories of U.S. Public Laws. Public Law 102-386. Federal Facilities Compliance Act of 1992, 106 Stat. 1505, 244-254.

Congressional Quarterly Almanac, One-Hundred-and-Second Congress, First Session, 1991. "Federal Facilities Cleanup." Volume 47: 222-223.

Congressional Quarterly Almanac, One-Hundred-and-Second Congress, First Session, 1992. "Federal Agencies Liable for Waste Violations." Volume 48: 261, 100-H

Craig, Jack R., Jr., James A. Saric, Thomas Schneider, and Michael K. Yates. February 1995. "Status Report: Fernald Site Remediation." A paper presented at the 1995 Waste Management Conference, Tucson, AZ.

Cramer, Jerome, B. Russell Leavitt, and J. Madeleine Nash. "They Lied to Us: Unsafe, Aging U.S. Weapons Plants Are Stirring Fear and Disillusion." *Time,* October 31, 1988, 60-65.

Crawford v. National Lead Company, 784 F.Supp. 439 (S.D. Ohio 1989).

Crosby, Ned, Janet M. Kelly, and Paul Schaefer. 1986. "Citizen Panels: A New Approach to Citizen Participation." *Public Administration Review,* 46: 170-178.

Crowfoot, James E. and Julia M. Wondolleck. 1990. *Environmental Disputes: Community Involvement in Conflict Resolution.* Washington, DC: Island Press.

Cunningham, James V. 1972. "Citizen Participation in Public Affairs." *Public Administration Review,* Special Issue, 32: 589-602.

Dalton, Russell J. 1988. *Citizen Politics in Western Democracies: Public Opinion and Political Parties in the United States, Great Britain, West Germany, and France.* Chatham, NJ: Chatham House Publishers, Incorporated.

Davis, Robert C., Jr. 1991. "Environmental Liability for Federal Lands and Facilities." *Natural Resources and Environment,* 6: 31-33 and 66-67.

Denhardt, Robert B. 1993. *Theories of Public Organization, Second Edition.* Belmont, CA: Wadsworth Publishing Company.

DeSario, Jack and Stuart Langton. 1987. *Citizen Participation in Public Decision Making.* Westport, CT: Greenwood Press.

Dixon, John. 1975. "How Can Public Participation Become Real?" *Public Administration Review,* 35: 69-70.

Duffield, Jennifer J. and Stephen P. Depoe. "Lessons from Fernald: Reversing NIMBYism Through Democratic Decision-Making." *Inside EPA's Risk Policy Report,* February 21, 1997, 31-34.

Edley, Christopher F., Jr. 1990. *Administrative Law: Rethinking Judicial Control of Bureaucracy.* New Haven: Yale University Press.

Eisner, Marc Allen. 1993. *Regulatory Politics in Transition.* Baltimore: The Johns Hopkins University Press.

English, Mary, et al. September 1993. *Stakeholder Involvement: Open Processes for Reaching Decisions About the Future Uses of Contaminated Sites: Final Report.* Knoxville: Waste Management Research and Education Institute, The University of Tennessee, Knoxville.

ENR (Engineering News Record). "Dingell Flays DOE Over ERMC Plan." September 14, 1992, 229: 7.

ENR (Engineering News Record). "DOE Auditors Target Fernald and Hanford." May 24, 1993, 230: 22-23.

ENR (Engineering News Record). "DOE Plans to Tighten Outside Contractor Liability." February 11, 1991, 226: 7.

ENR (Engineering News Record). "Huge Cleanup Contract Spelled Out by DOE." August 19, 1991, 227: 12-13.

Entman, Robert M. 1989. *Democracy Without Citizens: Media and Decay of American Politics.* New York: Oxford University Press.

Environmental Law Reporter. "Legal Environmental Assistance Foundation, Incorporated v. Hodel." May 1984, 14: 10209.

Epstein, Paul. 1987. "How Citizen Participation Spruces Up Performance." *National Civic Review,* 76: 147-151.

Feiertag, Joseph. "Eighty-Four Citations Documented at Fernald's Waste Transfer Site." *The Hamilton Journal-News,* July 18, 1995, A1.

Feiertag, Joseph. "Fernald Panel to Mull Radium Recovery Issue." *The Hamilton Journal-News,* September 2, 1995, A7.

Feiertag, Joseph. "Fernald Waste Shipping Plan Called Balanced." *The Hamilton Journal-News,* August 3, 1995, A5.

Feiertag, Joseph. "FMPC Waste: No Quick Fix in Store: Cleanup May Not Mean Material Leaves Site." *The Hamilton Journal-News,* June 24, 1990, B1.

Feiertag, Joseph. "Officials Endorse Radium Extraction." *The Hamilton Journal-News,* September 24, 1995, A1.

Feiertag, Joseph. "Studies: Useful Material Can Be Retrieved from Fernald's Waste Silos." *The Hamilton Journal-News,* July 20, 1995, A1, A2.

Feiertag, Joseph. "Trustees Support Radium Efforts." *The Hamilton Journal-News.* August 24, 1995, A3.

Feinberg, Kenneth R. 1990. "In the Shadow of Fernald: Who Should Pay the Victims?" *The Brookings Review,* 8: 41-46.

Fernald Citizens Task Force. "Citizen Advisory Group Created at Fernald." September 15, 1993, 1-4.

Fernald Citizens Task Force. October 1994. *The Focused SSAB: Key Issues and Activities from the Fernald Experience—Interim Report.*

Fernald Citizens Task Force. "Minutes from the May 10, 1997 Meeting." May 10, 1997, 1-5.

Fernald Citizens Task Force. July 1995. *Recommendations on Remediation Levels, Waste Disposition, Priorities, and Future Use.* Fernald, OH: U.S. Department of Energy.

Fernald Environmental Restoration Management Corporation. June 1996. *Fernald Environmental Management Project: 1995 Site Environmental Report.* Fernald, OH: Fernald Environmental Restoration Management Corporation, Site Restoration Services Department.

Fernald Environmental Restoration Management Team. "Fernald ERMC Typifies New Partnership Between Contractors and Feds." *ENR (Engineering News Record),* April 12, 1993, 230: E10-E14.

Fiorino, Daniel J. 1990. "Citizen Participation and Environmental Risk." *Science, Technology, and Human Values,* 15: 226-243.

Fiorino, Daniel J. 1989. "Environmental Risk and Democratic Process: A Critical Review." *Columbia Journal of Environmental Law,* 14: 501-547.

Fischer, Frank. 1990. *Technology and the Politics of Expertise.* Newbury Park, CA: Sage Publications.

Foley, Dolores. 1998. "We Want Your Input: Dilemmas of Citizen Participation." in *Government is Us: Public Administration in an Anti-Government Era,* edited by Cheryl Simrell King and Camilla Strivers, 140-157. Thousand Oaks, CA: Sage Publications.

Formaini, Robert. 1990. *The Myth of Scientific Public Policy.* London: Transaction Publishers.

FRESH Incorporated (Fernald Residents for Environmental Safety and Health). *FRESH News.* March 2000, Volume 28.

FRESH, Incorporated (Fernald Residents for Environmental Safety and Health). *FRESH News Newsletter.* May 1997, Volume 18.

Gallagher, Mike. "Agency Failed to Detect Problems: Energy Department Says It Is Hampered by Lack of Manpower." *The Cincinnati Enquirer,* February 14, 1996, A4.

Gallagher, Mike. "Audit Skewered FERMCO: Fernald Manager Repaid $768,000 to Government." *The Cincinnati Enquirer,* September 14, 1996, B1, B9.

Gallagher, Mike. "Construction Firm Files $15M Defamation Suit Against FERMCO: Action Claim Company Being Made 'Scapegoat.' " *The Cincinnati Enquirer,* July 26, 1996, C4.

Gallagher, Mike. "DOE Penalizes Fernald Manager: Project Cost Data in Error." *The Cincinnati Enquirer,* May 2, 1996, A1, A4.

Gallagher, Mike. "DOE Plan to Save Radium Is Praised: Fernald Cleanup Won't be Delayed." *The Cincinnati Enquirer,* September 9, 1995, B2.

Gallagher, Mike. "DOE Report: Warnings Ignored." *The Cincinnati Enquirer,* July 17, 1997, A1.

Gallagher, Mike. "FERMCO Accused of Intimidation: Company Ignored Safety, Workers Say." *The Cincinnati Enquirer,* May 5, 1996, A1, A10.

Gallagher, Mike. "FERMCO Can't Find Records." *The Cincinnati Enquirer,* March 24, 1996, A1, A10.

Gallagher, Mike. "Faster Fernald Cleanup Planned? 10-Year Plan Given Tentative Approval." *The Cincinnati Enquirer,* June 7, 1996, A1, A4.

Gallagher, Mike. "Fernald Cleanup Imperils Cancer Breakthrough." *The Cincinnati Enquirer,* August 6, 1995, A1.

Gallagher, Mike. "Fernald Cleanup Rolls on Despite Radium Cache: Element Coveted for Cancer Research." *The Cincinnati Enquirer,* July 16, 1995, A1, A17.

Gallagher, Mike. "Fernald Contractor Loses Big Job: Pilot Project Stripped from Fluor Daniel." *The Cincinnati Enquirer,* March 21, 1997, A1, A8.

Gallagher, Mike. "Fernald Faults Confirmed, But Energy Teams Reject 'Deceit' Label." *The Cincinnati Enquirer,* April 3, 1996, B1, B6.

Gallagher, Mike. "Fernald Firm Awarded a New Contract: Fluor-Daniel Set to Clean Washington Site." *The Cincinnati Enquirer,* August 7, 1996, A1.

Gallagher, Mike. "Fernald Mess Back to Square 1: New Disposal Methods May Be on the Table." *The Cincinnati Enquirer,* May 16, 1997, A1, A9.

Gallagher, Mike. "Fernald Neighbors Question Possible Delay." *The Cincinnati Enquirer,* August 9, 1995, A1, A6.

Gallagher, Mike. "Fernald Neighbors to Meet with DOE." *The Cincinnati Enquirer,* August 8, 1995, A4.

Gallagher, Mike. "Fernald Pilot Plant Cost Jumps: Problems Add $14M." *The Cincinnati Enquirer,* May 17, 1996, A1, A7.

Gallagher, Mike. "Fernald Project Shut Down: Leak in Melter Spews Ton of Molten Material at Plant." *The Cincinnati Enquirer,* December 31, 1996, B1, B6.

Gallagher, Mike. "Fluor Docked $4M: Penalty Stems from Troublesome Pilot Project." *The Cincinnati Enquirer,* February 1, 1997, C1, C9.

Gallagher, Mike. "Fluor Will Lose $6.6M: Penalties Pile Up for Fernald Firm." *The Cincinnati Enquirer,* July 8, 1997, A1, A6.

Gallagher, Mike. "Gold, Rare Radium in Fernald's Waste: Experts Race to Recover Treasures." *The Cincinnati Enquirer,* July 2, 1995, A1, A16.

Gallagher, Mike. "Key Project at Fernald Plagued by Problems: Design Flaws, Excessive Costs Cited in Energy Dept. Report." *The Cincinnati Enquirer,* March 25,1996, A1.

Gallagher, Mike. "Lack of Oversight: Agency Failed to Detect Problems: Energy Department Says It Is Hampered by Lack of Manpower." *The Cincinnati Enquirer,* February 14, 1996, A1.

Gallagher, Mike. "Plan Allows for Fast Recovery of Radium: Scientist Says Fernald Cleanup Could Stay on Track." *The Cincinnati Enquirer,* July 27, 1995, B1, B6.

Gallagher, Mike. "Radium in Small Amounts at U.S., European Sites: Fernald Cleanup Won't Be Delayed." *The Cincinnati Enquirer,* September 13, 1995, B2.

Gallagher, Mike. "Tank Cleanup Riddled with Problems, Delays, Design Errors, Contamination Reported." *The Cincinnati Enquirer,* March 5, 1996, A1, A4.

Gallagher, Mike. "Taxpayers Bilked in Fernald Cleanup." *The Cincinnati Enquirer,* February 11, 1996, A1, A6, and A7.

Gallagher, Mike. "Trusting Agency Pays $15 Million Without Receipts." *The Cincinnati Enquirer,* February 11, 1996, A7.

Gallagher, Mike and Tim Bonfield. "Audit: Cleanup Botched, Millions Wasted: Congressmen Want Changes Before Renewal." *The Cincinnati Enquirer*, March 19, 1997, A1, A6.

Gallagher, Mike and Tim Bonfield. "Fernald Critics Energized: Neighbors Want 'Action Not Promises.' " *The Cincinnati Enquirer*, March 20, 1997, A1, A12.

Gallagher, Mike and Tim Bonfield. "Scientists Backpedal: Fernald Risk Real. Lung Cancer Study Now Seen as Accurate." *The Cincinnati Enquirer*, July 11, 1997, A1.

Gittell, Marilyn. 1983. "The Consequences of Mandating Citizen Participation." *Policy Studies Review*, 3: 90-95.

Goetz, Kristina, "Vision for Fernald: Learning Center; Residents Want Site's Past Examined." *The Cincinnati Enquirer*, November 4, 2000, B2.

Golightly, Eric J. January 1993. *Site History of the Fernald Environmental Management Project, Draft*. Washington, DC: U.S. Department of Energy, History Division.

Gordon, George J. 1986. *Public Administration in America, Third Edition*. New York: St. Martin's Press.

Gore, Al. 1993. *Creating a Government That Works Better and Cost Less: The Report of the National Performance Review*. New York: Penguin Books USA, Incorporated.

Grassley, Charles E. and Charles Pou, Jr. 1992. "Congress, the Executive Branch, and the Dispute Resolution Process." *Missouri Journal of Dispute Resolution*, 1992: 1-24.

Hamilton, Minard. 1990. "Countdown in the Bomb Factories: Workers Fighting for Their Jobs, Fighting for Their Lives." *The Progressive*, 54: 30-33.

Harrigan, John J. 1993. *Political Change in the Metropolis, Fifth Edition*. New York: HarperCollins.

The Harrison Press. "Fernald Group Formed to Advise DOE on Socioeconomic Issues." August 14, 1996, 3.

Heclo, Hugh. 1978. "Issue Networks and the Executive Establishment." In *The New American Political System*, edited by Anthony King, 85-124. Washington, DC: American Enterprise Institute.

Hibbing, John R. and Elizabeth Theiss-Morse. 1995. *Congress as Public Enemy: Public Attitudes Toward American Political Institutions*. New York: Cambridge University Press.

Huntington, Samuel P. 1975. "The United States." In *The Crisis of Democracy*, edited by Samuel P. Huntington, Michael Crozier, and Joji Watanuki, 59-118. New York: New York University Press.

Ichniowski, Tom. "DOE Contractor Scrutinized." *ENR (Engineering News Record)*, December 13, 1993, 31: 8, 10.

Ichniowski, Tom and Debra K. Rubin. "DOE Lets Big Cleanup RFP." *ENR (Engineering News Record)*, January 6, 1992, 228: 14.

Ichniowski, Tom and Debra K. Rubin. "Fluor Cleanup Chief Is Out." *ENR (Engineering News Record)*, January 3, 1994, 32: 11.

Ingram, Helen and Steven Rathgeb Smith. 1993. *Public Policy for Democracy*. Washington, DC: Brookings Institution.

Jackson, Elayne. "Fernald Residents Wary of Radium Claim." *The Cincinnati Post*, August 9, 1995, 6A.

Jones, Charles O. 1998. *Passages to the Presidency*. Washington, DC: Brookings Institution Press.

Jonson, Nicholas G. "Authors Defend Study: Some Health Risks Exaggerated, But Conclusion Stands, Scientists Say." *The Hamilton Journal-News*, February 12, 1997, A1.

Jonson, Nicholas. "Fernald Study Gauges Risks: CDC Assess Theoretical Danger to Nearby Residents." *The Hamilton Journal—News*, August 23, 1996, A1.

Jonson, Nicholas G. "Fernald: Wildlife Haven--DOE Toys with Restoration Ideas." *The Hamilton Journal-News*, September 23, 1998, A1, A2.

Kathlene, Lyn and John A. Martin. 1991. "Enhancing Citizen Participation: Panel Designs, Perspectives, and Policy Formation." *Journal of Policy Analysis and Management*, 10: 46-63.

Keefe, William J. 1994. *Parties, Politics, and Public Policy in America, Seventh Edition.* Washington, DC: Congressional Quarterly.

Kerwin, Cornelius M. 1983. "Assessing the Effects of Consensual Processes in Regulatory Programs: Methodological and Policy Issues." *American University Law Review*, 32: 401-423.

Kerwin, Cornelius M. 1994. *Rulemaking: How Government Agencies Write Law and Make Policy.* Washington, DC: Congressional Quarterly.

Keystone Center. April 1996. *Final Report of the Federal Facilities Environmental Restoration Dialogue Committee: Consensus Principles and Recommendations for Improving Federal Facilities Cleanup.* Washington, DC: U.S. Government Printing Office.

Keystone Center. February 1993. *Interim Report of the Federal Facilities Environmental Restoration Dialogue Committee: Recommendations for Improving the Federal Facilities Environmental Restoration Decision making and Priority-Setting Processes and Setting Priorities in the Event of Funding Shortfalls.* Washington, DC: U.S. Government Printing Office.

King, Cheryl Simrell, Kathryn M. Feltey, and Bridget O'Neill Susel. 1998. "The Question of Participation: Toward Authentic Public Participation in Public Administration." *Public Administration Review*, 58: 317-326.

The Knoxville News-Sentinel. "Activist Group Slams DOE in Report on Public Participation." July 28, 1998, C2.

The Knoxville News-Sentinel. "DOE Cut Involves N-Plant Cleanups." December 15, 1994, A1.

Kosowatz, John J. "Fernald Breaks New Ground in Energy Dept.'s Cleanup Plan." *ENR* (*Engineering News Record*), November 25, 1991, 227: 36.

Kweit, Mary Grisez and Robert W. Kweit. 1987. "Citizen Participation: Enduring Issues for the Next Century." *National Civic Review*, 76: 191-198.

Kweit, Mary Grisez and Robert W. Kweit. 1981. *Implementing Citizen Participation in a Bureaucratic Society: A Contingency Approach.* New York: Praeger Publishers.

Kweit, Robert W. and Mary Grisez Kweit. 1980. "Bureaucratic Decision Making: Impediments to Citizen Participation." *Polity*, 12: 646-666.

Lang, Tony. "1,050 Acre Money Pit." *The Cincinnati Enquirer*, March 28, 1997, A18.

Lee, Gary. "Government Flunks Environmental Test." *The Washington Post*, April 26, 1994, A13.

Legal Environmental Assistance Foundation, Incorporated vs. Hodel, 586 F. Supp. 1163, 20 ERC (BNA) 2246, 14 ELR 20425 (United States District Court for the Eastern District of Tennessee, Northern Division, April 13, 1984).

Lippman, Thomas W. "A Fine Fight with EPA Over Fernald Plant." *The Washington Post*, February 12, 1991, A17.

Lippman, Thomas W. "Energy's 'Mountain Building Up': Super Collider, Cleanup Costs Likely to Shortchange Other Programs." *The Washington Post*, February 12, 1991, A17.

Lippman, Thomas W. "Ohio Nuclear Weapons Plant Closing Delayed." *The Washington Post*, March 17, 1993, A7.

Lipset, Seymour Martin. 1964. "Ostrogorski and the Analytical Approach to the Comparative Study of Political Parties." In *Democracy and the Organization of Political Parties, Volume II: The United States,* edited by Moisei Ostrogorski, ix-lxviii. Garden City, NY: Anchor Books.

Lipset, Seymour Martin and William Schneider. 1983. *The Confidence Gap: Business, Labor, and Government in the Public Mind.* New York: The Free Press.

The Los Angeles Times. "Jacobs Wins Uranium Cleanup Contract." May 30, 1991, D2.

Lowi, Theodore J. 1979. *The End of Liberalism: The Second Republic of the United States, Second Edition.* New York: W. W. Norton and Company.

Lowi, Theodore J. 1967. "The Public Philosophy: Interest Group Liberalism." *The American Political Science Review*, 61: 5-24.

Luttbeg, Norman R. and Michael M. Gant. 1995. *American Electoral Behavior: 1952-1992, Second Edition.* Itasca, IL: F. E. Peacock Publishers.

Lynn, Frances M. and George J. Busenberg. 1995. "Citizen Advisory Committees and Environmental Policy: What We Know, What's Left to Discover." *Risk Analysis,* 15: 147-162.

MacNair, Ray H., Russell Caldwell, and Leonard Pollane. 1983. "Citizen Participants in Public Bureaucracies: Foul-Weather Friends." *Administration and Society,* 14: 507-524.

Mahood, H. R. 1990. *Interest Group Politics in America: A New Intensity.* Englewood Cliffs, NJ: Prentice-Hall, Incorporated.

McAllister, Kristen. Fernald Health Group Disbands." *The Hamilton Journal-News*, August 23, 2001, A1, A2.

McCabe, Amy Snyder. 1987. *Open Systems of Environmental Decision Making: The MRS Nuclear Waste Siting Case in Tennessee.* Ph.D. Dissertation. Knoxville: The University of Tennessee, Knoxville.

McCabe, Amy Snyder, E. William Colglazier, and Michael R. Fitzgerald. 1993. "Public Acceptance of Nuclear Waste." *Proceedings of the National Conference on Waste Management '92:* 245-249, Tucson, AZ.

McCabe, Amy Snyder and Michael R. Fitzgerald. 1987. "Open Decision Making and Citizen Participation in Environmental Policy: The DOE Attempt to Site a Nuclear Waste Facility in Tennessee." A paper presented at the annual conference of the Southern Political Science Association, Charlotte, NC.

Meiners, Roger E. and Bruce Yandle. 1989. *Regulation and the Reagan Era: Politics, Bureaucracy, and the Public Interest.* New York: Holmes and Meier Publishers, Incorporated.

Melcer, Rachel. "Different Futures Seen for Fernald; Some Label Park, Museum Plans Unsafe." *The Cincinnati Enquirer*, April 22, 1999, B3.

Melcer, Rachel. "Fernald Fixing Waste Shipments." *The Cincinnati Enquirer,* September 3, 1998, B1.

Melcer, Rachel. "Fernald Prepares to Resume Shipping: Radioactive Waste Gets New Containers." *The Cincinnati Enquirer*, December 31, 1998, B1.

Melcer, Rachel. "Fernald Waits for OK to Ship Waste to Nevada: Inspectors Expect to Give Findings in August." *The Cincinnati Enquirer,* July 30, 1998, B2.

Melcer, Rachel. "Fernald Waste Is Ready for Shipping: Court Quashes Suit Over Bids." *The Cincinnati Enquirer,* May 16, 1998, B8.

Melcer, Rachel. "Fernald Waste to Ride the Rails: Plan Underway to Empty Pits." *The Cincinnati Enquirer,* May 31, 1998, A1, A7.

Melcer, Rachel. "Fernald Waste Will Head West by Spring; Residents Worry; Officials Say There Is Nothing to Fear." *The Cincinnati Enquirer*, November 27, 1998, A1.

Melcer, Rachel. "Indians Propose Fernald Plan; Tribal Alliance Wants Plant Site for Burial Ground." *The Cincinnati Enquirer*, October 5, 1998, B1.

Melcer, Rachel. "Showdown Is Looming at Fernald; Uranium Cleanup Method Divides." *The Cincinnati Enquirer*, November 19, 1999, D1.

Melcer, Rachel. "Tests Ready for 2nd Try at Fernald: Four Companies Get Contracts for Experiments." *The Cincinnati Enquirer*, June 9, 1998, A1, A4.

Melcer, Rachel. "Worries Don't Halt Plan OK; Fernald Panel Backs Process." *The Cincinnati Enquirer*, January 16, 2000, B4.

Miller, Nick. "Pits Leak into Aquifer at Fernald." *The Cincinnati Post*, October 14, 1993, 1A, 4A.

Moynihan, Daniel P. 1969. *Maximum Feasible Understanding: Community Action in the War on Poverty*. New York: The Free Press.

Munger, Frank. "Critics Fume Over Out-of-State Waste: Shipments to Ridge Called 'Outrageous.' " *The Knoxville News-Sentinel*, November 11, 1996, A1, A5.

Munger, Frank. "DOE to Improve Monitoring at Waste Incinerator: Governor Directed State Regulators to Consider Not Renewing Permits." *The Knoxville News-Sentinel*, May 4, 1997, B1, B7.

Munger, Frank. "Governor's Panel Hears From Sick Workers at K-25." *The Knoxville News-Sentinel*, June 27, 1997, A1, A3.

Munger, Frank. "Health Woes Recited to Panel: K-25 Incinerator Blamed by Witnesses." *The Knoxville News-Sentinel*, July 25, 1997, A1, A6.

Munger, Frank. "Incinerator's Future Is Up in the Air." *The Knoxville News-Sentinel*, July 1, 1998, A14.

Munger, Frank. "Panel Clears Incinerator, Urges Health Care." *The Knoxville News-Sentinel*, November 27, 1997, A17.

Munger, Frank. "Stats Won't Solve Incinerator Debate." *The Knoxville News-Sentinel*, July 30, 1997, A8.

Munger, Frank. "Three Leave DOE's Environmental Advisory Board." *The Knoxville News-Sentinel*, February 24, 1998, A3.

The Nashville Tennessean. "They Call Themselves 'The Exposed.' Oak Ridge Chronicles: Worker Wins Ruling, Gives Others Hope." February 11, 1997, 4A.

National Academy of Sciences. 1997. *A Review of the Radiological Assessments Corporation's Fernald Dose Reconstruction Report*. Washington, DC: National Academy Press, January.

National Academy of Sciences, Committee on International Security and Arms Control. 1993. *Management and Disposition of Excess Weapons Plutonium*. Washington, DC: National Academy Press.

National Commission on Civic Renewal. 1998. *A Nation of Spectators: How Civic Disengagement Weakens America and What We Can Do About It*. Washington, DC: NCCR

National Performance Review. October 1997. *Putting Customers First '97: Standards for Serving the American People*. Washington, DC: National Performance Review.

National Research Council, Committee to Provide Interim Oversight of the DOE Nuclear Weapons Complex Commission on Physical Sciences, Mathematics, and Resources. 1989. *The Nuclear Weapons Complex: Management for Health, Safety, and the Environment*. Washington, DC: National Academy Press.

Neal, Mark Newbold. "Public Hearing Set on Renewing TSCA Incinerator Permit." *The Oak Ridger*, June 27, 1997, 8A.

Neal, Mark Newbold. "State Review Panel Comes to OR; Adams: Continuous Emission Monitoring Not Available." *The Oak Ridger*, June 27, 1997, 5A.

Neal, Mark Newbold. "TSCA Panel: More Issues Than Time." *The Oak Ridger,* June 30, 1997, 1A, 8A.

The New York Times. "Energy Department to Pay Fine for A-Plant Cleanup." May 12, 1991, 19 (L).

Nichols, Dennis. "EMA Director Supports Extracting Fernald Radium for Cancer Treatment." *The Hamilton Journal-News,* September 11, 1995, A3.

Nisbet, Robert. 1975. *Twilight of Authority.* New York: Oxford University Press.

Nolan, John. "Neighbors of Fernald 'Peeved': Group Upset at Not Being Consulted on Fine." *The Hamilton Journal-News,* August 27, 1997, 1.

Nolan, John. "Task Force: Clean Up Fernald in Ten Years." *The Hamilton Journal-News,* July 8, 1995, A1, A2.

Nye, Joseph S., Jr., Philip D. Zelikow, and David C. King. 1997. *Why People Don't Trust Government.* Cambridge: Harvard University Press.

Obmascik, Mark. "Flats Sued, Taxpayers Pay: Ex-Operators' Legal Fees Hit $20 Million." *The Denver Post,* April 7, 1996, 1A.

O'Brien, Robert M., Michael Clarke, and Sheldon Kamieniecki. 1984. "Open and Closed Systems of Decision Making: The Case of Toxic Waste Management." *Public Administration Review,* 44: 334-340.

Ohio Environmental Protection Agency, Office of Federal Facilities Oversight. 1996. *1995 Annual Report to the Public on the Fernald Environmental Management Project.* Dayton, OH: Ohio Environmental Protection Agency.

Ohio Environmental Protection Agency, Office of Federal Facilities Oversight. *Radium Issues at Fernald: October 1995.* Available, online: http://offo2.epa.ohio.gov/fou4rad.htm (July 28, 1997).

O'Leary, Rosemary, et al. 1999. *Managing for the Environment: Understanding the Legal, Organizational, and Policy Challenges.* San Francisco: Jossey-Bass.

Osborne, David and Ted Gaebler. 1993. *Reinventing Government: How the Entrepreneurial Spirit Is Transforming the Public Sector.* New York: Plume Books.

Owendorf, James M. 1997. "DOE Restores Trust in Post-Cold War Era." *Forum for Applied Research and Public Policy,* 11: 110-112.

Owendorf, James M. "Letter to Mr. John S. Applegate, Chair, Fernald Citizen advisory Board." Washington, DC: U.S. Department of Energy, June 12, 1998.

Ozawa, Connie and Lawrence Susskind. 1985. "Mediating Science Intensive Policy Disputes." *Journal of Policy Analysis and Management,* 5: 23-39.

Paine, Anne. "Legislators Call for Hearings: Energy Department, State at Odds Over Burn Plan." *The Nashville Tennessean,* February 12, 1997, 1A, 6A.

Panel on Civic Trust and Citizen Responsibility. June 1999. *A Government to Trust and Respect: Rebuilding Citizen-Government Relations for the Twenty-first Century.* Washington, DC: National Academy of Public Administration.

Pasternak, Douglas and Peter Cary. "A $200 Billion Scandal (Department of Energy's Nuclear Waste Disposal Program) (Special Report)." *U.S. News and World Report,* December 14, 1992, 113: 34-47.

Patterson, Thomas E. 1999. *The American Democracy, Fourth Edition.* Boston: McGraw-Hill College.

Petersen, James C. 1984. *Citizen Participation in Science Policy.* Amherst: The University of Massachusetts Press.

Petrie, Laurie. "Chesley Prepares for Fernald Fight." *The Cincinnati Post,* August 24, 1996, 13A.

Petruno, Tom. "Cleanup Contract May Benefit Jacobs the Most." *The Los Angeles Times,* August 17, 1992, D5.

Powers, David. "Lending Guidance on Fernald Cleanup: New Group's Role." *Harrison Press,* June 9, 1993, 1A, 12A.

Radiological Assessments Corporation. August 1996. *The Fernald Dosimetry Reconstruction Project—Draft Report: Task 6: Radiation Doses and Risks to Residents From Feed Materials Production Center Operations From 1951-1988, Volume I.* Neeses, SC: Radiological Assessments Corporation.

Radiological Assessments Corporation. 1997. *A Review of the Radiological Assessments Corporation's Fernald Dose Reconstruction Report.* Washington, DC: National Academy Press.

"Radium: Don't Abandon Fernald Cleanup." *The Cincinnati Enquirer,* August 11, 1995, A10.

Rauch, Jonathan. 1994. *Demosclerosis: The Silent Killer of American Government.* New York: Times Books, Random House, Incorporated.

Reagan, Michael D. 1987. *Regulation: The Politics of Policy.* Boston: Little, Brown, and Company.

Reeves, Linda Dono. "Task Force Chews on Problem: Grazing May Not Be Allowed Near Fernald After Cleanup." *The Cincinnati Enquirer,* November 13, 1994, B1, B11.

Rose-Ackerman, Susan. 1992. *Rethinking the Progressive Agenda: The Reform of the American Regulatory State.* New York: The Free Press.

Rosenbaum, Nelson M. 1978. "Citizen Participation and Democratic Theory." In *Citizen Participation in America: Essays on the State of the Art,* edited by Stuart Langton, 43-54. Lexington, MA: Lexington Books.

Rosenbaum, Walter A. 1983. "The Politics of Public Participation in Hazardous Waste Management." In *The Politics of Hazardous Waste Management,* edited by James P. Lester and Ann O' M. Bowman, 176-195, Durham, NC: Duke University Press.

Rosenstone, Steven J. and John Mark Hansen. 1993. *Mobilization, Participation, and Democracy in America.* New York: Maxwell Macmillan International

Rubin, Debra K. "EPA and DOE at Odds Over Fernald Cleanup Deadlines." *ENR* (*Engineering News Record*), March 8, 1993, 230: 24.

Rubin, Debra K., Steven W. Setzer, John J. Kosowatz, and Tom Ichniowski. "After the Bomb, A War Against Waste: DOE, Contractors, Target Waste Cleanups." *ENR* (*Engineering News Record*), November 25, 1991, 227: 35-41.

Ryan, Clare M. 1994. "Implementing Theories and Practices of Mediation: Regulatory Negotiation at the U.S. Environmental Protection Agency." A paper presented at the annual meeting of the American Society for Public Administration, Kansas City, MO.

Schlesinger, Arthur M., Jr. 1946. *The Age of Jackson.* Boston: Little, Brown, and Company.

Schneider, Keith. "Estimate of Uranium Dust Emissions Is Increased." *The New York Times,* December 19, 1991, B22 (L).

Schneider, Keith. "Study of Nuclear Workers Finds High Cancer Rates." *The New York Times,* April 13, 1994, A16 (L).

Scrimgeour, Donald P. and Lisa Hanson. April 1993. *Advisory Groups in the U.S. Department of Energy Environmental Cleanup Process: A Review and Analysis.* Golden: Colorado Center for Environmental Management.

Seidman, Harold and Robert Gilmour. 1986. *Politics, Position, and Power: From the Positive to the Regulatory State, Fourth Edition.* New York: Oxford University Press.

The Steering Committee on Advisory Board Formation of the DOE Stakeholders' Forum. June 15, 1994. *A Report to the Stakeholders Concerning a Citizen advisory Board for the Oak Ridge Reservation.* Oak Ridge, TN: U.S. Department of Energy, Oak Ridge Reservation.

Stewart, William H., Jr. 1976. *Citizen Participation in Public Administration.* Birmingham, AL: University of Alabama Bureau of Public Administration.

Strange, John H. 1972. "The Impact of Citizen Participation on Public Administration." *Public Administration Review,* 32: 457-470.

Straub, Bill. " 'Body Snatching' Promoted in the 1950s: Fernald Workers Were Part of Study." *The Cincinnati Post,* June 16, 1995, 10A.

Straub, Bill. "Price Tag for Fernald Could Drop." *The Cincinnati Post,* April 4, 1995, 5A.

Susskind, Lawrence. 1994. "Overview of Developments in Public Participation." In *Public Participation in Environmental Decision making: ABA Standing Committee on Environmental Law,* edited by Elissa C. Lichtenstein and Ben H. Harris, Jr., 2-7. Washington, DC: American Bar Association.

Susskind, Lawrence and Connie Ozawa. 1983. "Mediated Negotiation in the Public Sector: Mediator Accountability and the Public Interest Problem." *American Behavioral Scientist,* 27: 255-279.

Switzer, Jacqueline Vaughn and Gary Bryner. 1998. *Environmental Politics: Domestic and Global Issues, Second Edition.* New York: St. Martin's Press.

Thomas, John C. 1995. *Public Participation in Public Decisions: New Skills and Strategies for Public Managers.* San Francisco: Jossey-Bass.

Thomas, Susan, Laura Frank, and Anne Paine. "Taking the Nations' Poisons." *The Nashville Tennessean,* February 9, 1997, 1A, 15A.

Timney, Mary M. 1998. "Overcoming Administrative Barriers to Citizen Participation: Citizens as Partners, not Adversaries." In *Government Is Us: Public Administration in an Anti-Government Era,* edited by Cheryl Simrell King and Camilla Strivers, 88-101. Thousand Oaks, CA: Sage Publications.

United States Code Congressional and Administrative News: One Hundredth and Second Congress—Second Session, 1992, Legislative History: Public Laws 102-244 to 102-484. Federal Facility Compliance Act of 1992, Public Law 102-386. Volume 4: 1287-1337, 1337-1 to 1337-3.

United States Department of Energy v. Ohio, 689 F.Supp. 760 (S.D. Ohio 1988).

United States Department of Energy v. Ohio, 904 F.2d. 1058 (6th Cir. 1990).

United States Department of Energy v. Ohio, 112 S. Ct. 1627 (1992).

United States Statutes at Large, One-Hundred-and Second Congress, Second Session, 1992. Public-Law 102-386, October 6, 1992, Federal Facilities Compliance Act. Volume 106: Part 2, 1505-1519.

U.S. Congress. "March 18, 1997, For Immediate Release: Lawmakers Release Report." Washington, DC: Congress of the United States, Press Release.

U.S. Congress, Congressional Budget Office. May 1994. *Cleaning Up the Department of Energy's Nuclear Weapons Complex.* Washington, DC: U.S. Congressional Budget Office.

U.S. Congress, House. October 5, 1989. *Environmental Crimes at DOE's Nuclear Facilities.* Hearing Before the Subcommittee on Transportation and Hazardous Materials of the Committee on Energy and Commerce, House of Representatives, One Hundred and First Congress, First Session. Washington, DC: U.S. Government Printing Office.

U.S. Congress, Office of Technology Assessment. February 1993. *Hazards Ahead: Managing Cleanup Worker Health and Safety at the Nuclear Weapons Complex.* Washington, DC: U.S. Government Printing Office.

U.S. Congress, Office of Technology Assessment, Congressional Board of the One Hundred and First Congress. February 1991. *Complex Cleanup: The Environmental Legacy of Nuclear Weapons Production.* Washington, DC: U.S. Government Printing Office.

U.S. Congress, Office of Technology Assessment, Congressional Board of the One Hundred and First Congress. February 1991. *Complex Cleanup: The Environmental Legacy of Nuclear Weapons Production-Summary.* Washington, DC: U.S. Government Printing Office.

U.S. Congress, Senate. Committee on Energy and Natural Resources. July 29, 1993. *Department of Energy's Nuclear Weapons Cleanup Program.* Hearing Before the Committee on Energy and Natural Resources, United States Senate, One Hundred and Third Congress, First Session. Washington, DC: U.S. Government Printing Office.

U.S. Department of Energy. June 1997. *Accelerating Cleanup: Focus on 2006, Discussion Draft.* Washington, DC: U.S. Department of Energy, Office of Environmental Management.

U.S. Department of Energy. August 10, 1998. *A Look Ahead: A Publication for Fernald Stakeholders.* Cincinnati, OH: U.S. Department of Energy.

U.S. Department of Energy. July 2, 1998. "DOE-Ohio Awards Waste Disposal Contract." U.S. Department of Energy, Miamisburg, OH, Regional Office, News Release: 1.

U.S. Department of Energy. August 1993. *Draft Report to Congress on Citizen Advisory Groups for Environmental Restoration and Waste Management.* Washington, DC: U.S. Government Printing Office.

U.S. Department of Energy. January 1993. *Environmental Restoration and Waste Management Five-Year Plan: Fiscal Years 1994-1998.* Springfield, VA: U.S. Department of Commerce, National Technical Information Service.

U.S. Department of Energy. June 1997. *Executive Summary, Accelerating Cleanup: Focus on 2005, Discussion Draft.* Miamisburg, OH: U.S. Department of Energy, Ohio Field Office.

U.S. Department of Energy. September 1998. *Fact Sheet: Request for Input on Final Land Use of the Fernald Site.* Cincinnati, OH: U.S. Department of Energy, Fernald Environmental Management Project.

U.S. Department of Energy. July 29, 1996. *Fall 1995 Site-Specific Advisory Board Exchange.* Available, online: http://www.em.doe.gov/stake/ssabst.htm#WM96.

U.S. Department of Energy. June 23, 1997. *A Look Ahead, A Publication for FEMP Stakeholders.* Cincinnati, OH: U.S. Department of Energy, Fernald Environmental Management Project.

U.S. Department of Energy. August 1998. *Fernald Report.* Cincinnati, OH: U.S. Department of Energy, Fernald Environmental Management Project.

U.S. Department of Energy. August 1997. *Fernald Report.* Cincinnati , OH: U.S. Department of Energy, Fernald Environmental Management Project.

U.S. Department of Energy. January 2000. *Fernald Report.* Cincinnati, OH: U.S. Department of Energy, Fernald Environmental Management Project.

U.S. Department of Energy. July 1998. *Fernald Report.* Cincinnati, OH: U.S. Department of Energy, Fernald Environmental Management Project.

U.S. Department of Energy. May 1997. *Fernald Report.* Cincinnati, OH: U.S. Department of Energy, Fernald Environmental Management Project.

U.S. Department of Energy. October 1997. *Fernald Report.* Cincinnati, OH: U.S. Department of Energy, Fernald Environmental Management Project.

U.S. Department of Energy, January 1997. *Fernald Report.* Cincinnati, OH: U.S. Department of Energy, Fernald Environmental Management Project.

U.S. Department of Energy. June 1997. *Narratives, Accelerating Cleanup: Focus on 2005, Discussion Draft.* Miamisburg, OH: U.S. Department of Energy, Ohio Field Office.

U.S. Department of Energy. September 3, 1997. *Oak Ridge Reservation Environmental Management Site Specific Advisory Board, FY 1997 Annual Report.* Oak Ridge, TN: U.S. Department of Energy.

U.S. Department of Energy. July 31, 1996. *Ohio Field Office: Environmental Management Ten (Nine)-Year Plan 1996-2005, Field Draft.* Washington, DC: U.S. Department of Energy, Office of Environmental Management.

U.S. Department of Energy. January 1996. *Site Specific Advisory Board Guidance.* Washington, DC: U.S. Department of Energy.

U.S. Department of Energy. September 26, 2000. *The Third Future of Fernald Workshop.* Fernald, OH: U.S. Department of Energy.

U.S. Department of Energy, Office of Environmental Management. August 1996. *Site Specific Advisory Board Initiative Evaluation Survey Results, Supplementary Appendix: Summary of Individual Site Results.* Washington, DC: U.S. Department of Energy, Office of Environmental Management.

U.S. Department of Energy, Office of Environmental Management, Office of Strategic Planning and Analysis. January 1995. *Closing the Circle on the Splitting of the Atom: The Environmental Legacy of Nuclear Weapons Production in the United States and What the Department of Energy Is Doing About It.* Washington, DC: U.S. Department of Energy, Office of Environmental Management, Office of Strategic Planning and Analysis.

U.S. Department of Energy, Office of Intergovernmental and Public Accountability. September 1997. *Site-Specific Advisory Board Initiative, 1997 Evaluation Survey Results: Volume I, Summary Report.* Washington, DC: U.S. Department of Energy, Office of Intergovernmental and Public Accountability.

U.S. Department of Energy, Office of Intergovernmental and Public Accountability. September 1997. *Site-Specific Advisory Board Initiative, 1997 Evaluation Survey Results: Volume II, Summary Report.* Washington, DC: U.S. Department of Energy, Office of Intergovernmental and Public Accountability.

U.S. Environmental Protection Agency. August 1997. *EPA, DOE Settle Dispute for Fernald Environmental Management Project.* Chicago, IL: Region 5.

U.S. General Accounting Office. March 1997. *Department of Energy: Management and Oversight of Cleanup Activities at Fernald (GAO/RCED-97-63).* Washington, DC: U.S. General Accounting Office.

U.S. General Accounting Office. February 23, 1989. "Enormous Modernization and Cleanup Problems in the Nuclear Weapons Complex." *Statement of Charles A. Bowsher, Comptroller General of the United States. Before the Subcommittee on Transportation and Hazardous Materials, Committee on Energy and Commerce, House of Representatives.* Washington, DC: U.S. General Accounting Office.

U.S. General Accounting Office. October 27, 1993. *ERMC (Environmental Restoration Management Contractor) Follow-Up.* Washington, DC: U.S. General Accounting Office.

U.S. Office of the Federal Register, National Archives and Records Administration. *Code of Federal Regulations, The President, 1981 Compilation and Parts 100 and 101.* Executive Order 12291, Federal Regulation, February 17, 1981, 127-134.

U.S. Office of the Federal Register, National Archives and Records Administration. *Code of Federal Regulations, The President, 1978 Compilation and Parts 100 and 101.* Executive Order 12088, Federal Compliance with Pollution Control Standards, October 13, 1978, 243-246.

U.S. Office of the Federal Register, National Archives and Records Administration. *Weekly Compilation of Presidential Documents.* Executive Order 12898, Federal Actions to Address Environmental Justice in Minority Populations and Low-Income Populations, February 11, 1994, 30, 276-280.

U.S. Office of the Federal Register, National Archives and Records Administration. *Weekly Compilation of Presidential Documents.* Statement on the Executive Order on Environmental Justice, February 18, 1994, 30, 286.

Van Sant, Rick. "Resident Group: Fears Confirmed." *The Cincinnati Post*, August 23, 1996, A7.

Verba, Sidney and Norman H. Nie. 1972. *Participation in America: Political Democracy and Social Equality.* Chicago: The University of Chicago Press.

Vig, Norman J. and Michael E. Kraft. 1990. *Environmental Policy in the 1990s.* Washington, DC: Congressional Quarterly.

Vig, Norman J. and Michael E. Kraft. 1997. *Environmental Policy in the 1990s, Third Edition.* Washington, DC: Congressional Quarterly.

Wald, Matthew L. "Energy Department to Pay Fine for Cleanup." *The New York Times*, May 14, 1991, A14 (L).

The Wall Street Journal. "U.S. Will Pay Settlement in Factory-Radiation Suit." July 27, 1994, B6 (E).

Waste Control Specialists, LLC vs. United States Department of Energy, 141 F 3rd 564 (5th Cir. 1998).

Westneat, Danny. "Cloud Over New Hanford Operator Fluor Under Investigation in Ohio Nuclear Cleanup." *The Seattle Times,* August 7, 1996, A1, A11.

White, Robert. "How Clean Is Clean? Fernald Citizens Make a Sensible Call." *The Cincinnati Post,* August 12, 1995, 8A.

White, Robert. "Plenty of 'Process' at Fernald—But Cleanup's Still Not in Sight." *The Cincinnati Post,* September 18, 1993, 8A.

Williams, Bruce A. and Albert A. Matheny. 1995. *Democracy, Dialogue, and Environmental Disputes: The Contested Languages of Social Regulation.* New Haven: Yale University Press.

Williams, Walter Lee, Jr. 1999. *Citizen Participation in Environmental Decisionmaking: The Department of Energy Experience with Site Specific Advisory Boards.* Ph.D. Dissertation. Knoxville: The University of Tennessee, Knoxville.

Wilson, James Q. 1980. *The Politics of Regulation.* New York: Basic Books.

Wissner, Sheila. "Legislatures Call for Hearings: Oak Ridge Workers' Unexplained Illnesses and Transport of Toxic Wastes Raise Concerns." *The Nashville Tennessean,* February 12, 1997, 1A, 6A.

Wright, Andrew G. "Despite Apparent Advantages, Onsite Waste Cell Is Still a Hard Sell." *ENR* (*Engineering News Record*), April 24, 1995, 234: 24.

Wright, Andrew G. "Fernald Fix Starts to Fall in Place." *ENR* (*Engineering News Record*), April 24, 1995, 234: 22-25.

Yin, Robert K. 1989. *Case Study Research: Design and Methods, Revised Edition, Applied Social Research Methods Series, Volume 5.* Newberry Park, CA: Sage.

Zimmerman, Joseph F. 1972. *The Federated City: Community Control in Large Cities.* New York: St. Martin's Press.

Zimmerman, Joseph F. 1986. *Participatory Democracy: Populism Revisited.* New York: Praeger.

NEWSPAPERS

Cincinnati Enquirer
Cincinnati Post
Denver Post
Hamilton Journal-News (Ohio)
Harrison Press (Ohio)
Knoxville News-Sentinel
Los Angeles Times
Middletown Journal (Ohio)
Nashville Tennessean
New York Times
Oak Ridger (TN)
Seattle Times
Wall Street Journal
Washington Post

INTERVIEWS

Alvin Alm
John Applegate
French Bell
James Bierer
Eula Bingham
Sherry Black
Ron Bridgeman
Mary Bryan
Sandy Butterfield
William Childress
Marvin Clawson
Jack Craig
Lisa Crawford
Gary Davis
Steven Depoe
Pam Dunn
Mary English
Amy Fitzgerald
Laura Hafer
Jane Harper
Marianne Heiskell
Ralph Hutchison
Gene Jablonowski
Charles Jenkins
Nicholas Jonson
Michael Keyes
Earl Leming
Kristen McAllister
Rachel Melcer
Graham Mitchell
Ken Moore
Ken Morgan
Frank Munger
Tisha Patton
Elizabeth Peelle
Sandra Plant
Joy Sager
Douglas Sarno
Tom Schneider
Gary Stegner
Warren Strunk
Robert Tabor
Jeff Wagner
Thomas Wagner
Susan Walpole
Gene Willeke

Index

About the Author

WALTER LEE WILLIAMS, JR. is an independent scholar who has worked as an adjunct professor of political science at Pellissippi State Technical Community College. Dr. Williams' research interests include public and environmental policy and public administration.